IMAGES
of America

GADSDEN PUBLIC LIBRARY

100 YEARS OF SERVICE

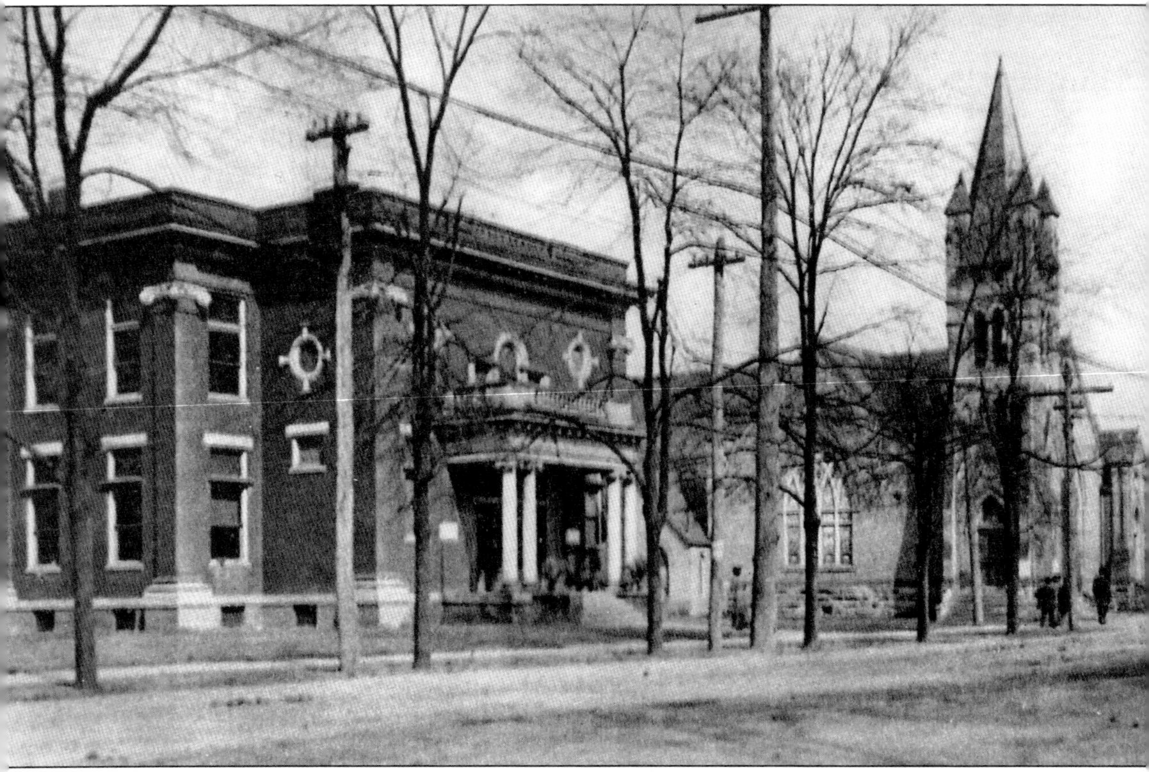

Gadsden Public Library has a rich history of 100 years of service to Etowah County and the surrounding areas. Established in 1906, the library's first home was in this building on the corner of Forrest Avenue and Seventh Street, next to the First Baptist Church. (Courtesy of Gadsden Public Library.)

On the Cover: At Gadsden Public Library's Alabama City branch, the number of books read per person in 1940 was twice the national average. Constructed in 1920, this landmark building reflects the beauty of Southern Colonial architecture and is still an essential part of Alabama City. (Courtesy of Gadsden Public Library.)

IMAGES
of America

GADSDEN PUBLIC LIBRARY
100 YEARS OF SERVICE

Library History Committee

ARCADIA
PUBLISHING

ISBN 978-0-7385-5385-6

Published by Arcadia Publishing
Charleston SC, Chicago IL, Portsmouth NH, San Francisco CA

Printed in the United States of America

Library of Congress Catalog Card Number: 2007942648

For all general information contact Arcadia Publishing at:
Telephone 843-853-2070
Fax 843-853-0044
E-mail sales@arcadiapublishing.com
For customer service and orders:
Toll-Free 1-888-313-2665

Visit us on the Internet at www.arcadiapublishing.com

We dedicate this book to the people who have shaped Gadsden Public Library's growth to its present place in history and hope it serves as a challenge to those who follow.

Contents

ACKNOWLEDGMENTS

Since its founding in 1906, hundreds of people have contributed to the preservation of Gadsden Public Library's history. It is impossible to recognize all of these people, but without their hard work and love of history, this book would not have been possible. The library's reference and local history departments house a treasure of information meticulously maintained through the years by diligent staff members. They paved the way for this book through their research, writing, and enthusiasm for local history, and fostered this interest in those who followed.

In addition to those named in this book, we gratefully acknowledge the contributions of all the many employees, board members, citizens, and community organizations that have played important roles in the library's development. We regret that lack of space and photographs prevented us from recognizing each of them.

We wish to thank local photographer Robert Scarboro for his devotion to preserving history for the enrichment of future generations. We owe a debt of gratitude to the many citizens who contributed photographs to his collection. The library was privileged to purchase the Scarboro collection with funds appropriated by Bobby Junkins. In addition, we are grateful to the reporters and photographers at the *Gadsden Times* for their excellent news coverage through the years and to the publisher for generously allowing the library to reproduce their images. Unless otherwise specified, all images are from the library's collection.

We would also like to thank Backstage Library Works for its timely assistance in developing many of the photographs from antiquated negatives. Without the company's efforts, many of the photographs could not have been included in this volume.

Although he was not an official member of the Library History Committee, Joshua Carlson played an integral part in the production of this book. Without his computer knowledge and willingness to help, this book would still be a work in progress.

"Thank you" does not seem adequate to express our appreciation to our editor at Arcadia Publishing, Brooksi Hudson, for her guidance, support, and patience.

The Library History Committee members enthusiastically contributed their time, research, and writing skills to this project. Committee members Anita Brooks, Glenda Byars, Danny Crownover, Julie Dobbins, and Bobby Junkins are pleased to commemorate Gadsden Public Library's centennial with this tribute to its past and present.

Introduction

With the opening dedication of a newly renovated facility in 2006, Gadsden Public Library celebrated 100 years of service to Etowah County and the surrounding areas. The vision shown by Mayor Steve Means and the Gadsden City Council in allocating funds for this vital project parallels the same vision shown by those who recognized the importance of a library in 1906.

In 1897, eight young women formed an alliance that evolved into the Thursday Study Club, which is still active today. One of their early goals was to establish a reading room or library for Gadsden. They enthusiastically began raising money to obtain books by holding fund-raisers such as oyster suppers, ice cream socials, doll shows, and steamboat excursions on the Coosa River. The cost of an outing on a steamboat was $1.25 per person, which included tea and sandwiches. Fines of 5¢ for being late to a meeting and 25¢ if a member failed to give a program generated money for the club. Through these efforts, club members raised $256 and, in 1900, began circulating books to the public. In December 1905, the club voted to close the reading room and to store the books until Gadsden's new library was ready.

In 1905, the Carnegie Foundation awarded a grant of $10,000 to the City of Gadsden to build a library. Lena Martin, a charter member of the Thursday Study Club, was chosen as the first librarian. The library had its formal opening on the evening of December 20, 1906. Most visitors were impressed, but one prominent citizen remarked, "This is not a reading town. People will not waste their time here. In two years, the YMCA will take over the building." Consequently, one of the early problems of the library was to sell itself to the community. Martin apparently succeeded in doing this. In 1907, registered borrowers totaled 832, and 10,500 books were checked out. As a result of Martin's diligence, the library flourished through two world wars and a depression. In the 1930s, when the American Library Association set a $1 per capita minimum expenditure, Gadsden's per capita expenditure was 12¢.

On October 22, 1936, in a report titled *Reminiscence of the Thursday Study Club*, Martin wrote the following: "In the spring of 1897 there came into being, quite without intent or purpose, without fanfare or trumpets, an organization which, tho an infant born of design or chance, according as you may look at life, has survived the adversities, the heat of summer, the cold of winters, the cruel pinch of three depressions, the loss of valuable members through death, has felt the wrench when intimate friends moved to distant cities. In fact, experienced most of the ills a human being would have encountered in thirty nine years of living. Now that it has attained its full stature we may look around and see the shadow it casts." Based on population, Gadsden Public Library had the second largest circulation in the state in 1937.

Remarkably, Martin served as the librarian until 1955, when Richard Covey became library director. He inherited a woefully inadequate building and worked hard to publicize the fact that Gadsden Public Library was far behind the times. Despite an addition constructed in the 1940s, the library had outgrown its quarters. Covey was succeeded in 1961 by Cecil Beach, who remained in the job until 1965. He benefited from Covey's efforts, and a new library was built during Beach's administration. It opened on June 29, 1964, and was considered immense for its time.

Col. Oscar Rymer followed Beach, and next came Bobby Junkins, who had worked as a stack boy during his school days. Junkins, also a state representative, was the library director from 1975 to 1988. Under Junkins's direction, the 1980s were a period of tremendous growth for Gadsden Public Library. In 1984, a wing to house the genealogy department was added and named in honor of Congressman Albert Rains. The children's division was expanded in 1987 to double its existing space.

Rebecca Buckner Mitchell became director after Junkins was elected probate judge of Etowah County. She served as the library's director from 1988 to 2001, a time period when services changed rapidly to meet the technological needs of the staff and community.

Lee Howington was appointed as director in June 2002. In 2004, the library began a $2.5-million renovation project. It represented the City of Gadsden's continued commitment to excellence in library services and belief that libraries play an important role in the future by making information available to people of all ages and incomes.

Amanda Jackson is the current director, serving since October 2006. As director, Jackson plans to build on patrons' enthusiastic response to newly renovated library facilities.

Throughout its history, Gadsden Public Library has sponsored a variety of programs and housed countless displays. There have been speakers, book clubs, classes, and reading programs for adults and children. Innovations, renovations, demonstrations, and ghostly encounters define the library's character. In spite of its many years of service, the library has had only eight directors. All either wrote articles for local newspapers or were the subject of articles in an effort to keep the community aware of special events scheduled at the library.

Gadsden Public Library stands as a monument to the initiative, creativity, and vision of the citizens of Gadsden, whose dreams of a library seemed to exceed their grasp. Hard work and perseverance saw a reading room grow from a small loft above a downtown store to a 40,000-square-foot facility with branches. It continues to grow toward tomorrow with the original vision of service always foremost in the eyes of those who lead. With a dedicated staff and supportive city government, the library will continue its tradition of encouraging lifelong learning. While great traditions remain unchanged, the role of the public library has grown to accommodate the changing times. Community demands and services now reflect the impressive technological innovations of the past 100 years. What will never change is the library's importance to the city and the joy of reading that is central to its mission.

One

Lena Martin 1906–1955

In 1897, eight young women formed a club called the Bachelor Girls to socialize and play cards. Soon, due to parental persuasion, weekly meetings became devoted to improving minds instead of playing cards. They changed the mission of their meetings, gave the programs structure, and adopted local causes. In 1899, the intellectual gathering evolved into the Thursday Study Club, which is still active today. One of the club's early goals was to establish a reading room for Gadsden. Members raised $256 for books and opened a public reading room in 1900. When Gadsden Public Library opened in 1906, some 456 volumes from the reading room formed the nucleus of the library's collection. Lena Martin, a charter member of the Thursday Study Club, was the first librarian and served for almost 50 years. During her years as librarian, Martin proved to be innovative and progressive. Thanksgiving 1908 marked the first story hour—with almost 500 in attendance. To help fund new materials, she offered a collection of books available to rent for a penny per day. The big news of 1913 was the addition of a telephone. Gas heat was installed in 1933, eliminating the need for coal. Martin became a synonym for "library" in the town as a second generation formed their reading tastes. Parents called to inquire whether it was fitting for a high school student to read novels by radical writers like John Steinbeck. Martin was often heard to say, "If I had a hundred lives to live, I should want to be a librarian in every one." In 1955, Martin was 82 with failing health. Newly elected mayor Hugh Patterson appointed a library board without consulting Martin. The chairman of the library board sent Martin a letter requesting her retirement. Understanding Martin's need to maintain ties to the library, he offered her a permanent place in the library and a special job of selecting the books to be received. However, this did not work out, and she resigned. After diligently serving almost half a century as library director, Martin accepted semi-retirement as graciously as possible. Mable Mosteller, an employee of the library, acted as head of the library until a new director was hired.

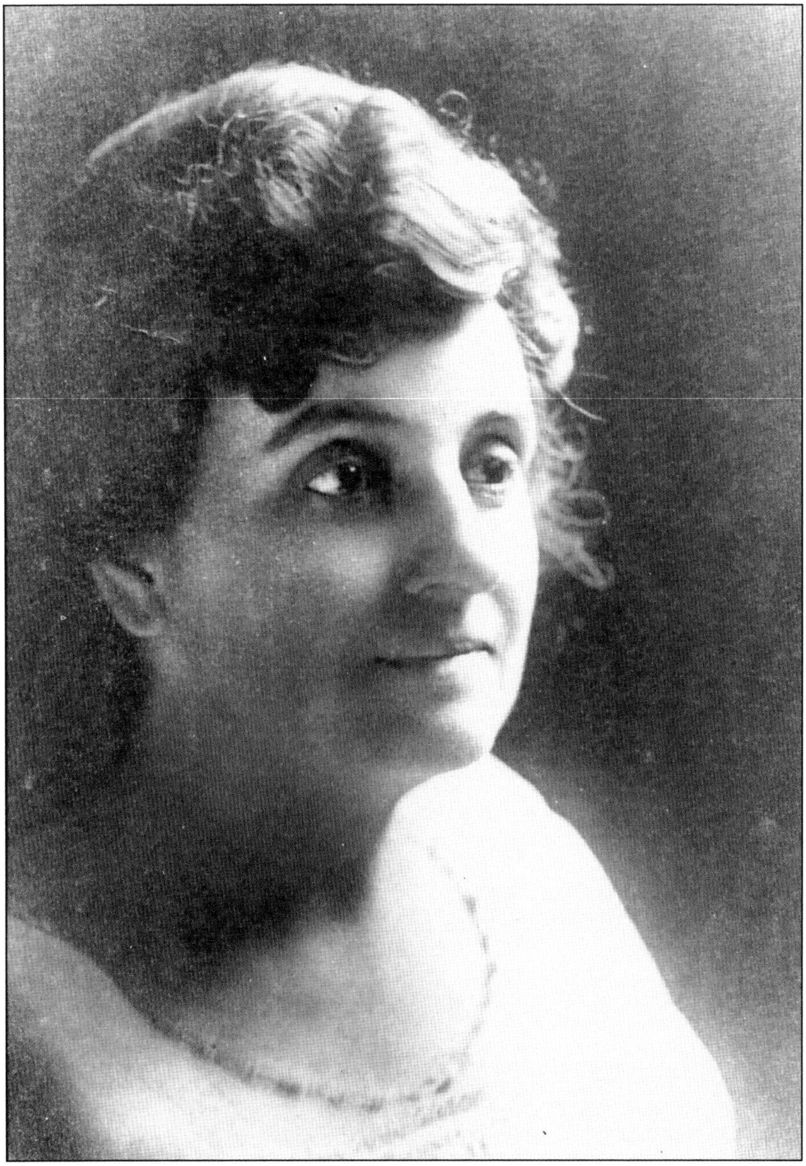

Because of her enthusiasm, love for books, and literary knowledge, at age 33, Lena Martin was chosen as Gadsden Public Library's first librarian. After her appointment on September 7, 1906, Martin attended a library school in Atlanta. From the beginning, Martin cherished and guarded her books. Everyone whispered in the library, and children tiptoed up the creaking stairs as carefully as they could, afraid to make any noise that would bring a frown from Martin. Despite her strictness, she cared for the library like it was her own child. The high quality of library service enjoyed in Gadsden today is a direct result of Martin's dedication. Martin, known to everyone simply as "Miss Lena," opened the door of learning for many Gadsden youngsters and contributed greatly to the entire community's love of good books. On October 25, 1945, the Woman's Club surprised Martin with a program in her honor at the Hotel Reich. Mayor Herbert Meighan presented her with a silver tray and candlesticks. The tray was inscribed "Presented to Lena Martin by the citizens of Gadsden, Alabama in appreciation of 45 years of devoted service to the Gadsden Public Library."

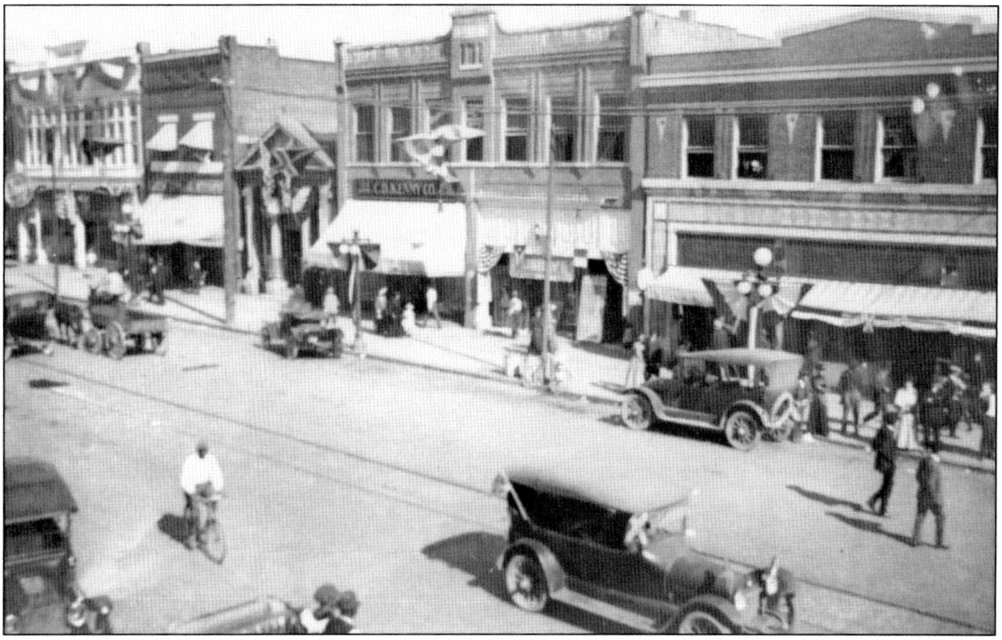

The first meeting of the Thursday Study Club took place in the spring of 1897. Charter members were Bianca Randall, Mathilde Bilbro, Etna Camp, Florrie Kyle, Annie Pentecost, Ada Pope, Minnie Turrentine, and Lena Martin. In December 1900, the Thursday Study Club opened a reading room, the first of its kind in Gadsden. The members paid $5 a month, six months in advance, to lease a little upstairs room in the new Moragne Building at 425 Broad Street, pictured second from right. Members of the club kept the reading room open four times weekly.

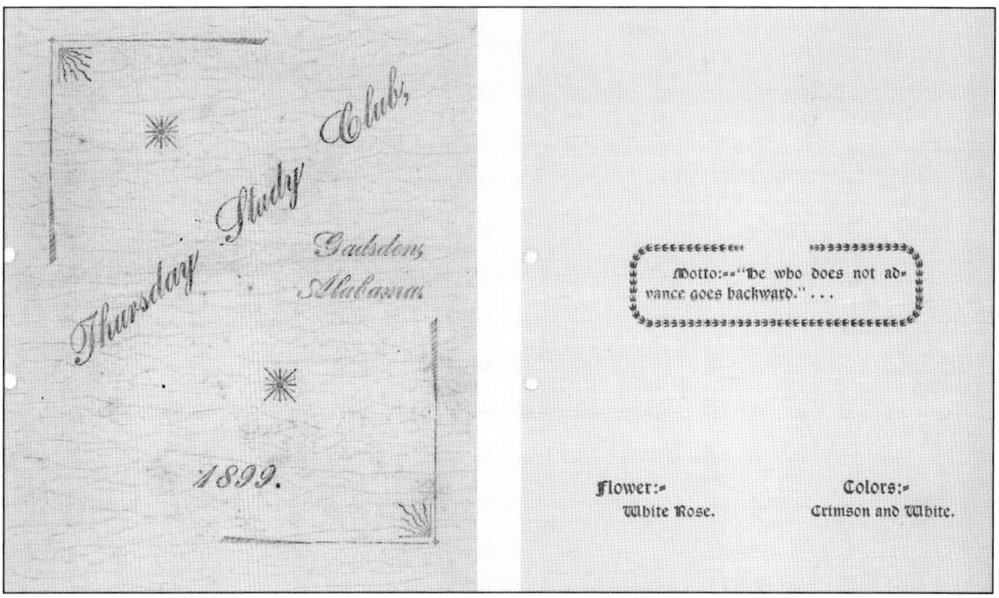

The Thursday Study Club's first printed yearbook, dated 1899, bears this motto: "He Who Does Not Advance, Goes Backward," which reflected the members' determination to improve their minds. The themes of programs throughout the club's history expressed a keen awareness of current events, as well as a true appreciation of literature and the arts in all forms.

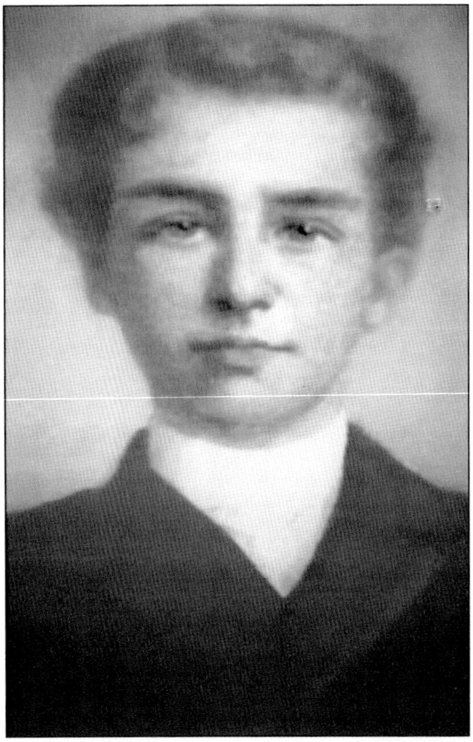

Neighboring Alabama City had what is believed to be the first public library in Alabama. The Nichols Library was built in 1902 by the Dwight Cotton Mill in memory of Howard Gardner Nichols, who lost his life at the age of 25 in an 1896 accident at the plant. It confined its readership to male cotton mill workers; neither children nor ladies were allowed. Challenged by the beautiful Howard Nichols Library, the Thursday Study Club vowed to see a full-time public library for Gadsden. The Nichols Library is now the home of the Northeast Alabama Genealogical Society and was added to the National Register of Historic Places in 1974.

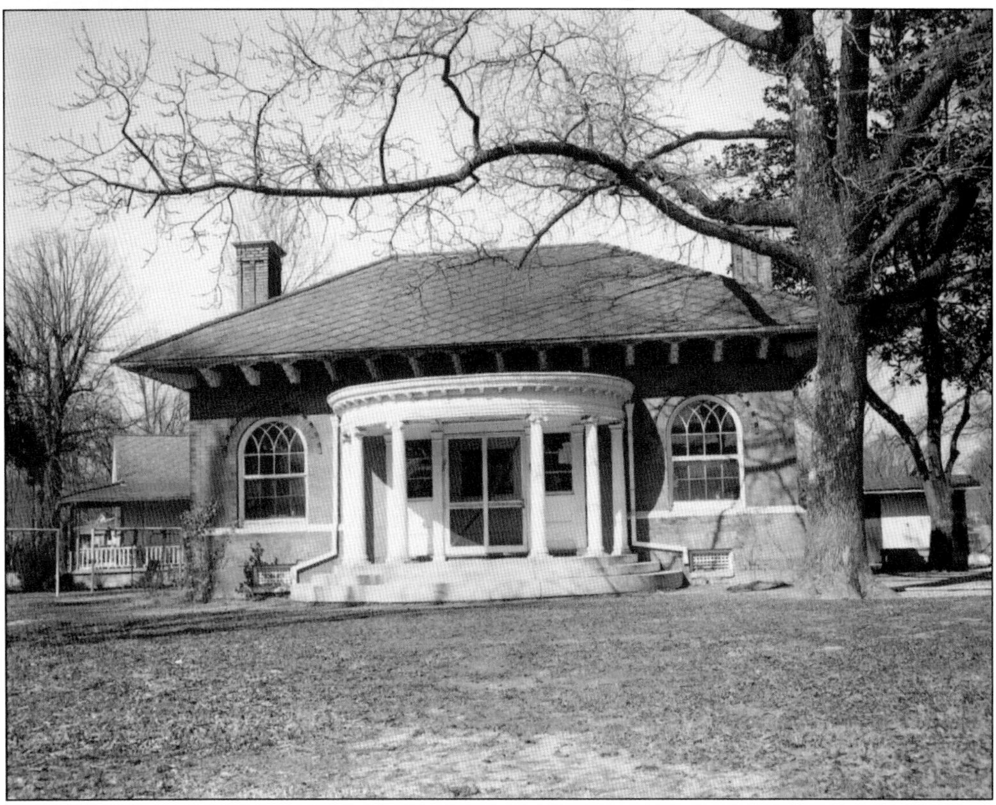

Andrew Carnegie funded the building of libraries throughout the country. Encouraged by the success of the Thursday Study Club's reading room, Prof. Walter E. Striplin approached the Carnegie Corporation about the necessary qualifications for a community to receive a grant for a library. Striplin and others raised money to purchase a northwest corner lot on Seventh Street and Forrest Avenue. An agreement was reached by Striplin and the Carnegie Corporation that provided Gadsden with a $10,000 grant to establish a public library. This portrait was a gift of the Carnegie Corporation of New York in 1935 and still hangs in the library.

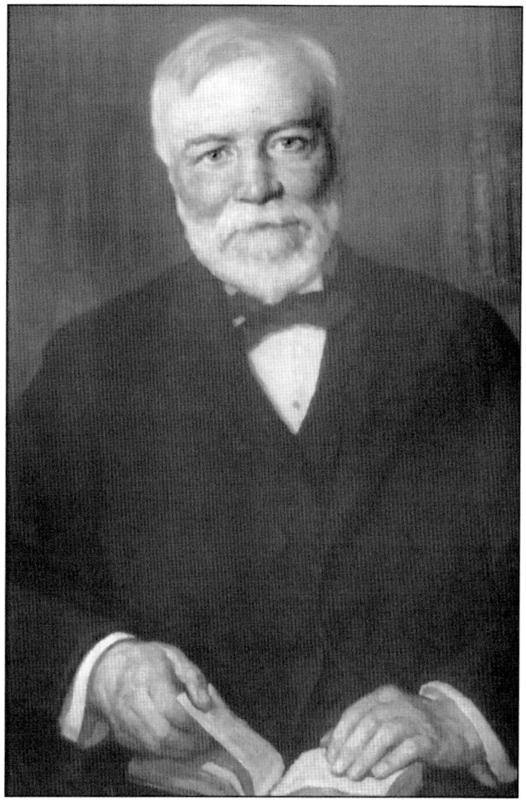

Gadsden's city hall was located on Fifth Street until 1960. In April 1904, the city council unanimously adopted Ordinance Number 741 to appropriate $1,000 annually to support a library. On May 4, 1905, they bought an additional lot in the rear of the Carnegie Library for $250. The board of education and the city worked together on plans for the Carnegie Library.

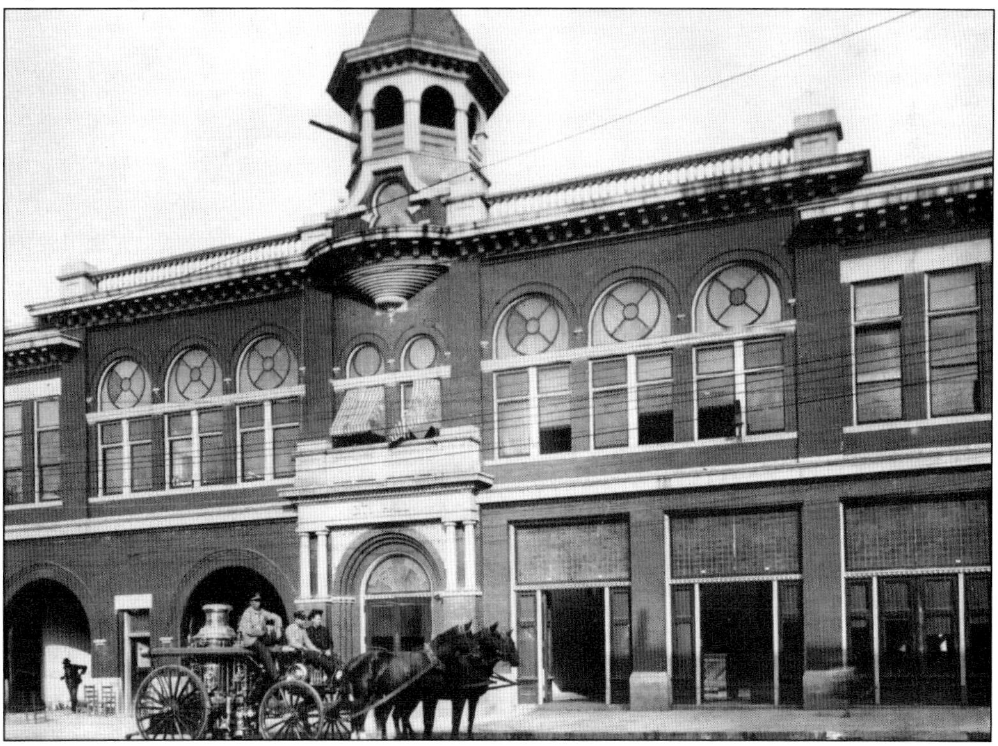

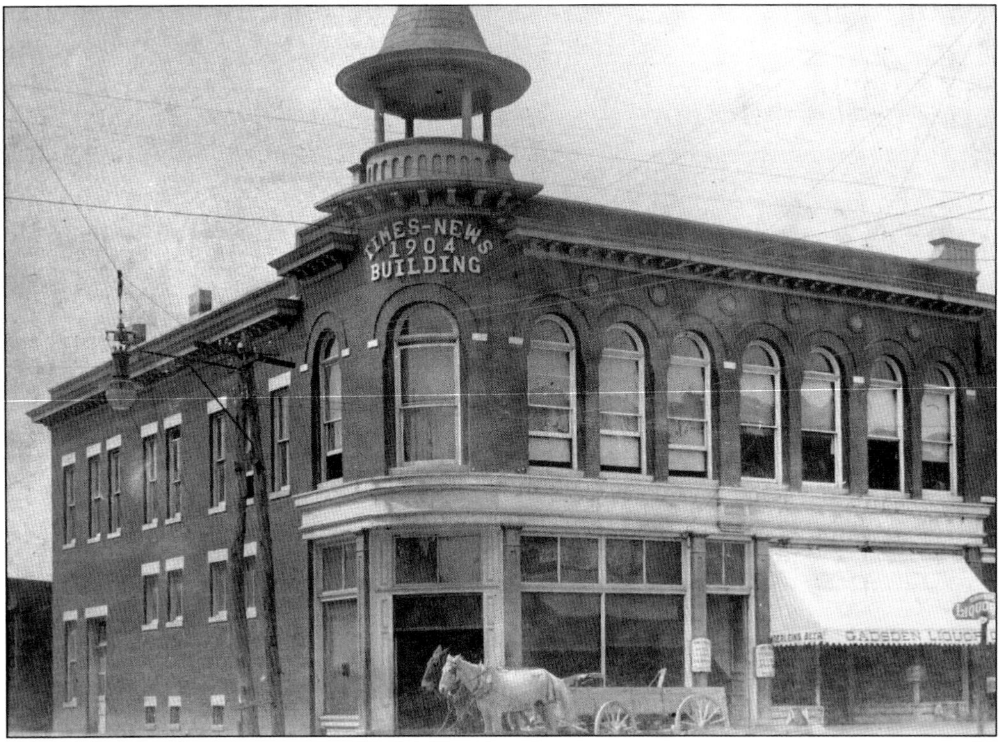

As excitement grew, the *Gadsden Times* frequently ran stories on the details of the library project. Etowah County's oldest employer, the *Gadsden Times* was established in 1867 and moved to this building in 1904. After the newspaper's owners relocated their business, the building was purchased for use as professional office space. It was renovated in 1981 and was added to the National Register of Historic Places in 1983. The extensive resources of Gadsden Public Library include the *Gadsden Times* on microfilm dating back to 1867.

GADSDEN PUBLIC LIBRARY IS OPENED UNDER MOST FLATTERING AUSPICES

The grand opening of the library made front-page news on December 21, 1906, with the headline "Gadsden Public Library Is Opened Under Most Flattering Auspices." Many members of the Thursday Study Club were there to assist with the reception. The city did not include any money for books when the new library opened because it already had 1,657 volumes. Donations included 456 volumes from the Thursday Study Club reading room, 342 from Gadsden public schools, and 230 from F. R. Abercrombie, with the rest received at book "showers."

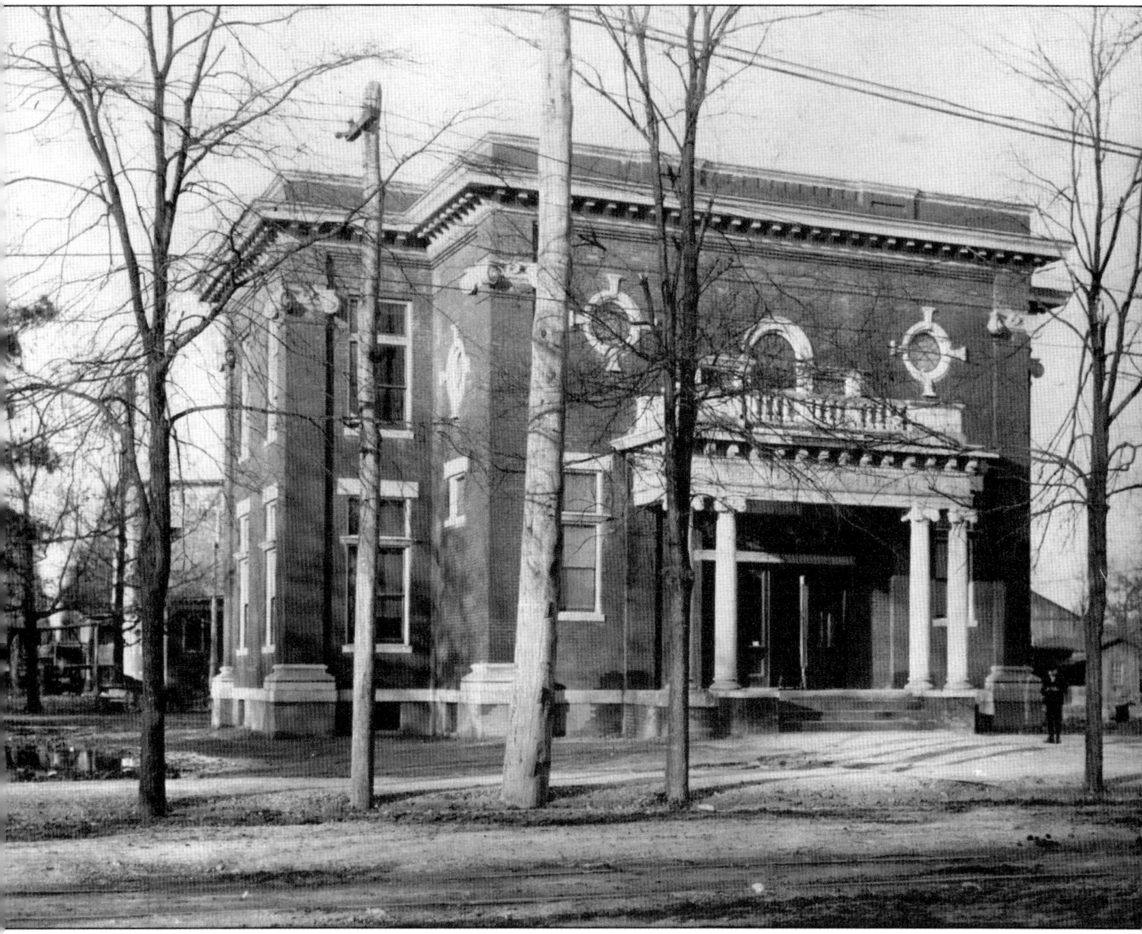

Built on the corner of Forrest Avenue and Seventh Street, this beautiful redbrick building with its lofty stone columns was a combination of Colonial and Italian architecture. Reading and reference rooms were on the first floor, and on the second floor was a spacious assembly room with a seating capacity of 400, which could be used for meetings and programs. New shrubs and flowers were planted by the Gadsden Beautiful Club and the Woman's Club with the help of Congressman John L. Burnett.

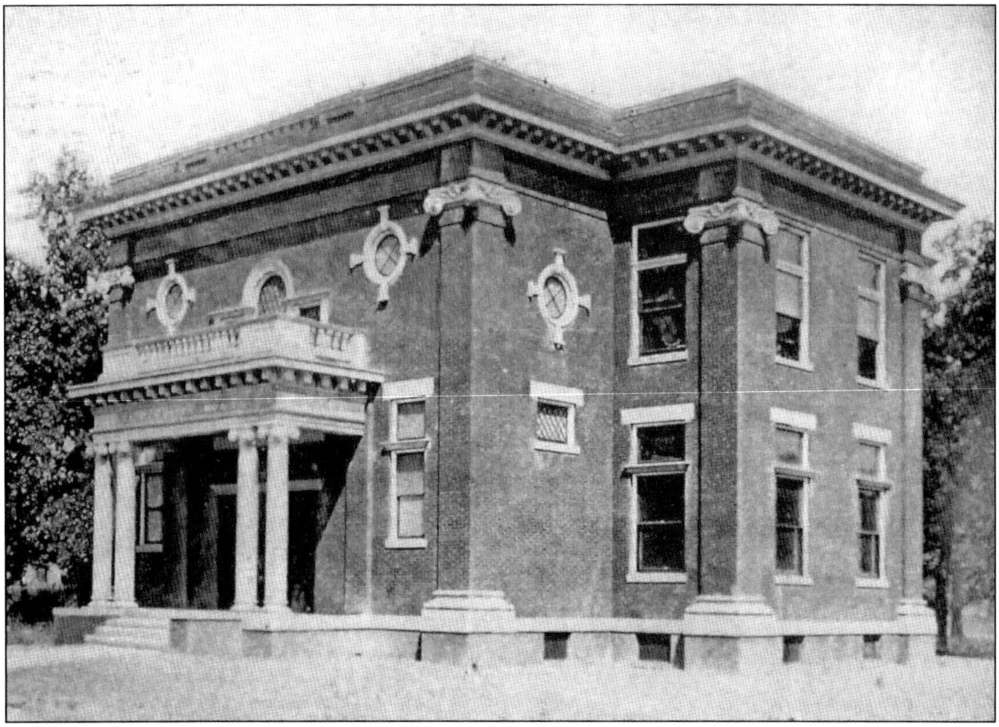

Lena Martin sent this postcard of the Carnegie Library to the superintendent of documents in Washington, D.C. It is dated June 8, 1907.

The library closed on May 26, 1912, out of respect for the untimely death of young Walter E. Striplin, superintendent of Gadsden City Schools, who had been instrumental in securing the original Carnegie grant for the library. At age 39, Striplin's death from pneumonia was a great shock and loss to the community.

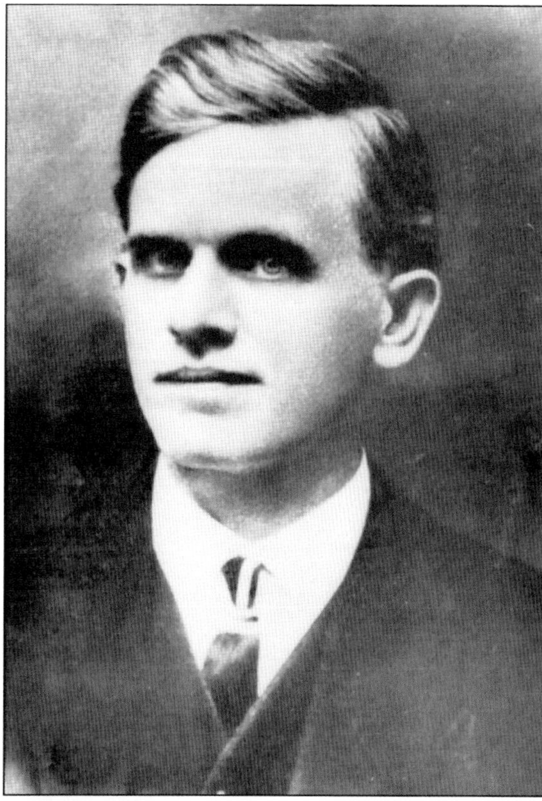

In 1913, an outreach program was instigated for the benefit of children at the Eleventh Street School who could not otherwise come to the library. The Eleventh Street School was erected in 1907. It closed when newer schools were built in this area. The aging structure was later renovated, and it now houses the Gadsden Board of Education. It is the only surviving school building of that era and was added to the National Register of Historic Places in 1984. Pictured is the 1910 second-grade class on the steps of the school.

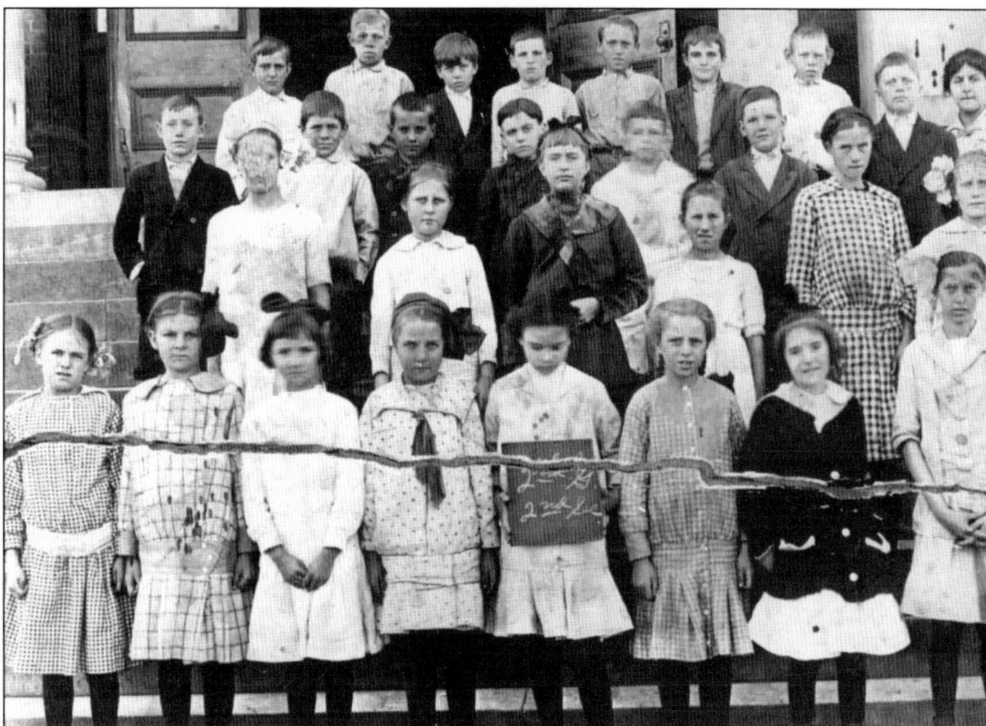

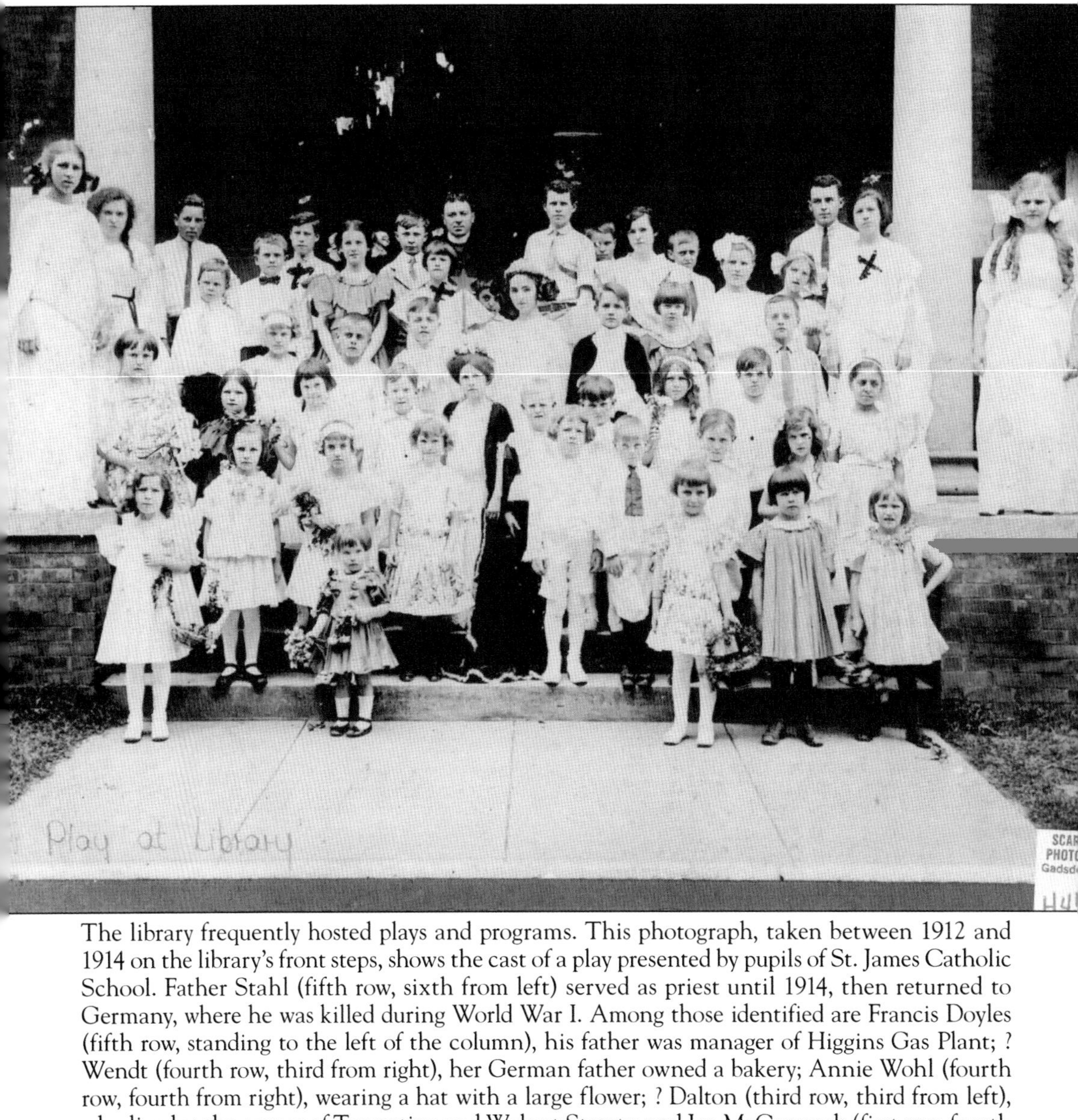

The library frequently hosted plays and programs. This photograph, taken between 1912 and 1914 on the library's front steps, shows the cast of a play presented by pupils of St. James Catholic School. Father Stahl (fifth row, sixth from left) served as priest until 1914, then returned to Germany, where he was killed during World War I. Among those identified are Francis Doyles (fifth row, standing to the left of the column), his father was manager of Higgins Gas Plant; ? Wendt (fourth row, third from right), her German father owned a bakery; Annie Wohl (fourth row, fourth from right), wearing a hat with a large flower; ? Dalton (third row, third from left), who lived at the corner of Turrentine and Walnut Streets; and Joe McCormack (first row, fourth from left), with the Buster Brown haircut. This picture was copied courtesy of Obal J. Christopher in October 1977. He is pictured on the fifth row, second from left column.

In 1915, Robert Fosdick presented to the library a collection of more than 1,000 rare and valuable volumes in memory of his mother, Anna Mortimer Fosdick. This bookplate was designed for the collection by Thursday Study Club member Isabelle W. Cumming.

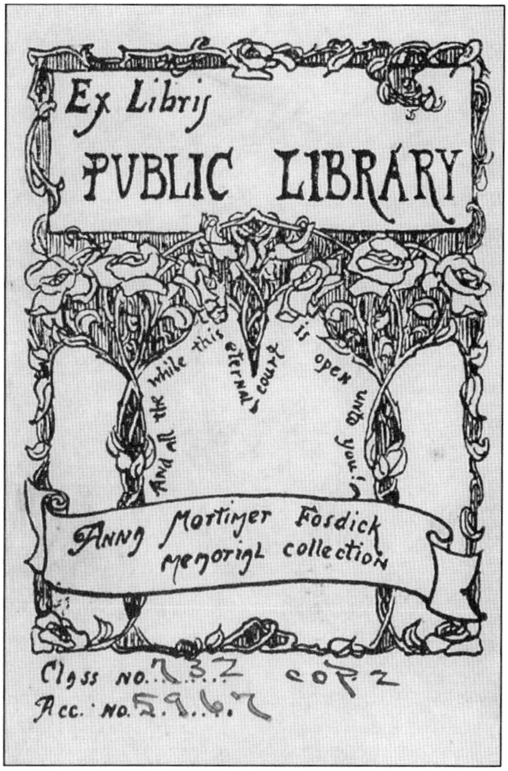

It had long been a goal of Lena Martin's to have a branch especially for the black community. Black teachers and students were allowed to use library materials by contacting Martin or Ruby Prater, a black maid who worked in the library. Their books were handed to them at the back door. In 1923, Martin finally succeeded in opening a branch library at Central High School especially for the black community. Funding was a problem, but Martin managed to interest people in making donations. Shown here is the Central High class of 1936 on the steps of the school. Carver High School was built on this site in 1936.

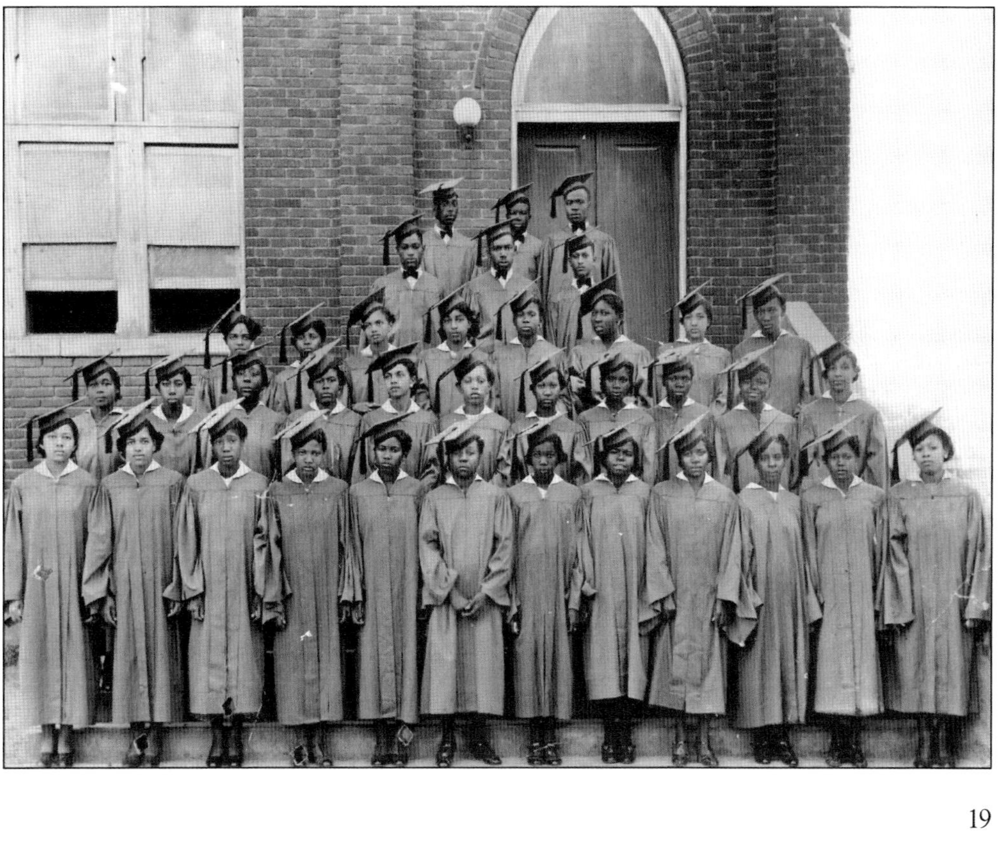

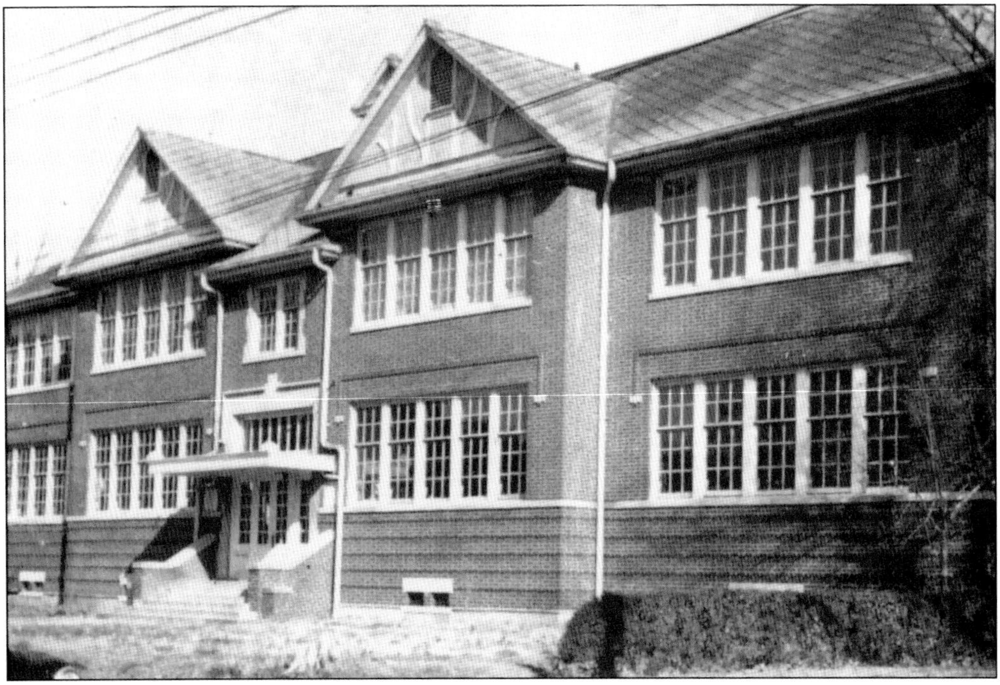

To encourage children to read, book lists were compiled and sent to the public schools. By 1927, more than 5,000 books were being circulated through the school branches. A total of 39,688 books were circulated through the main library and its branches. The new Henry Street School, pictured here, opened with an outreach library in 1929.

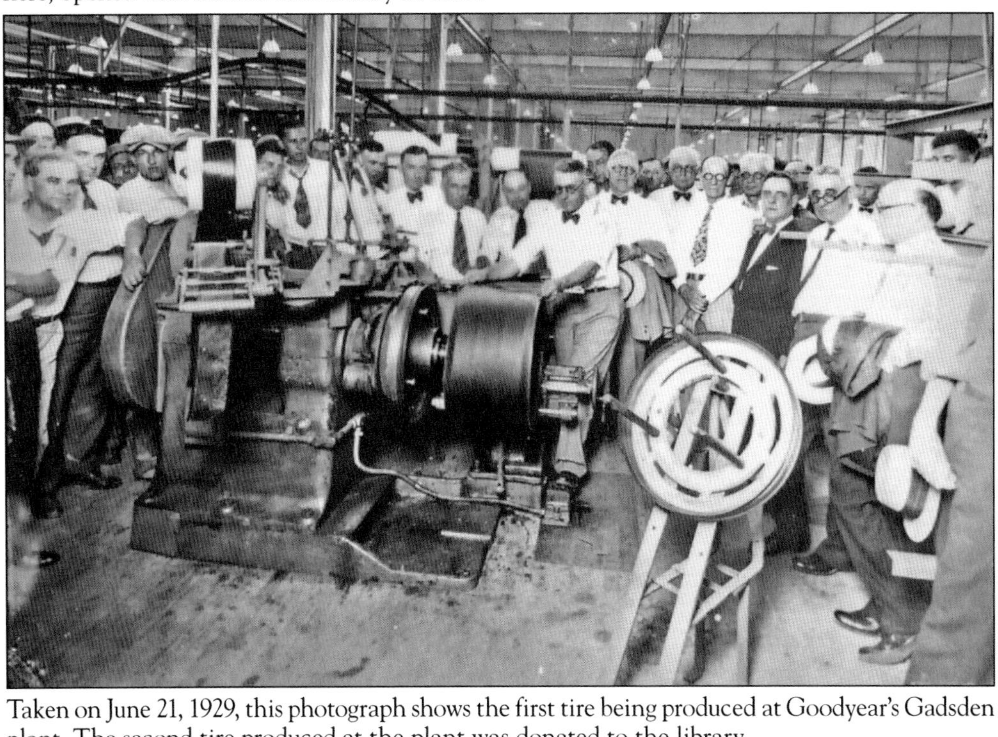

Taken on June 21, 1929, this photograph shows the first tire being produced at Goodyear's Gadsden plant. The second tire produced at the plant was donated to the library.

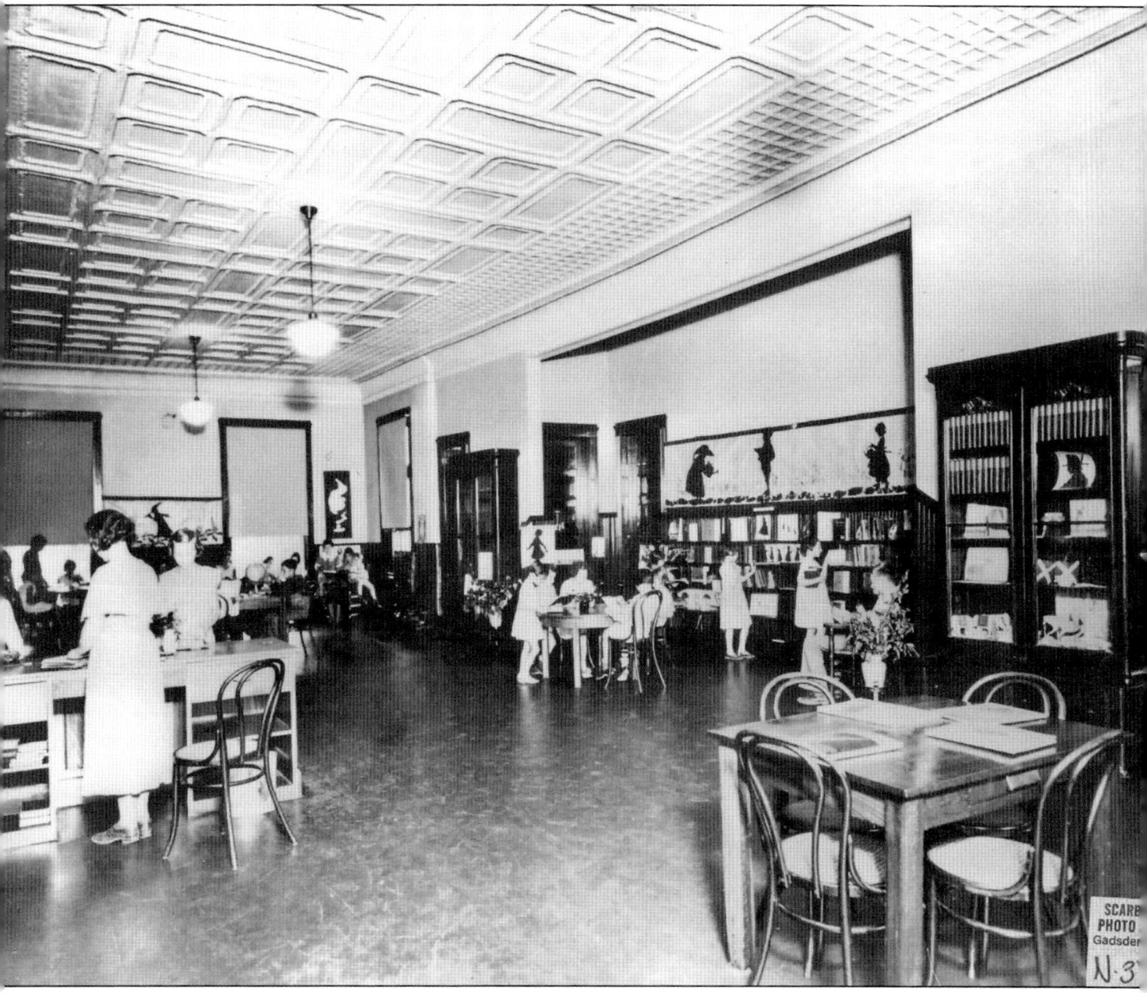

In 1931, the Gadsden Woman's Club donated books to establish a new children's department on the second floor. The oak charging desk was donated by Will Gwin. The *Gadsden Times* proclaimed, "Children flocked there for books." Vacation clubs and summer reading programs were organized for the children. This photograph was published in the *Gadsden Times* on November 13, 1932, with the headline, "Children's Room of Public Library One of Its Most Popular Features." At the right of the picture is one of two bookcases donated by Robert Fosdick that are still used for displays in the corridor of the main library.

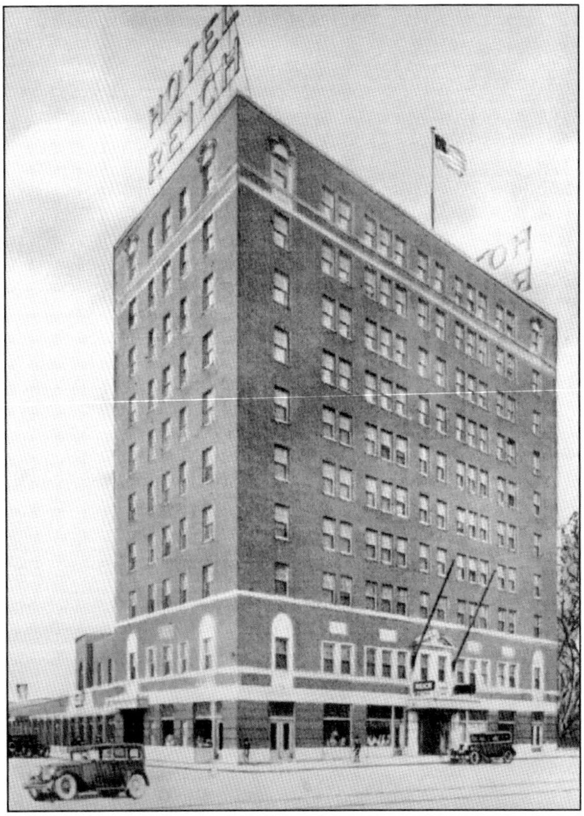

Known in library circles for its growth and extensive book collection, Gadsden Public Library was chosen to host the regional library meeting of the Alabama Library Association's biannual session in 1937. Dignitaries from across the state attended the meetings held at the Hotel Reich, located across the street from the library. Gadsden's first skyscraper, the 10-story hotel was built in 1929 by a group of investors headed by Adolph Reich and was operated for 50 years.

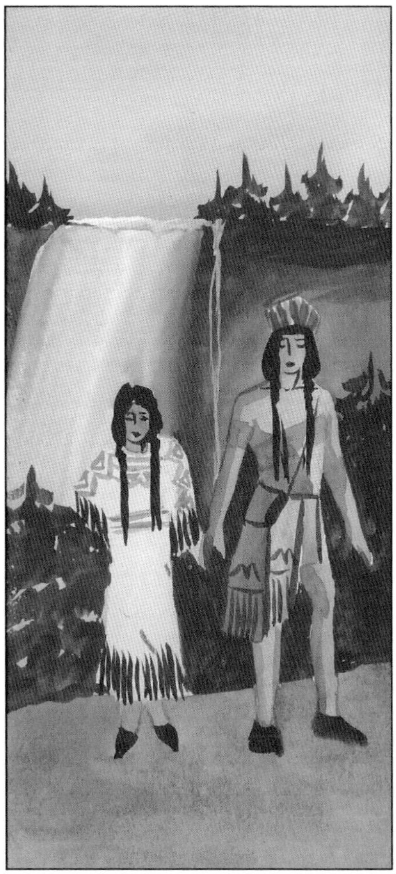

At the 1937 library meeting, the banquet favor next to each plate was a booklet titled *The Legend of Noccalula* by Mathilde Bilbro, with a beautiful hand-painted cover by Marjorie Plank.

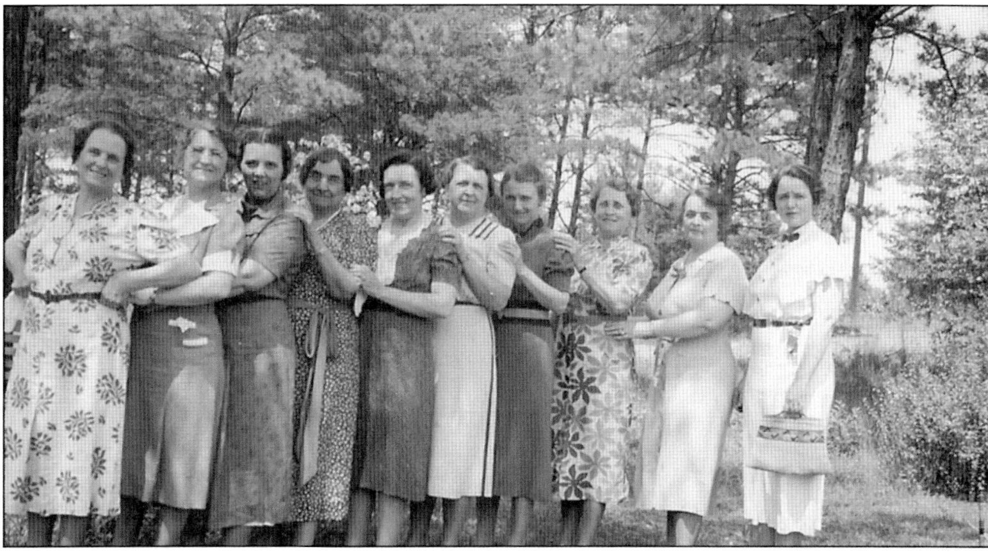

Thursday Study Club members are casually dressed to enjoy a picnic in 1938 at the Mentone summer home of Alice Inzer. They are, from left to right, Mrs. A. E. (Q. Johnson) Swanson, Mrs. H. W. (Edna) Neiderhauser, Mrs. Morgan (Ethel Line) McCall, Lena Martin, Mrs. Adolph (Nellie King Riddle) Reich, Mrs. Dee (Jessie Banks) Holloway, Mrs. Lucien (Hilda) Brown, Mrs. Howard (Daisy McDuffie) Thomas, Mrs. James C. (Alice) Inzer, and Mrs. George (Ella Watson) Vann.

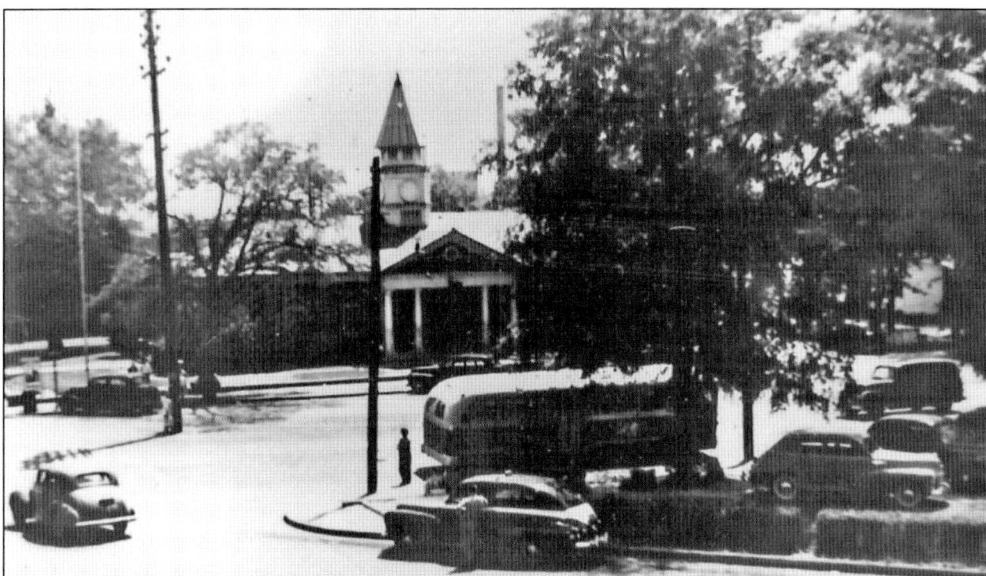

As Gadsden began annexing territory and experiencing population growth, the demand for branch libraries also grew. The city commission approved funding for an Alabama City branch of Gadsden Public Library on February 15, 1938. The old city hall, built in 1920 when Alabama City was a separate municipality, was selected as an ideal spot. After cleaning and painting, shelving was installed. The librarian's desk was formerly the city clerk's desk, the judge's bench was cut down to make a dictionary stand, and a magazine stand was previously used in one of the city's pool rooms. The library was housed in the abandoned courtroom, and a post office occupied the rest of the building.

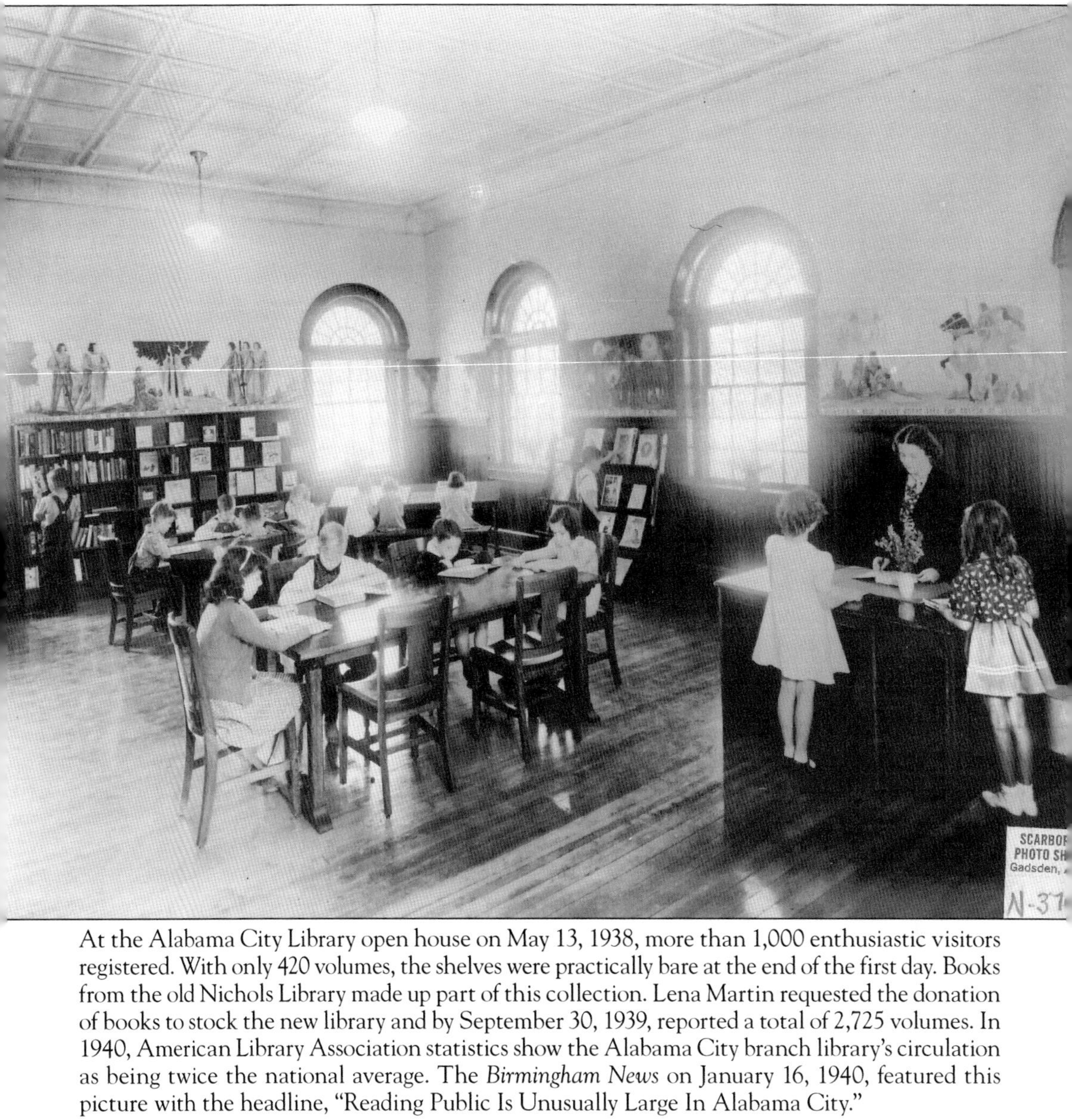

At the Alabama City Library open house on May 13, 1938, more than 1,000 enthusiastic visitors registered. With only 420 volumes, the shelves were practically bare at the end of the first day. Books from the old Nichols Library made up part of this collection. Lena Martin requested the donation of books to stock the new library and by September 30, 1939, reported a total of 2,725 volumes. In 1940, American Library Association statistics show the Alabama City branch library's circulation as being twice the national average. The *Birmingham News* on January 16, 1940, featured this picture with the headline, "Reading Public Is Unusually Large In Alabama City."

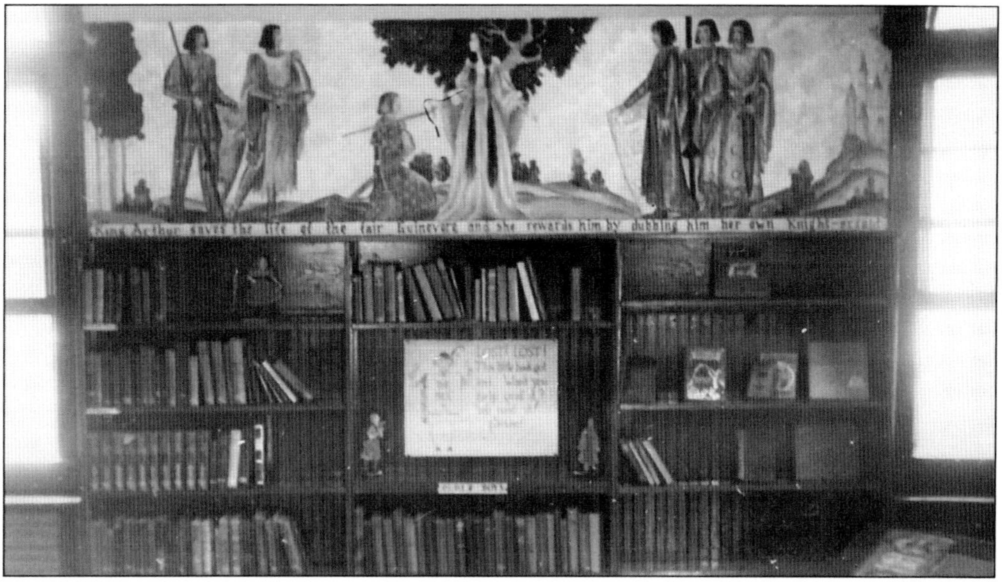

Beautiful murals depicting the Arthurian legends were painted at the Alabama City Library by Marjorie Plank. Materials were purchased by the Woman's Book Club, and Plank donated her time.

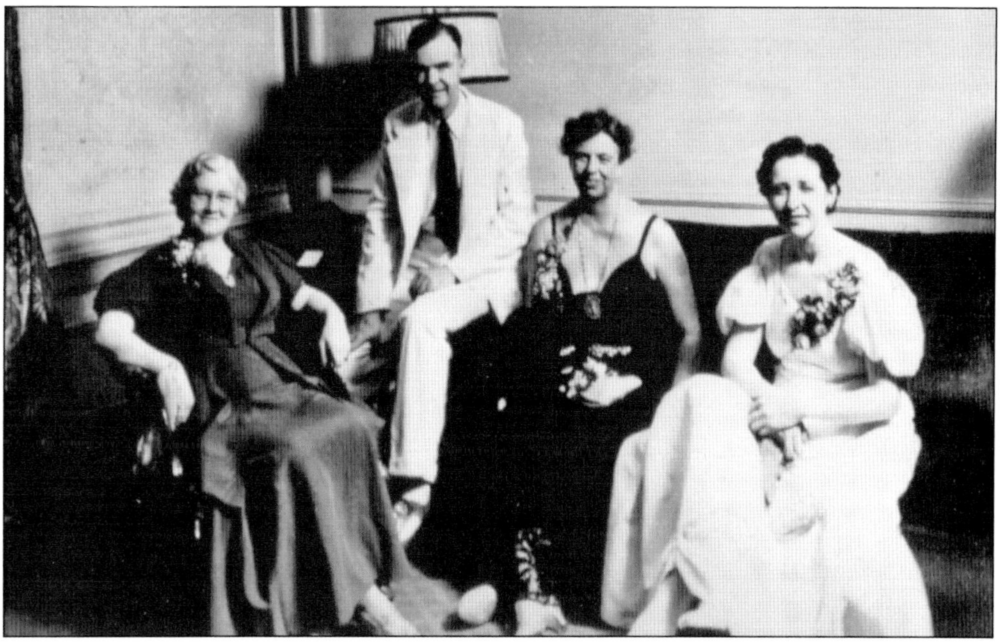

Lena Martin perfected a method to effectively bind old newspapers and magazines that drew widespread attention. On September 14, 1939, First Lady Eleanor Roosevelt inspected the mending and binding work at the Alabama City branch library while in Gadsden on a lecture tour. In a *Birmingham Post* article titled "My Day," Roosevelt said, "We visited a library in the post office of Alabama City, where big cotton mills are situated. Here they have about 2,600 books, but the circulation is so large that a very good educational job must have been done in the community to awaken a realization of the value of reading." Pictured here are Roosevelt, third from left; Mayor J. Herbert Meighan, and two unidentified women at a meeting in Gadsden's Hotel Reich.

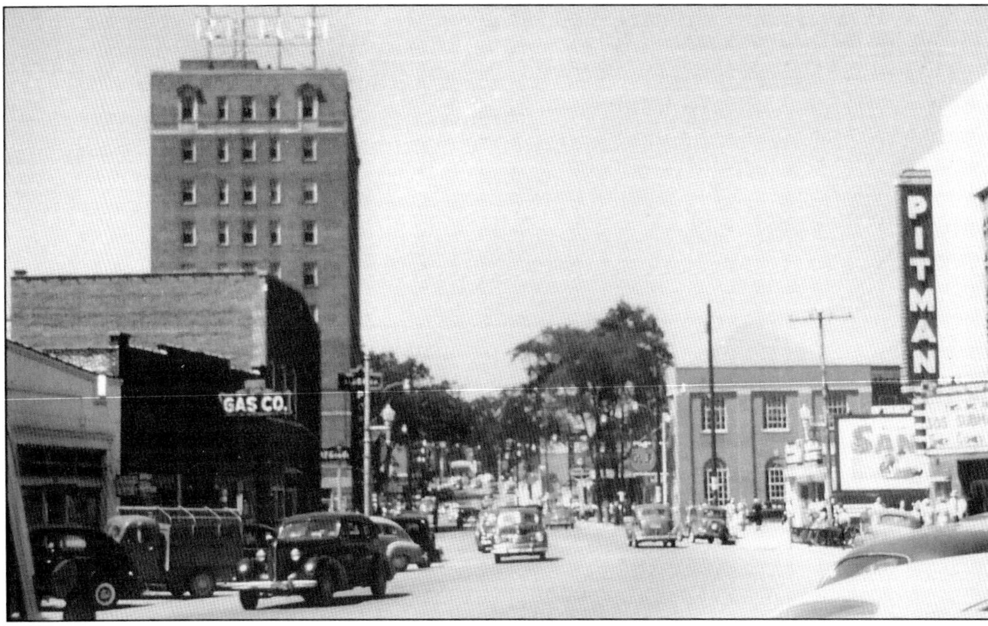

Downtown Gadsden was busy in the 1940s. Originally built to house 5,000 volumes, the library now had more than 23,000 volumes. The library was open 35 hours per week, with an annual circulation of 161,336 in 1940. Books were stacked in every possible space. The Woman's Club started a drive to increase the size of the library. Shown after the addition was complete, the library is the brick building on the right, across the street from the Hotel Reich.

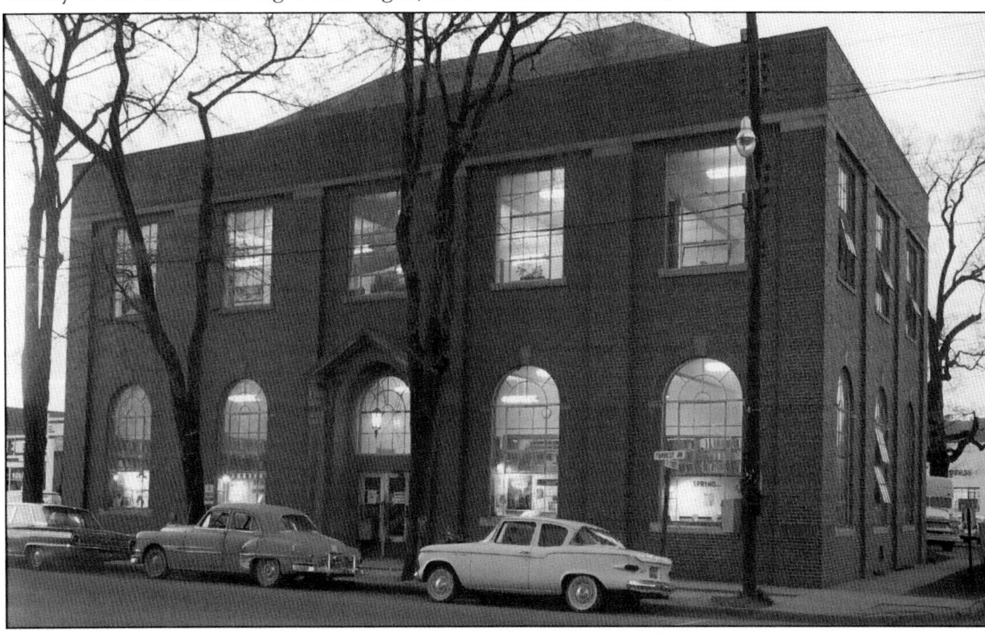

A Works Progress Administration grant provided $24,884 of the $49,884 needed for the expansion of the library. Two huge rooms were added in the Williamsburg style, and in 1941, Lena Martin directed the move to the new quarters. With so much expansion and progressiveness, it is little wonder Gadsden Public Library received an award of excellence from the American Library Association in 1942.

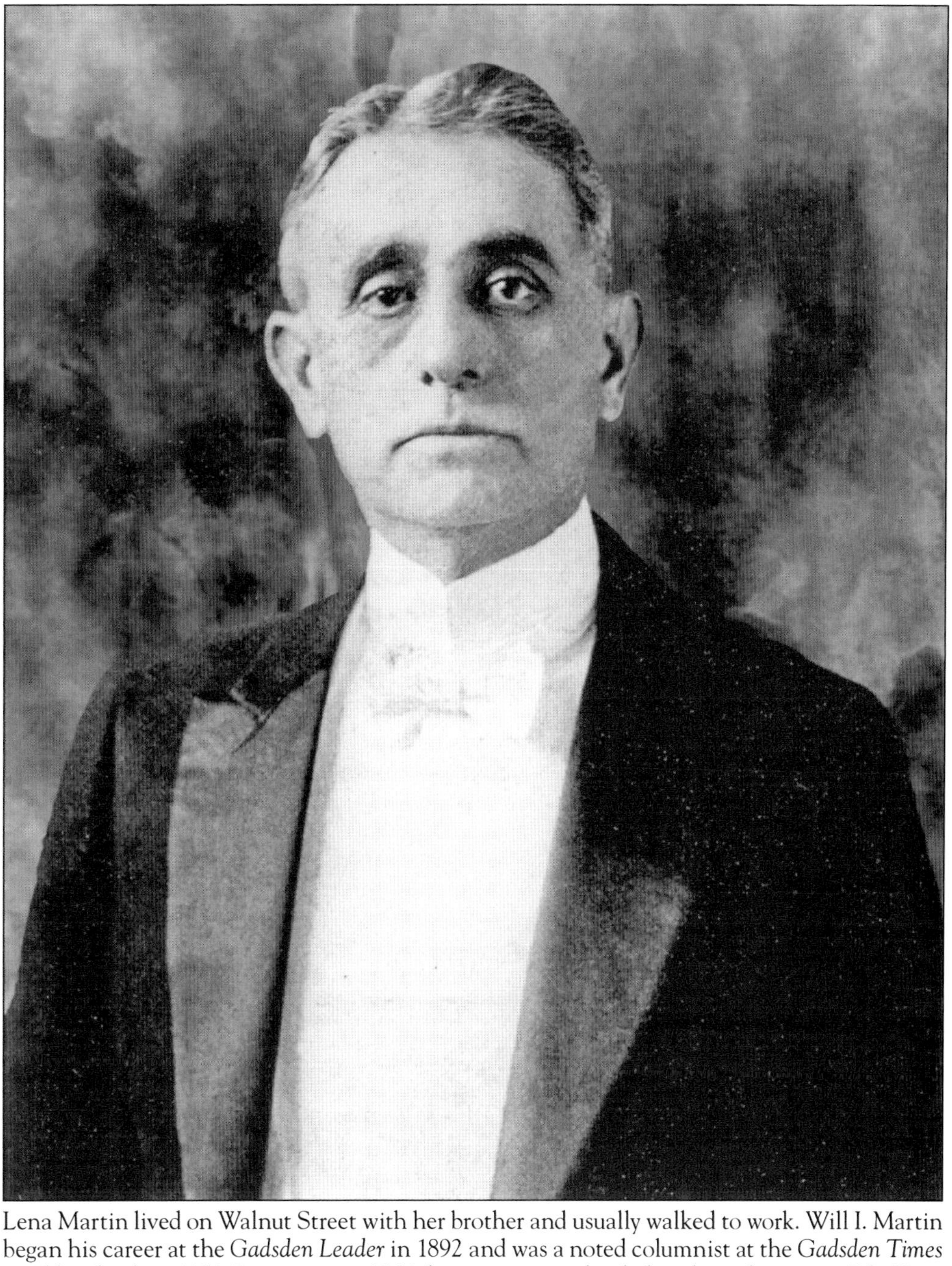

Lena Martin lived on Walnut Street with her brother and usually walked to work. Will I. Martin began his career at the *Gadsden Leader* in 1892 and was a noted columnist at the *Gadsden Times* until his death in 1954. Beginning in 1946, he wrote a popular daily column known as *Fifty Years Ago*. *If Memory Serves*, published in 1953, is a collection of 100 of Martin's newspaper columns. Approximately 4,000 of his columns were preserved by his sister in scrapbooks. Because of the deteriorating condition of the scrapbooks and a desire to share this local history, in the 1980s, the library's reference staff began typing and saving these columns on disc. It was a laborious task, complicated by ever-changing computer technology and format compatibility. Although not a professional product, what it lacks in quality is outweighed by hours of reading enjoyment.

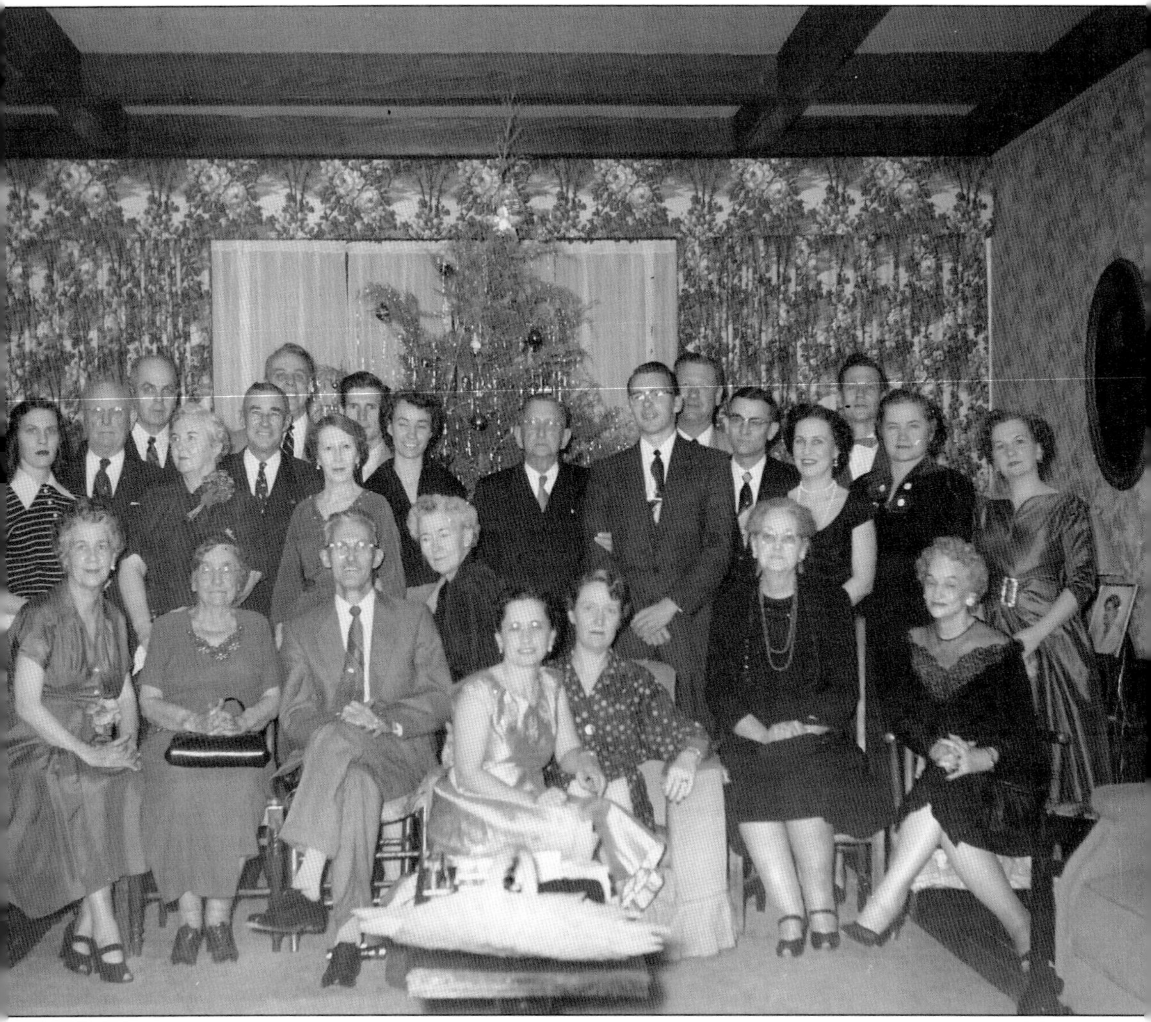

The Etowah Historical Society made Lena Martin an honorary member in 1954 in recognition of her lifetime spent contributing to research and local preservation. Pictured at their first annual Christmas party in December 1954, members from left to right are (first row, seated) Mary Harrison Lister, Lena Martin, R. H. Copeland, Mrs. R. H. Copeland, Mrs. W. O. (Kate) Briscoe, Hazel Oliver, Mrs. W. A. Leach, and Frances Underwood; (second row) Mrs. Pete (Ramona) Butler, Mrs. Tom (Irene) Sansom, Mrs. Russell Hooks, Mrs. Elbert (Ramona) Watson, George W. Floyd, Elbert Watson, W. O. Briscoe, Mrs. William C. Tolbert, Mrs. C. L. Manderson, and Mrs. Glenn Sedam; (third row) Marvin Small, Tom Sansom, Russell Hooks, Glenn Sedam, Pete Butler, C. L. Manderson, and William Tolbert.

Two

Richard Covey 1956–1960

Richard Covey was appointed the library director in October 1956. His immediate challenge was to raise public awareness about the needs of the library. As Lena Martin's physical condition had deteriorated, so had the condition of the library. Covey used statistics to compare Gadsden's library with the national average for cities of the same size. The concluding statement was that "no library does more to pull down the national average than the Gadsden Public Library." Obviously, Gadsden no longer had an award-winning library, but Martin was not entirely to blame. On average, cities of equal size spent more than five times more on their libraries. In his report, Covey stressed the importance of organizing a Friends of the Library association. The report was taken seriously by the city fathers, and plans went into effect for improvements. With Covey directing, Gadsden Public Library greatly expanded its services. Book programs flourished under the guidance of the newly formed Friends of the Library. Book lists were prepared, teas were given, and essay contests were sponsored by the Friends. National Library Week was launched in 1958, and more than 3,000 people visited the library during its observance. That year, 1,578 new library cards were issued. Covey attended the Library Building Institute at the University of Maryland in 1959, an event that was attended by participants from all over the world. Although he returned with a collection of plans of recently built libraries in other parts of the country, a building project was not to be in his future. The same *Gadsden Times* article that reported on his trip also pointed out how lucky Gadsden was to have a librarian with his training, vision, and originality. It stressed that, in spite of his capabilities, he could not improve the library on his own and needed the support of the community. The article even pointed out that such a librarian was high in demand and had unlimited possibilities elsewhere. The article proved prophetic as Richard Covey resigned one year later in September 1960 to become the library director in Huntsville.

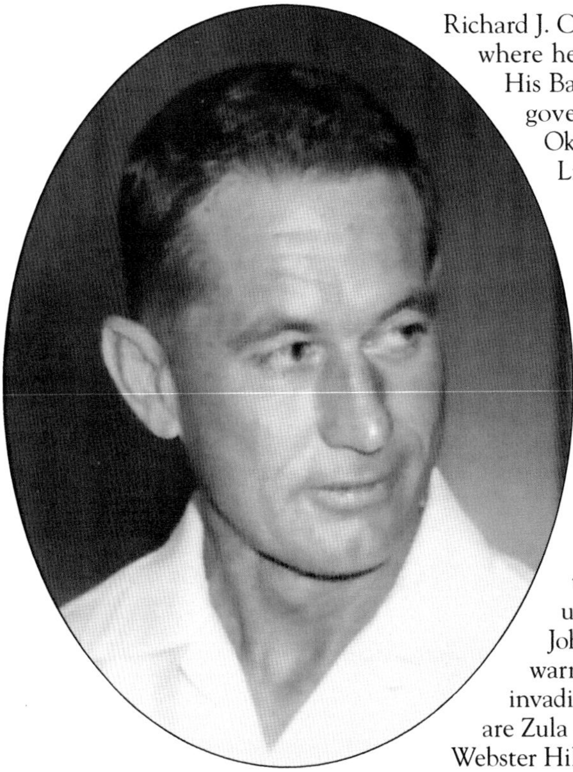

Richard J. Covey came to Gadsden from Oklahoma, where he was the library director in Muskogee. His Bachelor of Science degrees in library and government were from the University of Oklahoma. Later in life, Covey worked for the Library of Congress in Washington, D.C.

An oil painting of John Henry Wisdom, the Paul Revere of north Alabama, was unveiled at the library in September 1957. John Wisdom rode 67 miles from Gadsden to warn the citizens of Rome, Georgia, about the invading Union army. Pictured from left to right are Zula Roper, granddaughter of Wisdom; Henri Webster Hill, the artist; and Richard Covey.

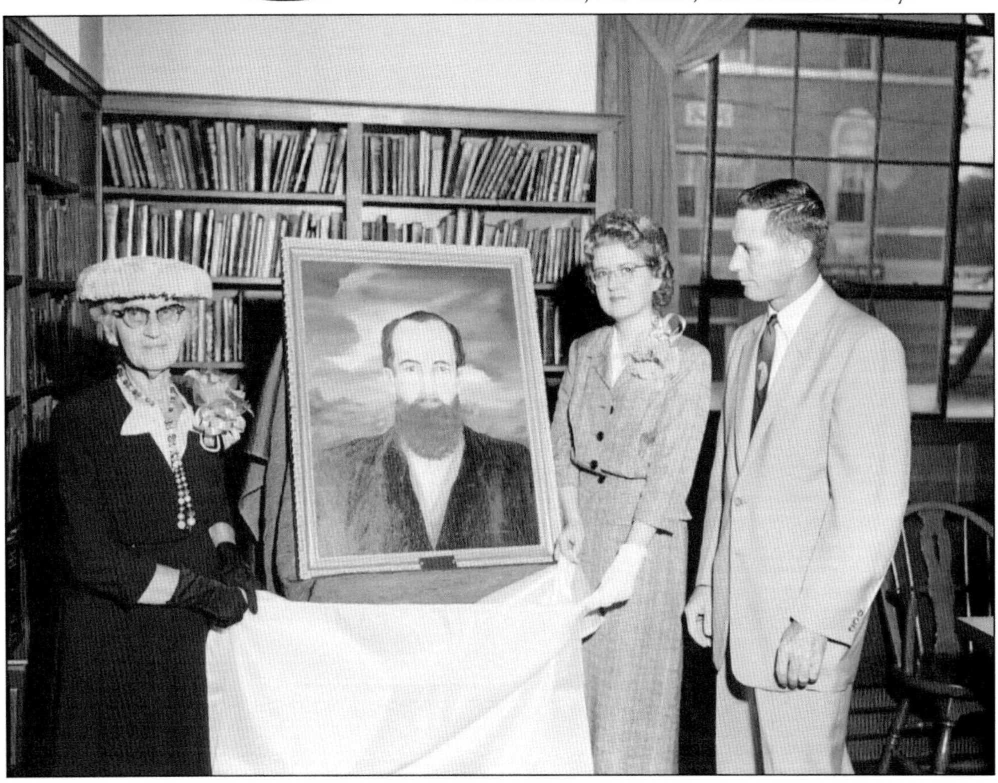

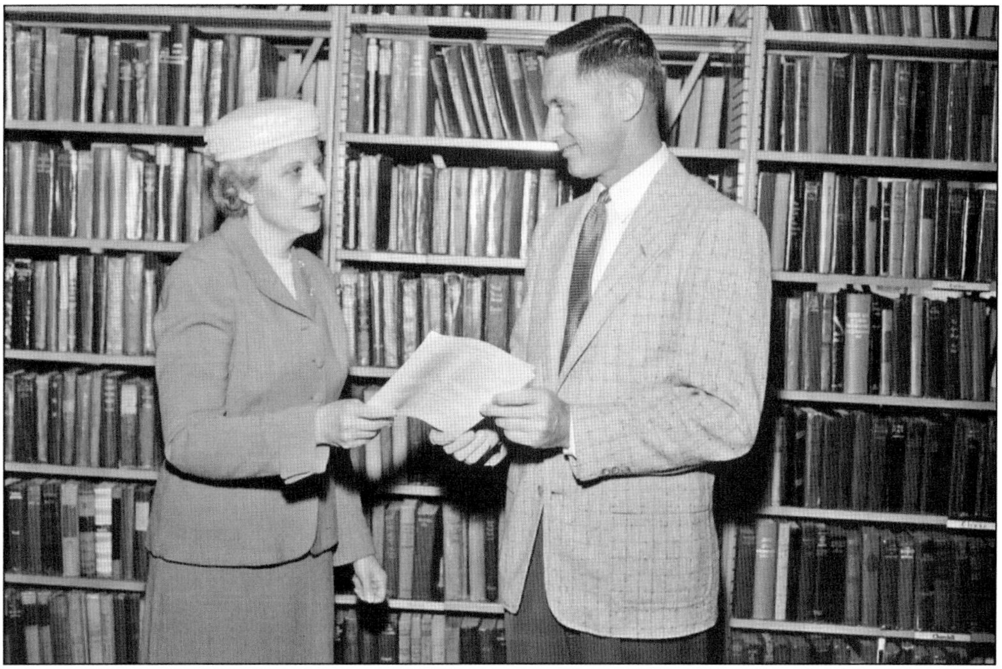

The B'nai B'rith Women's Chapter of Gadsden presented to Gadsden Public Library a vocational guidance kit containing the latest career information. Mrs. Sam Harris, chapter president, made the presentation to Richard Covey in April 1958. The B'nai B'rith Women's Chapter of Gadsden was a part of America's oldest and largest Jewish service organization.

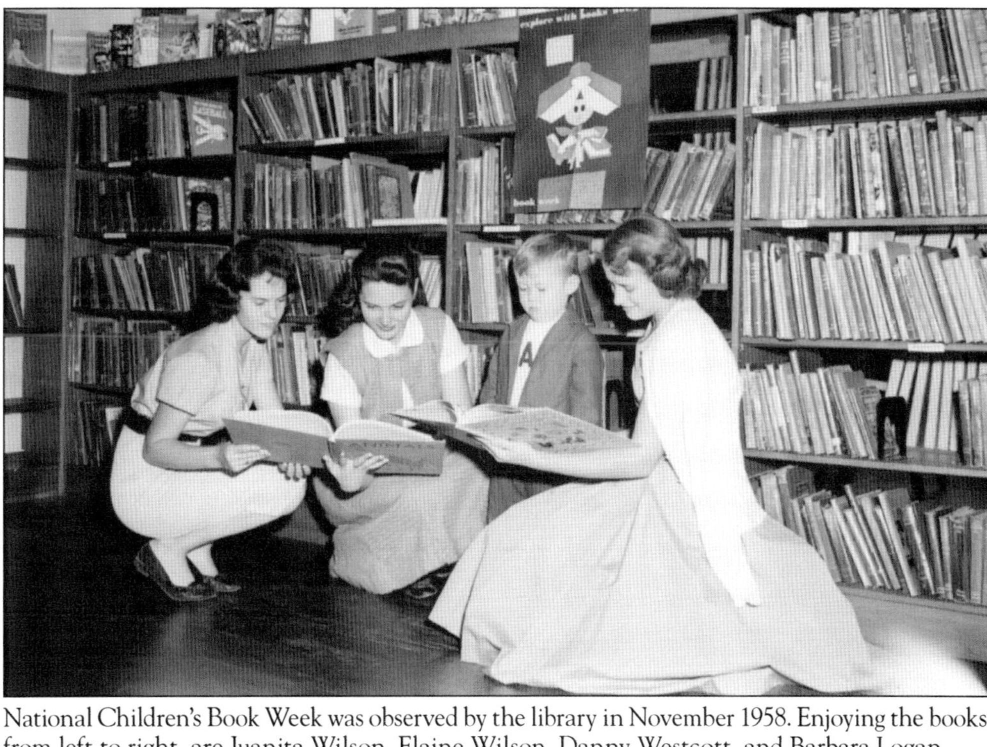

National Children's Book Week was observed by the library in November 1958. Enjoying the books, from left to right, are Juanita Wilson, Elaine Wilson, Danny Westcott, and Barbara Logan.

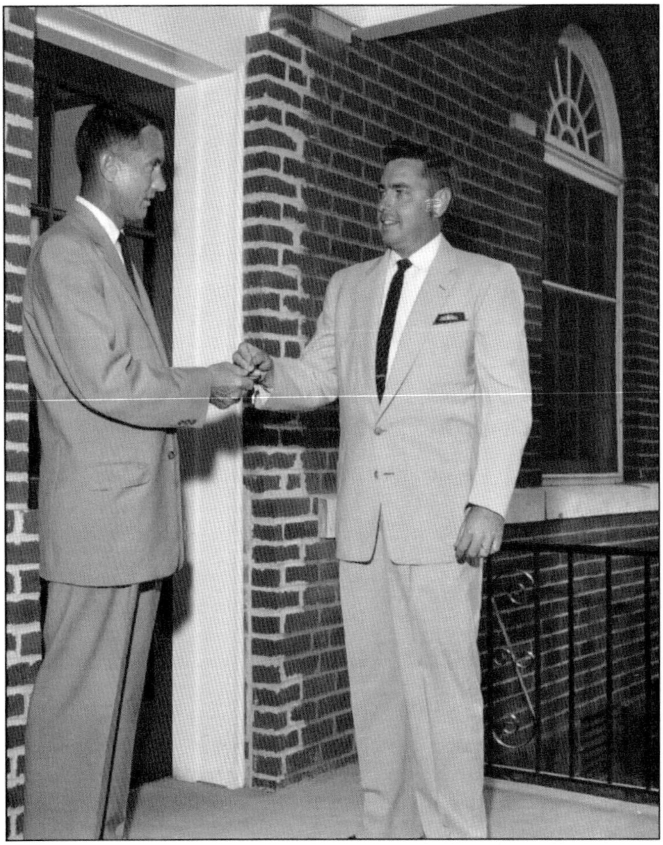

When the Nichols library was converted to a day care for the cotton mill workers during World War II, the books were moved to Gadsden Public Library's nearby Alabama City branch. In this May 18, 1958, photograph, director Richard Covey (left) receives the keys back from the contractor, Rod Cross, after the Alabama City branch was renovated and renamed the Nichols Memorial Library. In 1973, the original Nichols library building was purchased by the Northeast Alabama Genealogical Society with the help of Jerry B. Jones and was restored to its former glory. At that time, the Nichols name was returned, and the Alabama City branch went back to its original name.

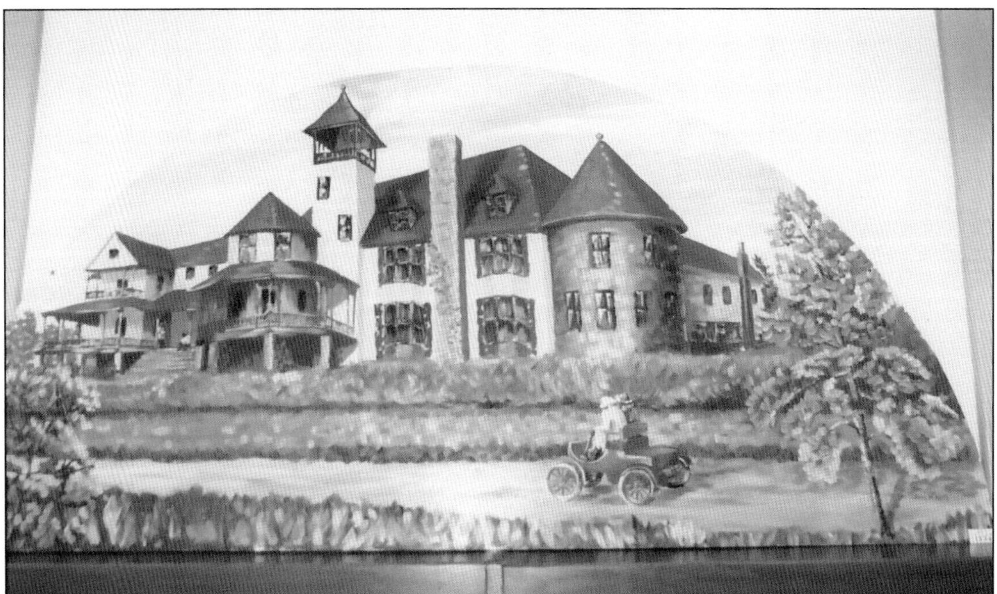

Eight murals depicting scenes in Alabama City were painted by the Noccalula Art League and were donated to the Alabama City Library in 1959. These paintings still decorate the library's walls. Pictured is a close-up of the Mineral Springs Hotel, painted by James Ashley.

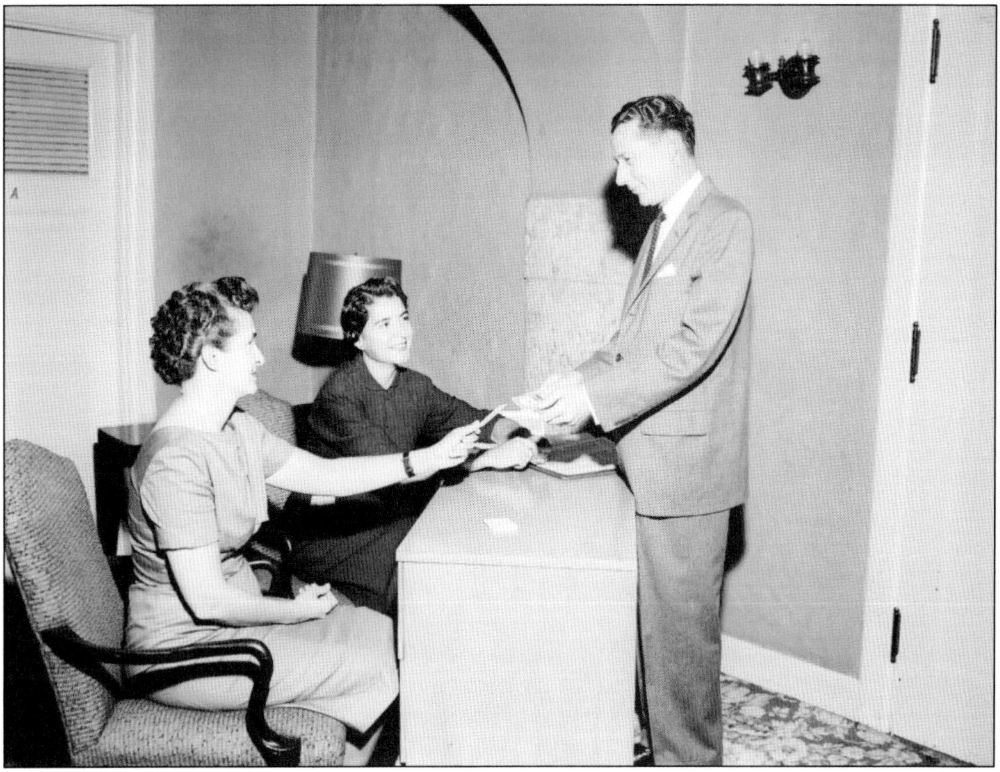

Mrs. George Hawkins (left) and Mrs. Aleck T. Greenwood, members of the Gadsden Woman's Club, are shown in December 1958 as they sell a membership to the Friends of the Library. With the table set up on the mezzanine of Hotel Reich, many bought memberships. Among them was Sidney Wolfe of New Orleans, a guest in the hotel.

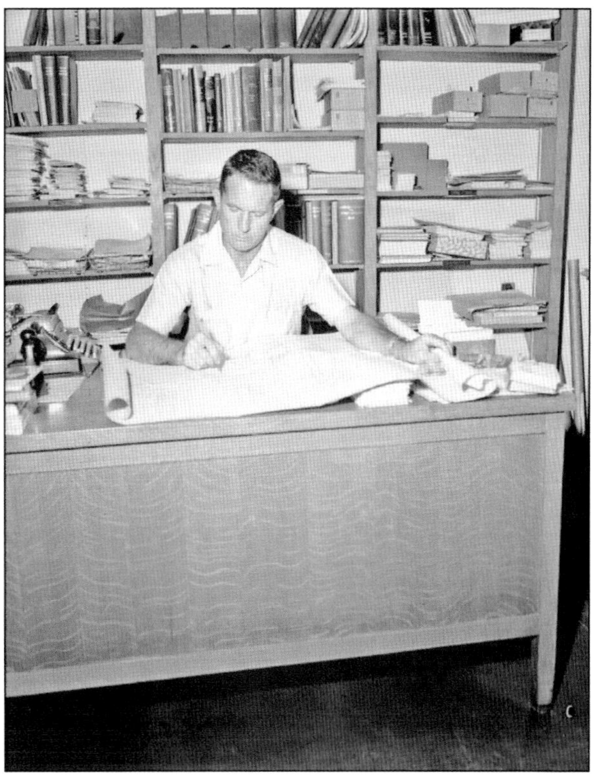

Thoroughly aware of the urgent need for a new library, Richard Covey studies blueprints of other newly constructed libraries. Under Covey's direction, the library saw phenomenal growth, but services were limited by building constraints.

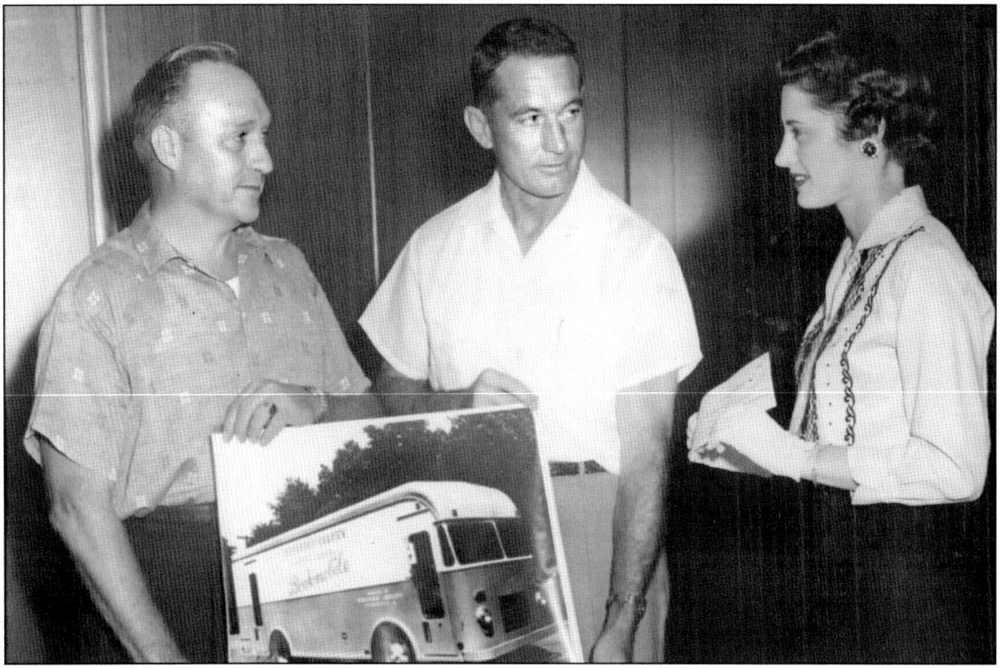

In 1958, the newly organized Friends of the Library began a community-wide effort to raise $15,000 for a bookmobile. Mrs. Wade Fadely, president of the Gadsden Altrusa Club, is shown presenting a check for $200 to Duane Heib (left), president of the Friends, and Richard Covey (center). While the Altrusa Club made the first donation, various groups and organizations planned events to help fund the bookmobile. One such event, called Operation Bookmobile, was a one-hour campaign in which adults and children went through their neighborhoods from 6:00 p.m. to 7:00 p.m., knocking on doors, to request $1 donations.

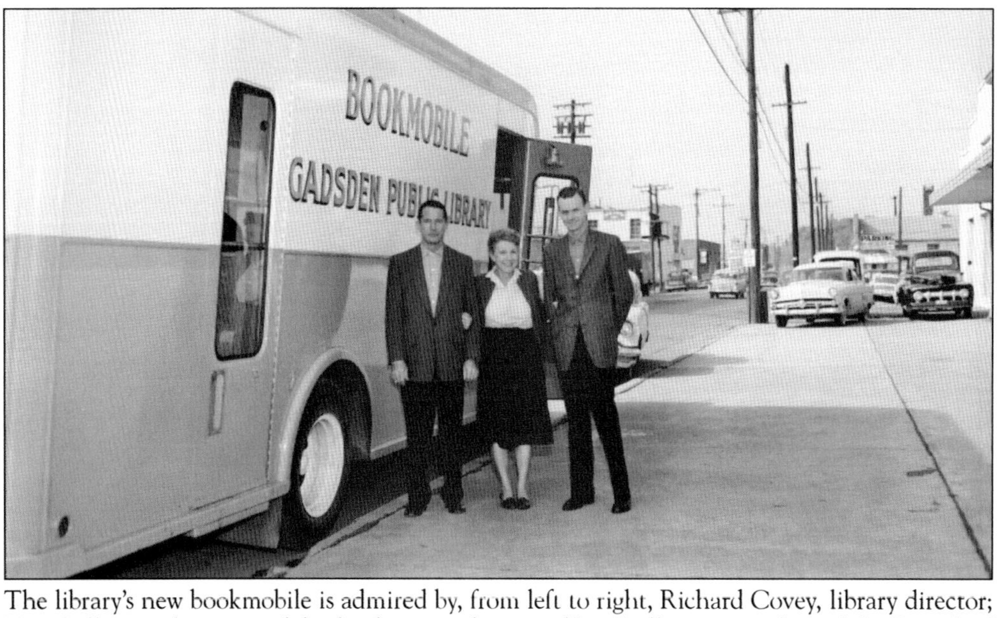

The library's new bookmobile is admired by, from left to right, Richard Covey, library director; Nan Callan, cochairman of the fund-raising drive; and Joe Ezell, vice president of the Friends of the Library. It began rolling into communities in December 1959.

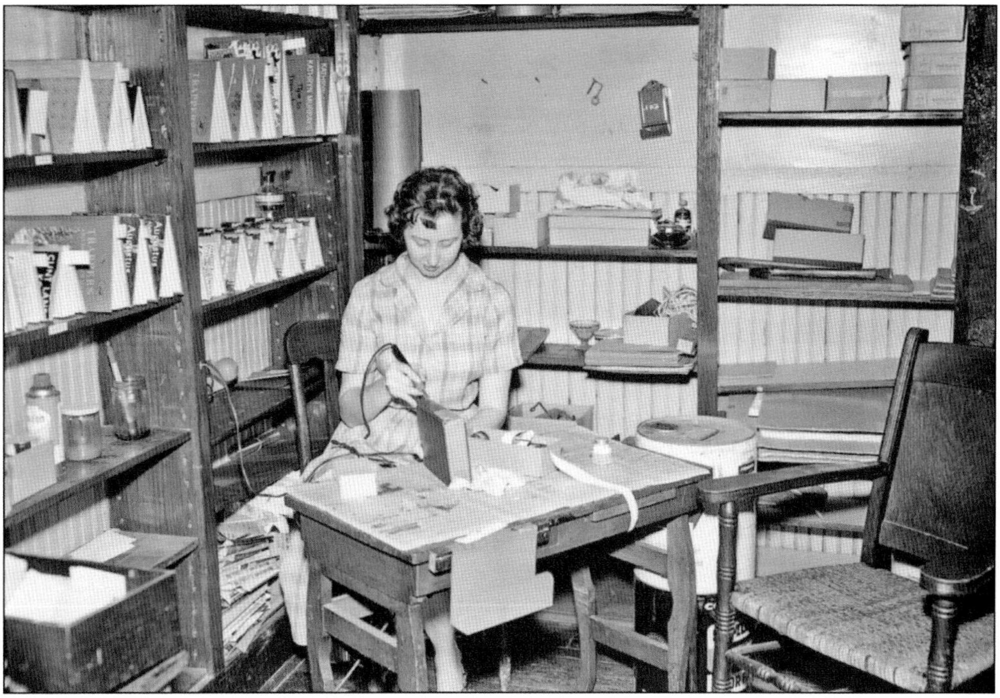

Editorials and letters to the editor began to appear in the local newspaper about the conditions in the old library: story hour attendance was down, and there was no air-conditioning, limited space, very little reading room area, and an absence of closets. The articles increased citizen support for building a new library. Joanna Evans is processing books in an unventilated room with illumination from one naked lightbulb in this 1960s photograph.

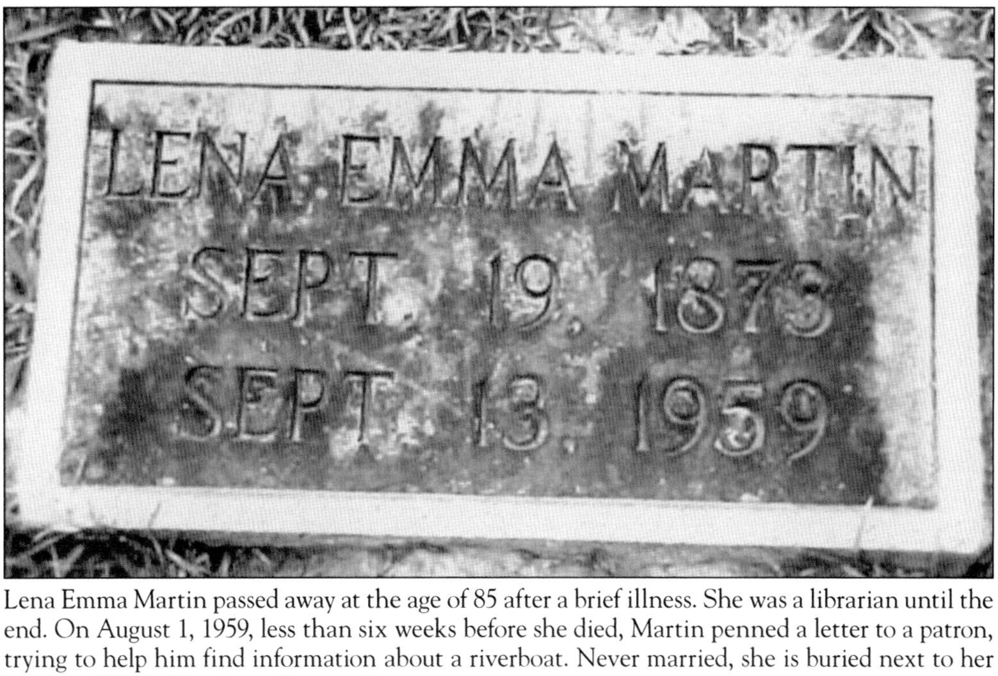

Lena Emma Martin passed away at the age of 85 after a brief illness. She was a librarian until the end. On August 1, 1959, less than six weeks before she died, Martin penned a letter to a patron, trying to help him find information about a riverboat. Never married, she is buried next to her brother, Will I. Martin, at Forrest Cemetery.

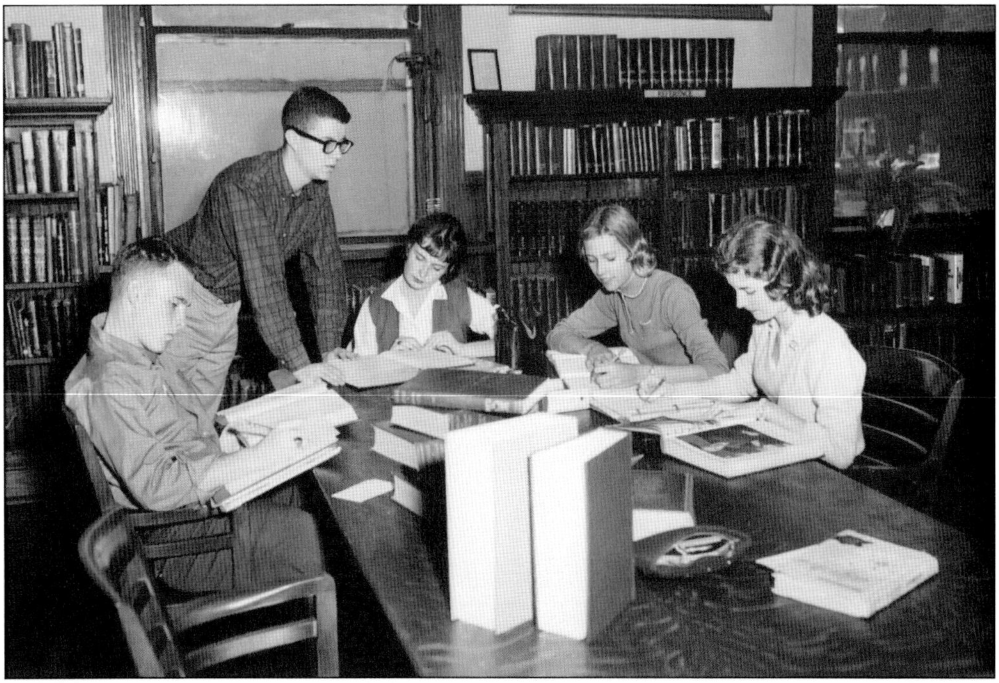

The library was a popular hangout at night for students in the late 1950s because stores and restaurants downtown closed at dark. Seated around the table doing reference work are, from left to right, Ferris Hall, Richard Leach, Martha Blackshear, Judy Parker, and Nancy Ellis.

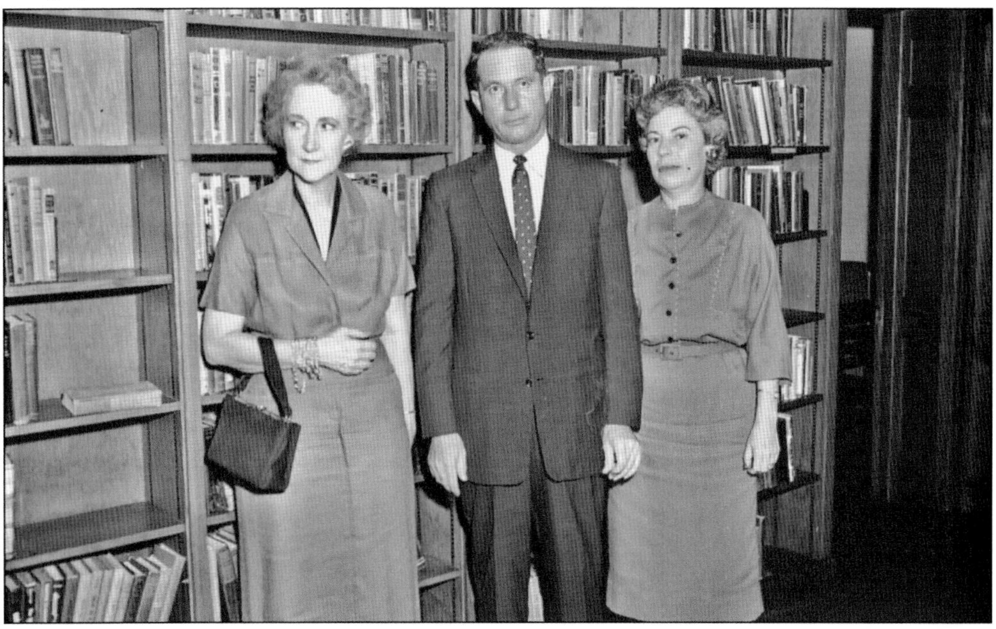

At the close of the September 1960 Friends program, Joe Ezell, president, read a resolution of appreciation for the efficiency of Richard Covey's work as library director and expressed regret at his leaving Gadsden for Huntsville. A gift of a silver tray and refreshment service was presented to Covey and his wife, Helen Covey, pictured with Helen Callan (left), president-elect of the Friends.

Three

CECIL BEACH 1961–1965

Cecil Beach began duties as the new library director in January 1961. In July, just six months after his arrival, a horrific thunderstorm damaged the library. The building was closed, and services were interrupted for 12 days because the interior of the library was flooded. There was discussion about whether the building was too old and damaged to be worth repairing. Inspectors found that no steel had been used in the addition and that the tie-in to the older building was faulty. Options were considered, but it was decided to stay in the current location, even though repairs would continue after the library reopened. By December, the building was rewired, and new fluorescent lights were installed. In 1962, the library acquired its own telephone line (no longer an extension of city hall) and air-conditioning. Beach continued to improve library services. Gadsden's Friends of the Library became the largest, most active group in the state, and a goal of 1,200 was set for membership. Plans for a new building continued with a greater sense of need. Money was raised by the community through various businesses, civic groups, schools, and regular mention by the newspaper in articles and advertisements. A total of $8,188 for furnishings was raised by the Friends of the Library. The new library, built and furnished at a cost of $750,000, was completely paid for when it opened in 1964. In the spring of 1965, Beach resigned to become director of a library community with 14 branches in Tampa, Florida. Circulation at the Gadsden Public Library had quadrupled during his tenure, as had community involvement. Monita Elliott served as temporary director until the fall, when a new director was hired.

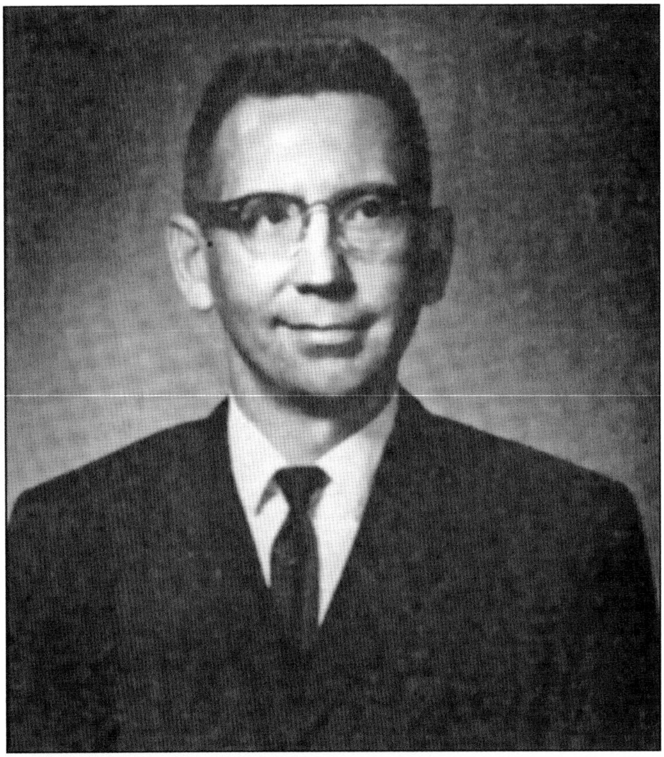

A native of Tennessee, Cecil Beach attended the University of Chattanooga, where he earned his Bachelor of Arts degree. He received his master's degree in library science from Florida State University. Before moving to Gadsden, Beach was the director of the Piedmont Regional Library in Georgia. Later in his career, Beach became the director of the Florida State Library.

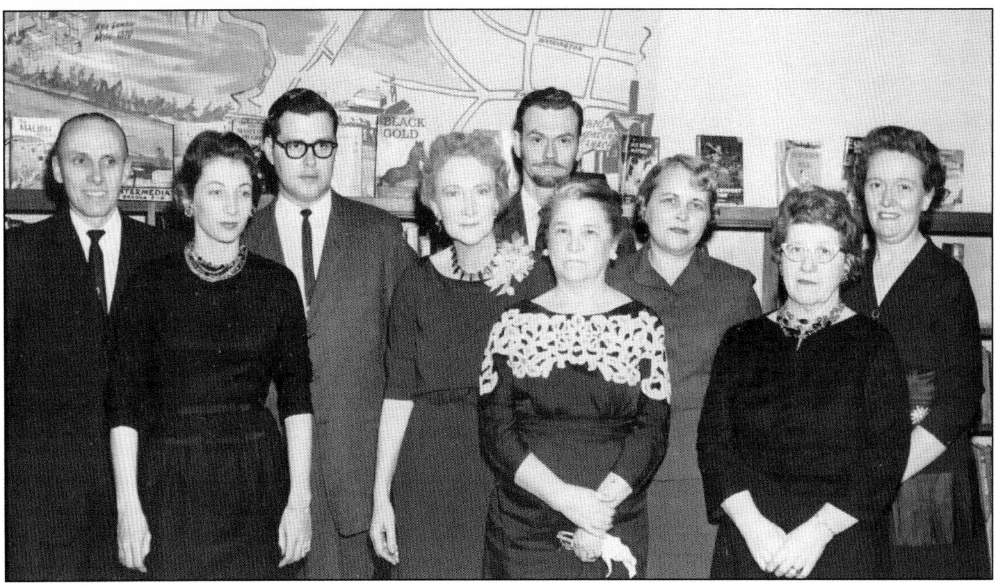

Election of officers took place at the annual meeting of the Friends of the Library on January 31, 1961. Officers and board members, from left to right, were Ed Keil, board member; Jean Cator, corresponding secretary; Rev. T. M. Carroll, first vice president; Helen Callan, president; Joe Ezell, board member; Mrs. L. L. (Irene) Sutherlin, second vice president; Mrs. Earl (Myrtle) Meador, treasurer; Mrs. Charles W. (Lillian) Barrett, parliamentarian; and Mrs. C. E. (Hazel) Oliver, recording secretary. Following the business meeting, a reception was given to honor new library director Cecil Beach.

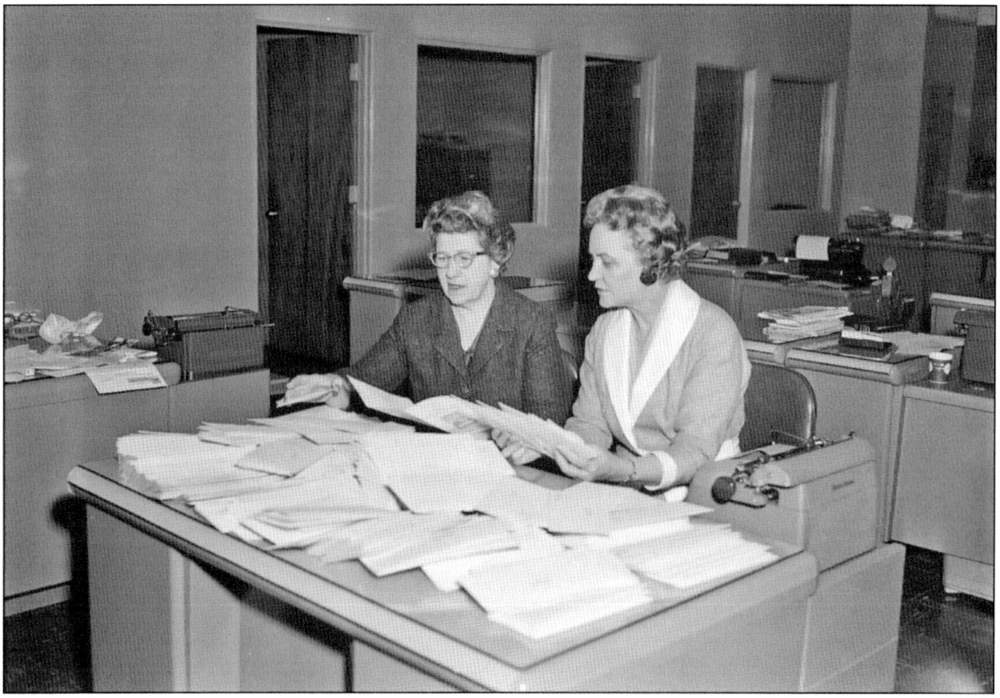

Mrs. Charles W. Barrett, left, and Mrs. R. W. Hicks, cochairmen of the Friends membership drive, are shown as they prepare 650 letters to mail out in April 1961.

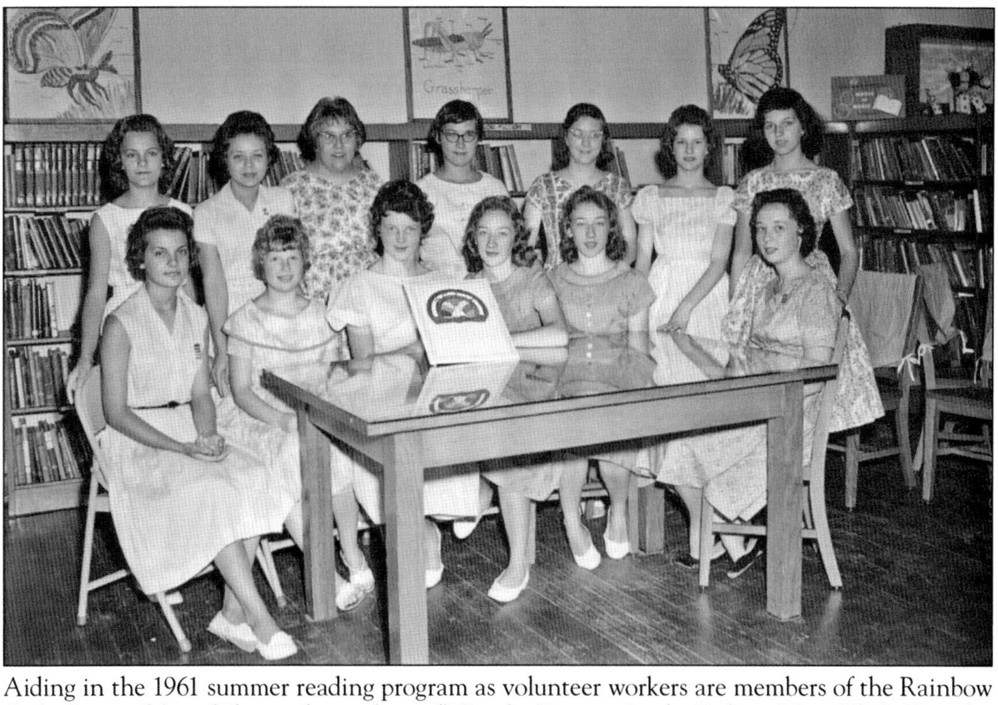

Aiding in the 1961 summer reading program as volunteer workers are members of the Rainbow Girls. Pictured from left to right are (seated) Cecilia Dorsett, Becky Bishop, Mary Clark, Dorothy Bernard, Barbara Barnard, and Evelyn Brannon; (standing) Imelda Dorsett, Kay Taliaferro, Kaye Berry, Barbara Gingras, Margaret Moon, Ginny Bender, and Charlene Vinson.

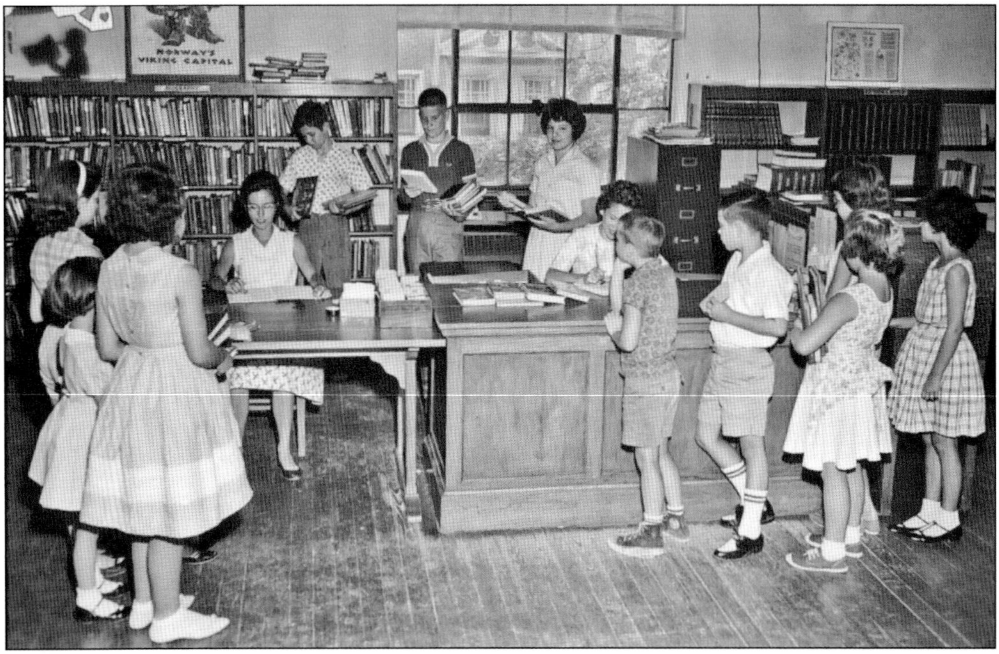

With children checking out as many as 400 books per day during the week of July 2, 1961, library staff members were grateful for student volunteers. From left to right are (checking in books) Michelle Bowers and Betty Hollingsworth; (standing) Ann Flannigan, slipping cards into books; and Buzz Bridges and Joseph Saxon, at the book cart.

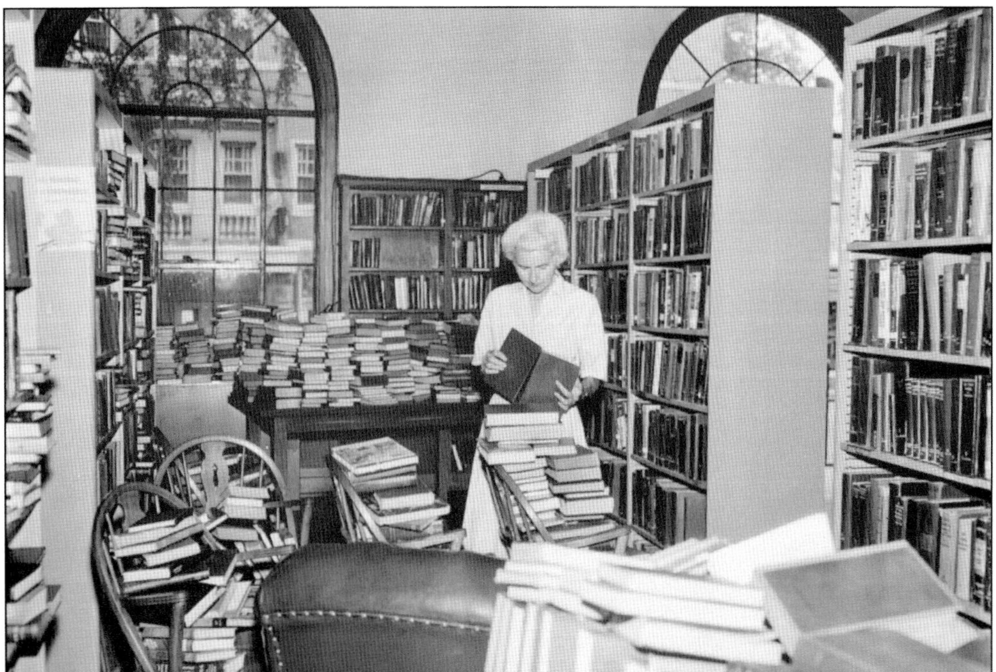

Gaynelle Brewer moves books and assesses damage in the library's children's department after a rainstorm flooded the building on July 13, 1961.

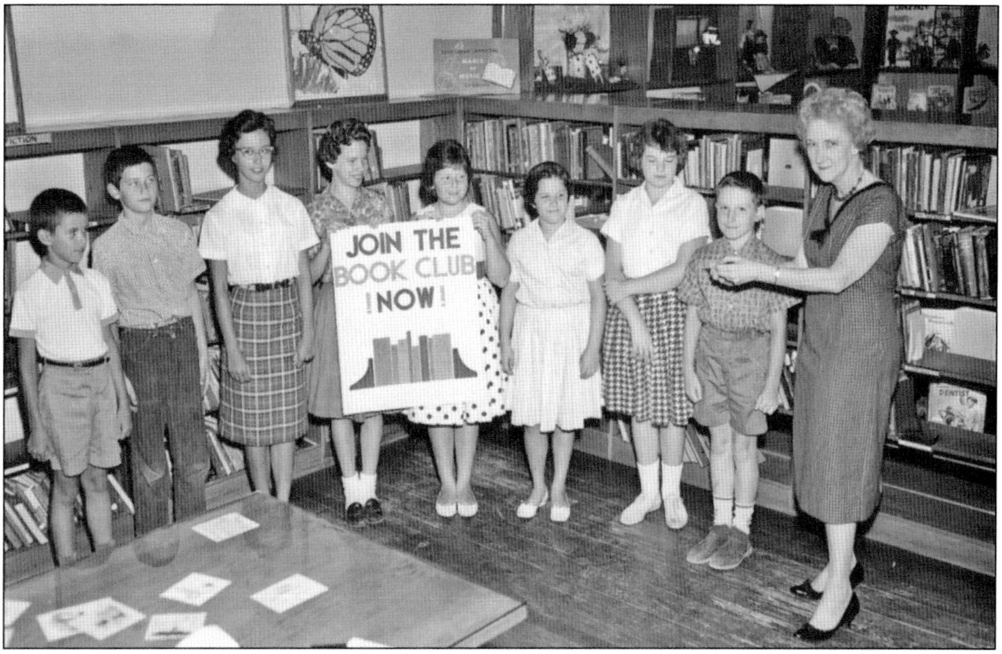

At the end of the 1961 summer reading program, the Friends of the Library gave bronze medals to those who read 12 books from a quality reading list. Friends president Helen Callan (right) is shown presenting medals to (from left to right) Jerry Bowers, Joseph Saxon, Michele Bowers, Betty Hollingsworth, Rosalie Harris, Patsy Flannigan, Ann Flannigan, and George Bowers.

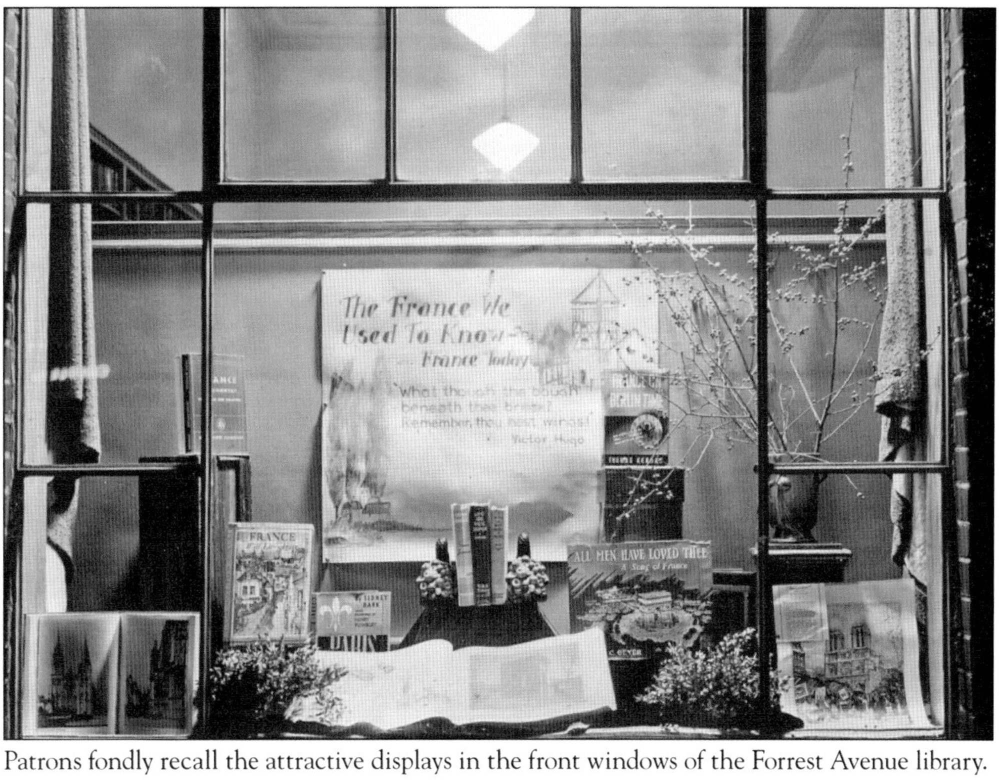

Patrons fondly recall the attractive displays in the front windows of the Forrest Avenue library.

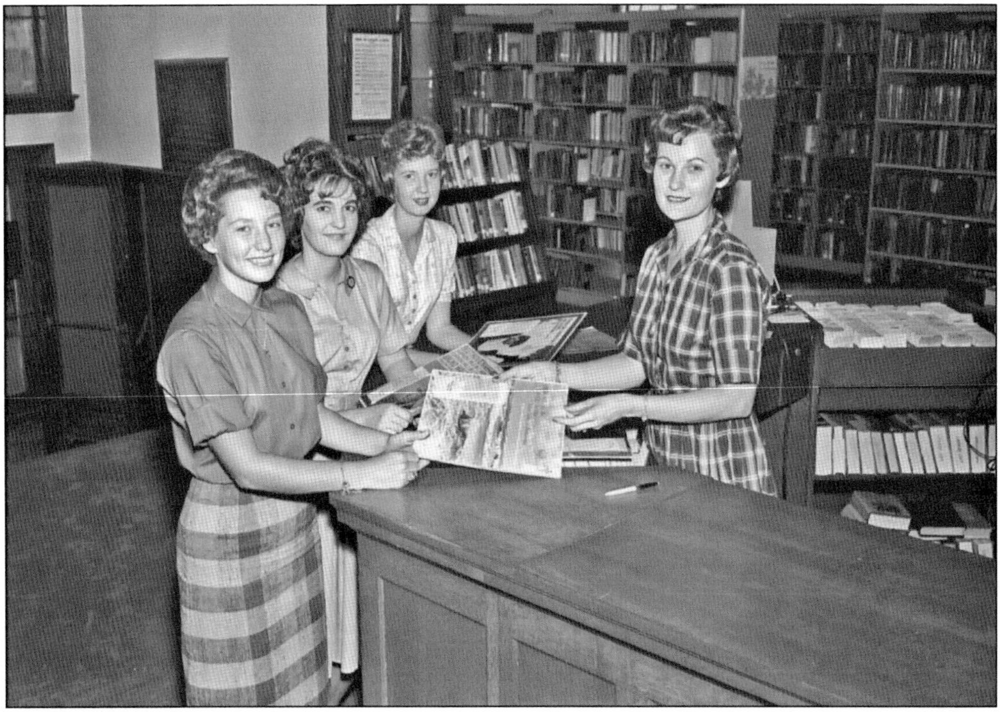

Patricia Martin (right), chairman of the 1961 drive for records for the library, is shown receiving donations of albums from (from left to right) Charlotte Beard, Nancy Floyd, and Judy Cole.

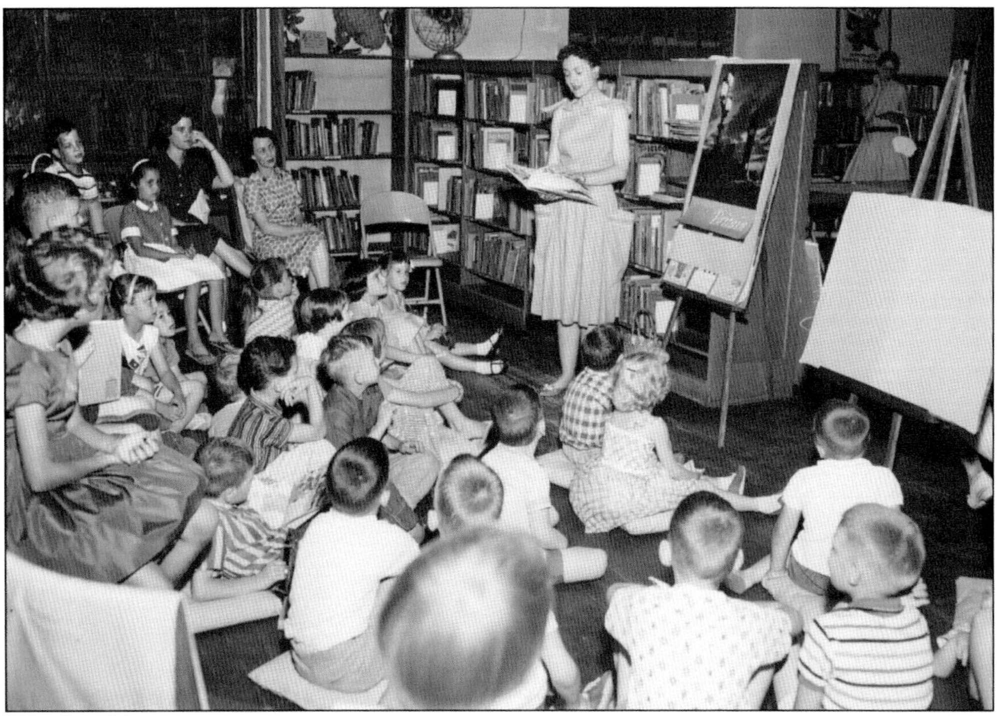

Mrs. W. W. Patterson is shown conducting story hour in June 1961. With her is part of a crowd of 70 children who came to take part in this summer vacation library program.

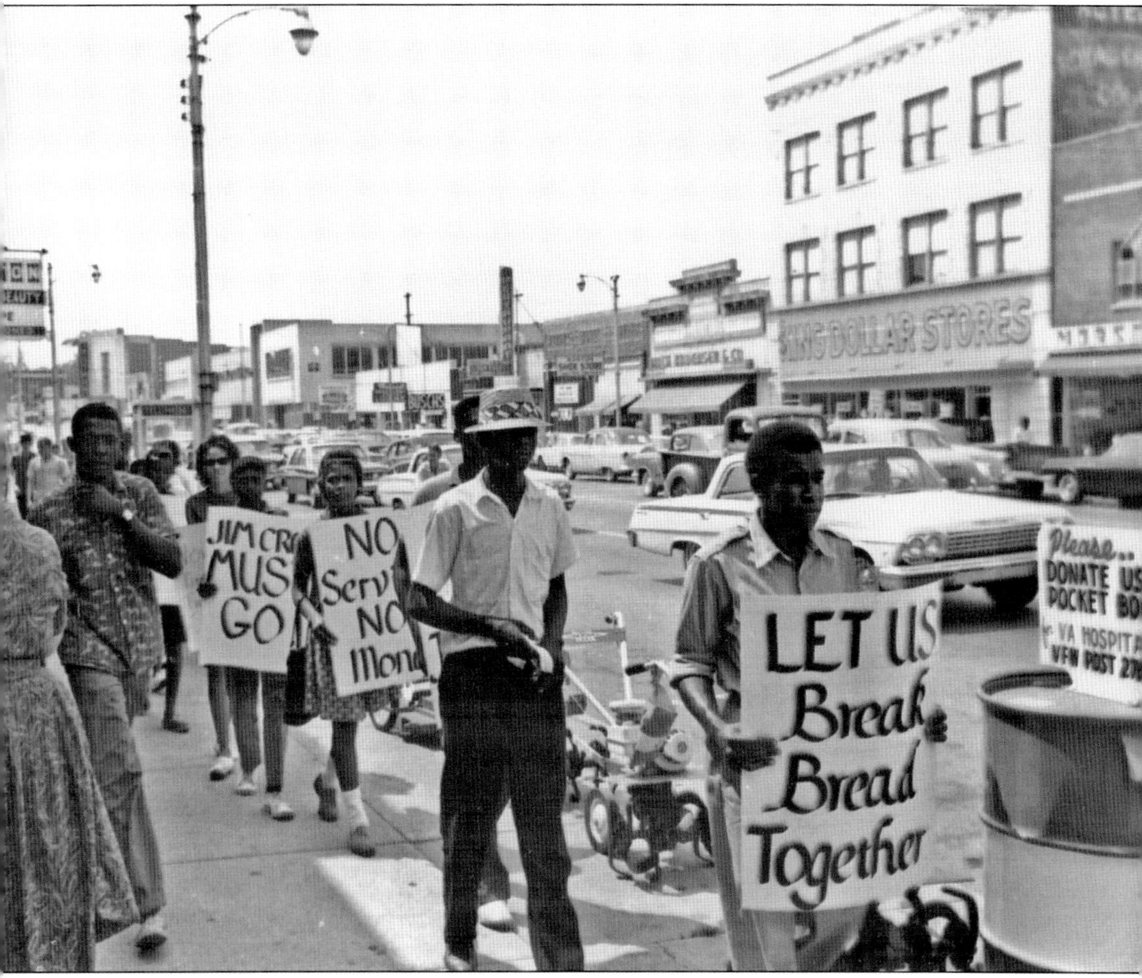

Gadsden went through an uneasy time during the early 1960s, as blacks marched and lined the streets in demonstrations protesting segregation laws. Lena Martin had been a longtime advocate of services to the black community. Blacks had previously been assigned two small reference tables at the library with signs on them reading "colored only." The reference room, which was already crowded, became a point of conflict. Doors in the library were blocked, and blacks lay in the main reading area of the library, protesting segregation. Gadsden's city attorney ruled that the library board could not deny service to blacks, and the library became officially integrated in 1962. The library is barely visible at the far end of the street.

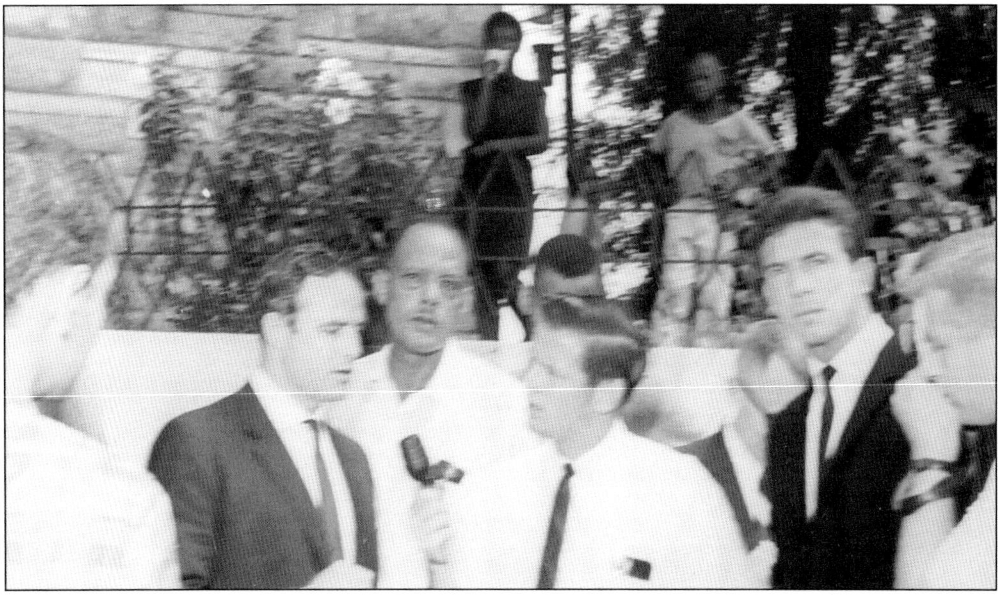

Under the leadership of individuals such as Q. D. Adams, the civil rights movement in Gadsden drew national attention. The Reverend Martin Luther King Jr. made several trips to Gadsden during this time, as did many actors and celebrities. With their support, inequalities in hiring practices and voting irregularities were corrected. Taken in Gadsden in the early 1960s, this photograph shows, from left to right, Marlon Brando, Q. D. Adams, an unidentified reporter, Tony Franciosa, and Paul Newman. (Courtesy of the Q. D. Adams collection.)

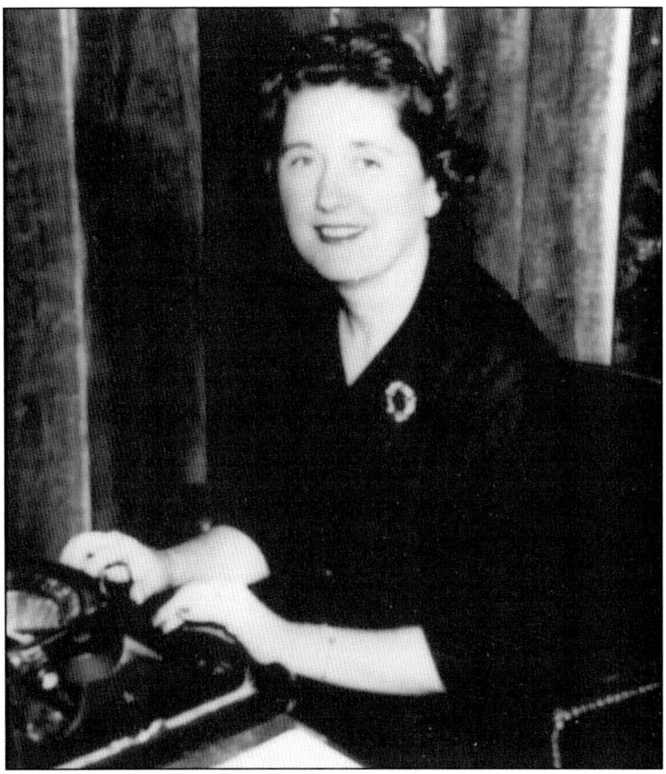

A former Gadsden resident became known as the white martyr of civil rights. Hazel Brannon Smith, born in Alabama City, was a 1930 graduate of Gadsden High School. She was the owner and editor of four weekly newspapers in rural Mississippi. Her editorials focused on unpopular causes, political corruption, and social injustice in Mississippi. After condemning in print the unprovoked July 1954 shooting of a black man by a local sheriff, Smith was ostracized by social peers, and her newspapers were boycotted by advertisers. In 1964, Smith was the first woman to receive the Pulitzer Prize for editorial writing.

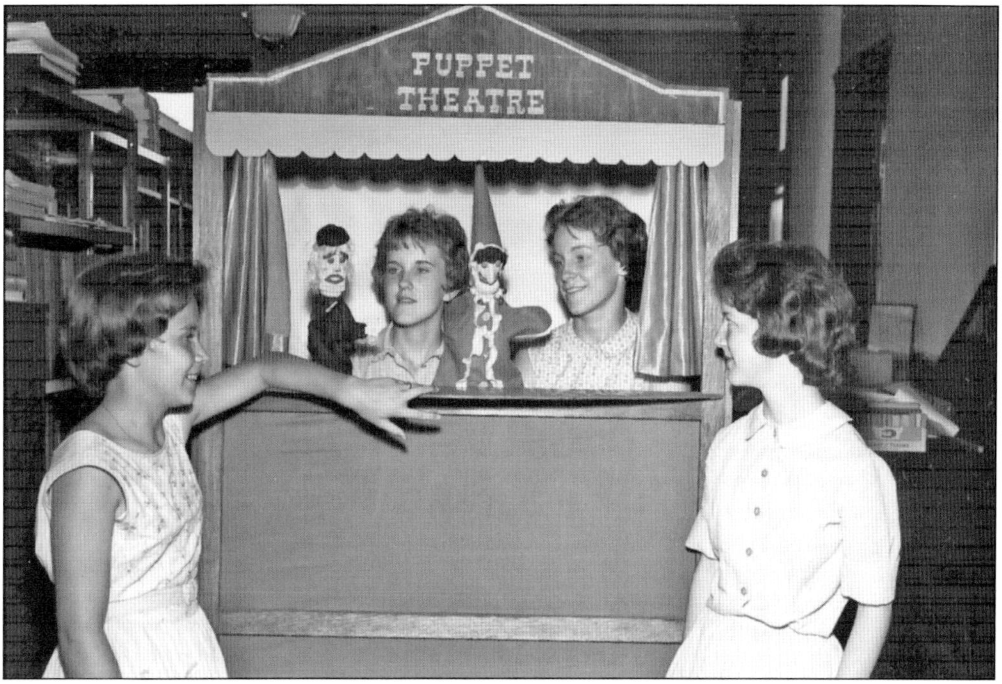

Punch and Judy, the world's most beloved puppet show, was one of the most popular features of the library's 1962 summer program. The young people who enacted the roles were, from left to right, Kay Deavor, Carolyn Allison, Carolyn Deavor, and Stephanie Ellis.

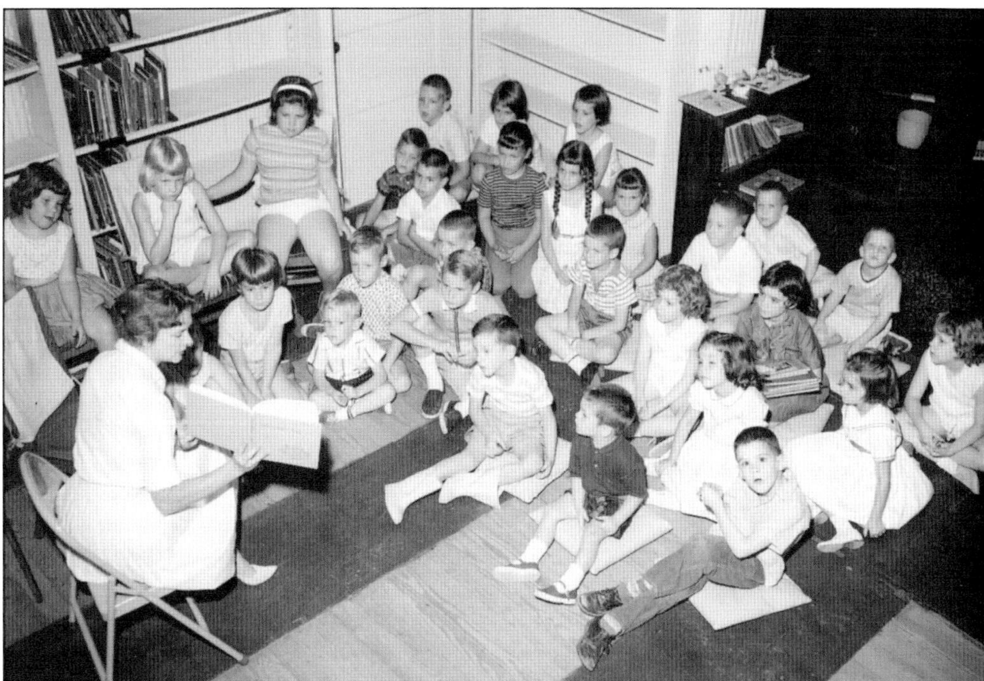

Story hour was a weekly feature of the 1962 summer program for children. Thirty-five children listen to a story read by Mrs. Gary Jordan.

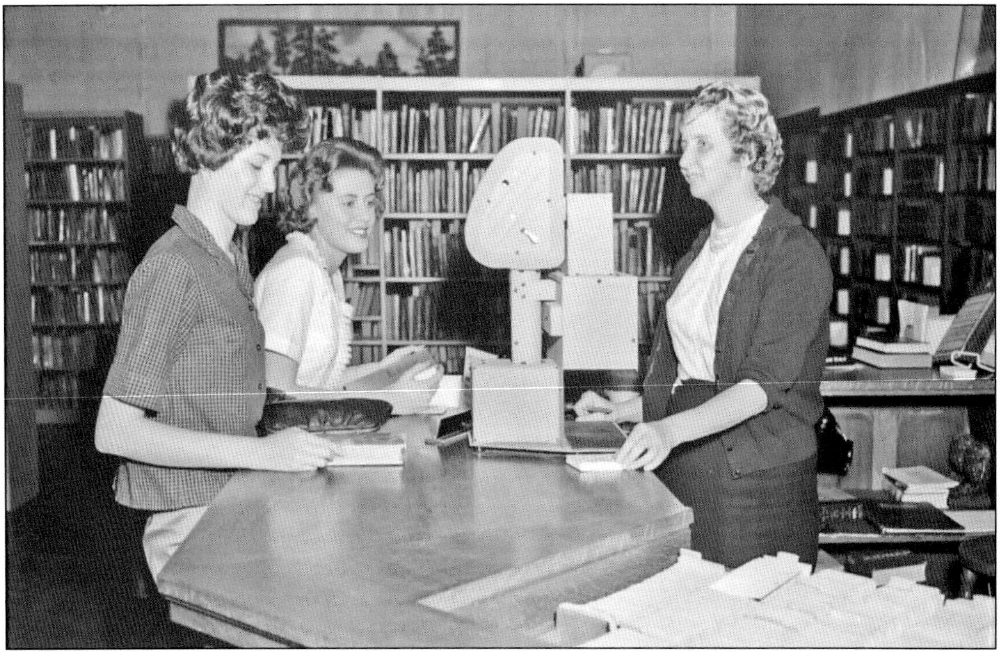

Pat Irwin (left) and Jan Moyer watch Joanna Evans check out their books using a new microfilm charging system. Installed in 1962, the camera took a photograph of the book, date due slip, and the borrower's card as a book was checked out. New patron cards were issued, and books were checked out for 28 days instead of 14.

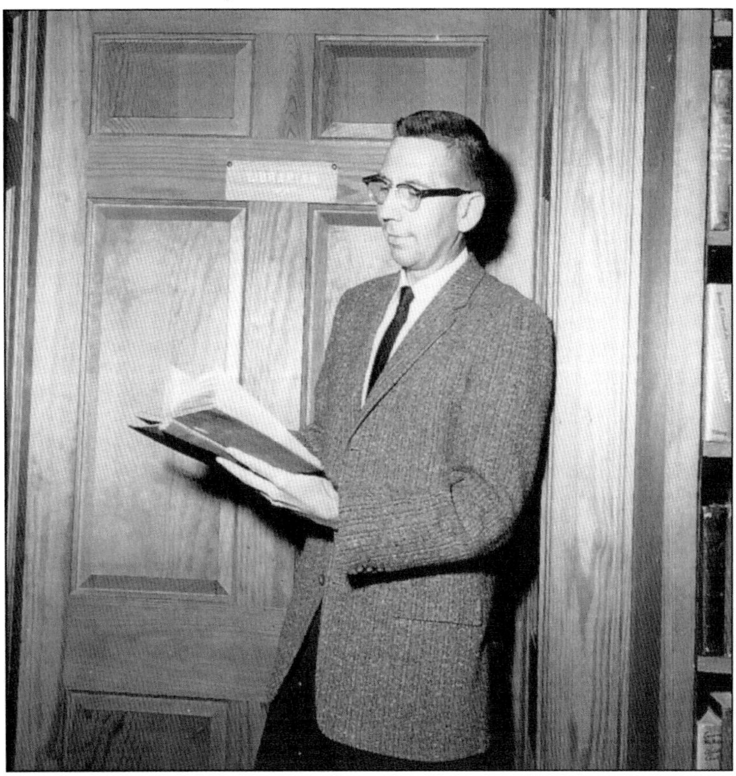

The addition of a drive-up book return on the Seventh Street side of the library resulted in the return of a book that was 40 years overdue. Cecil Beach inspects the book, *Ordeal of Honor*, which was checked out on October 28, 1922, and was returned on October 15, 1962.

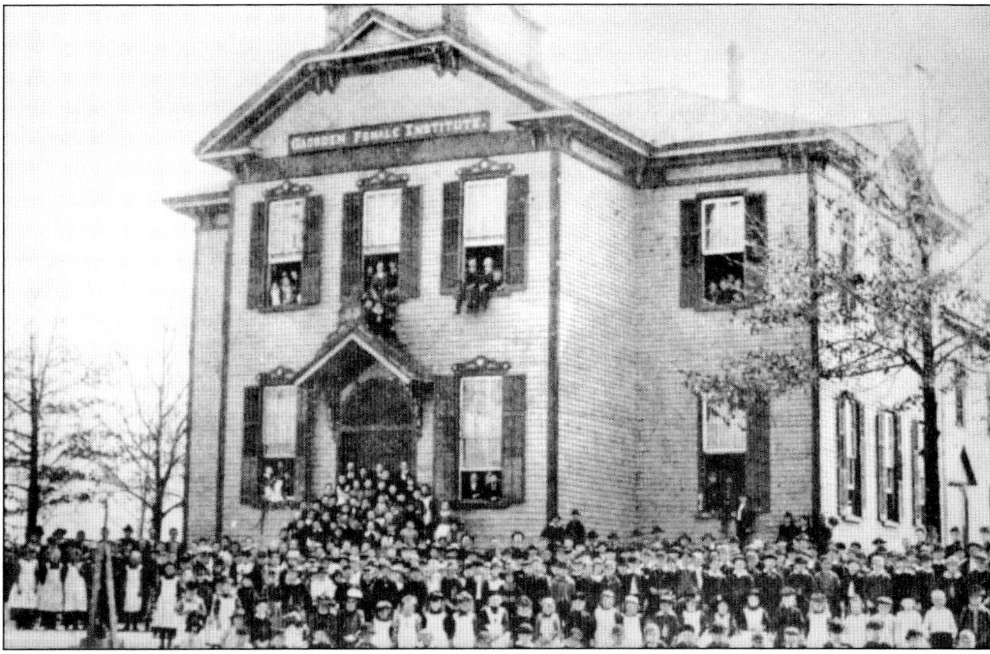

In November 1962, Gadsden was awarded an Accelerated Public Works Grant of $272,000 to match local money for a new library building. Fittingly, the new library would be located at 254 College Street on a site long devoted to learning. Gadsden's first public school, built here in 1880, was known as the Gadsden Public Institute. This school was attended by both boys and girls, including the library's first director, Lena Martin. The name was changed in 1881 to the Gadsden Female Institute. In later years, it was also known as Gadsden Normal School.

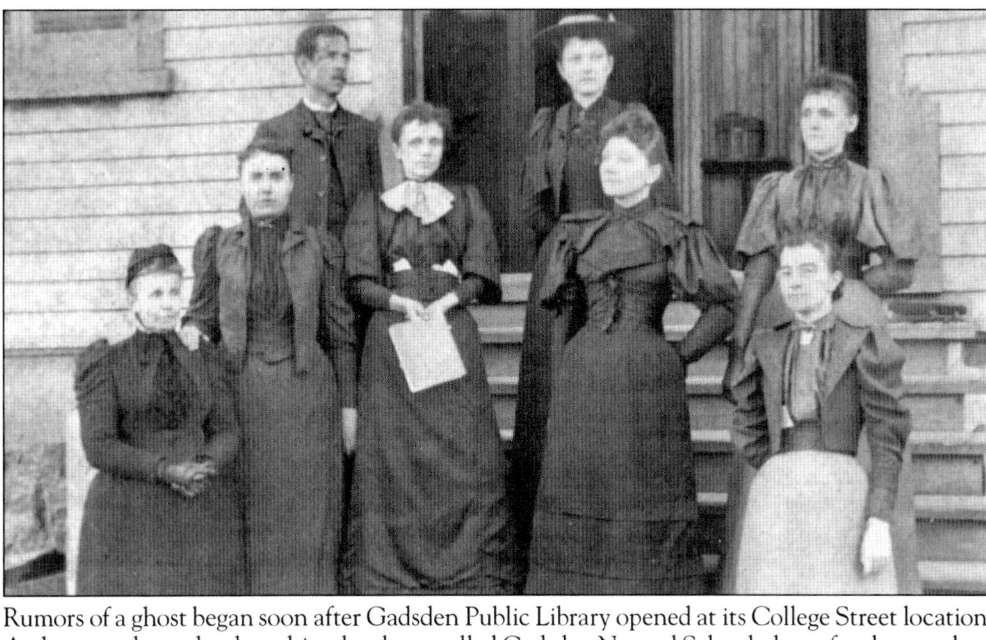

Rumors of a ghost began soon after Gadsden Public Library opened at its College Street location. A photograph, made when this school was called Gadsden Normal School, shows faculty members in front of the building. In 2003, one of these teachers (first row, fourth from left) would be identified as the ghost seen at the library.

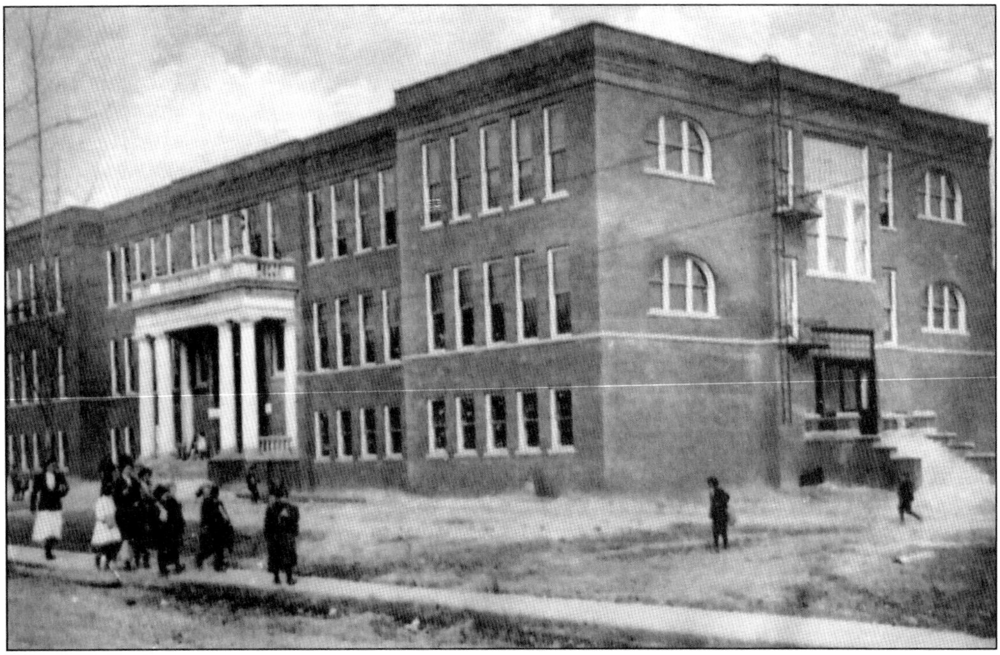

In 1910, Gadsden Normal School was replaced by Striplin School, which served the community at this location until 1962. It was torn down after a newer and more modern structure was built. It was originally known as the College Street School, until the name was changed in 1912 to honor Walter E. Striplin, who had done so much for the public schools and the library in Gadsden.

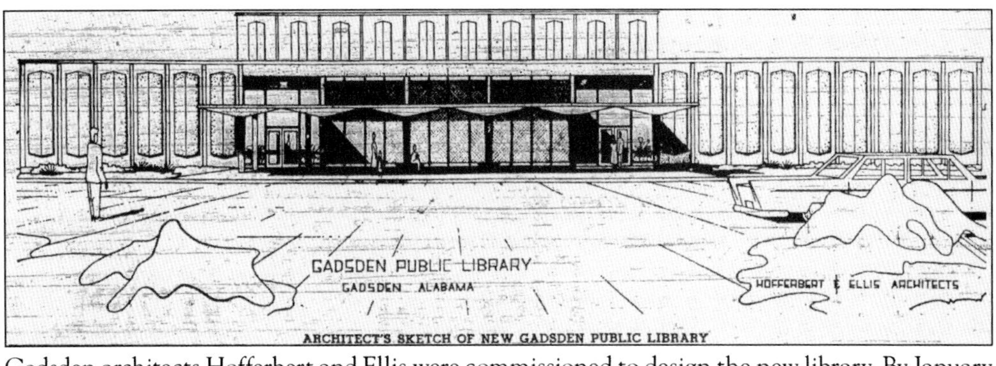

Gadsden architects Hofferbert and Ellis were commissioned to design the new library. By January 1963, architectural plans were approved, and it was determined that the new library would cost $544,000 to build. It was hoped that the sale of the old library property and the government grant would be sufficient to cover expenses. Roberts Brothers was awarded the contract to build the new structure with a base bid of $503,331. Construction of the library took 12 months.

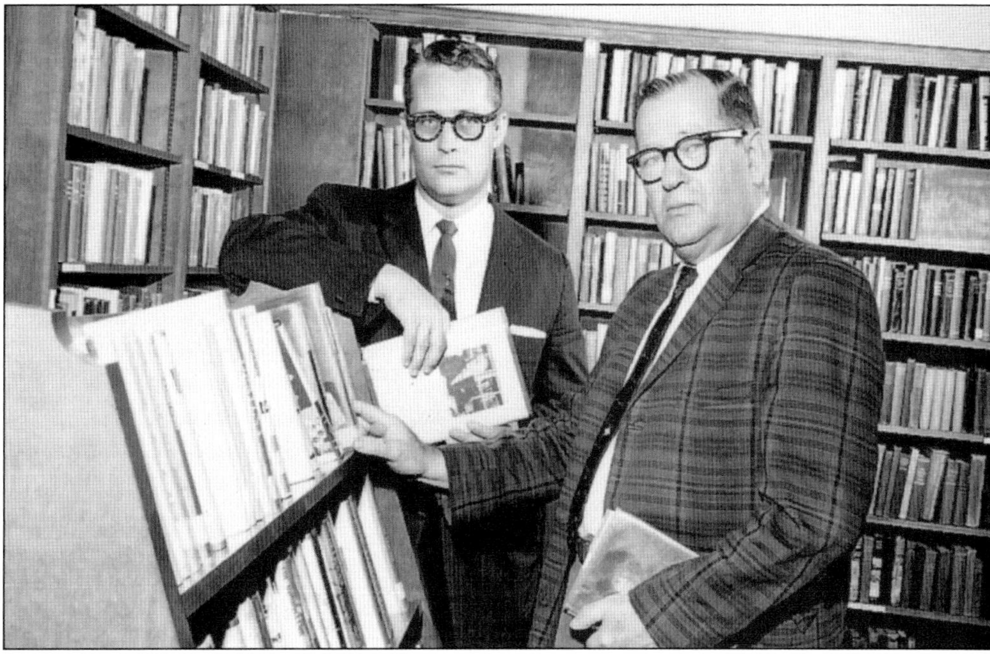

During National Library Week in April 1963, the Friends of the Library conducted its annual membership drive. Friends president Charles Cantrell (left) named Pinky Koss as chairman of the membership drive. With a membership of 500, the goal was to add 1,000 new members to the organization.

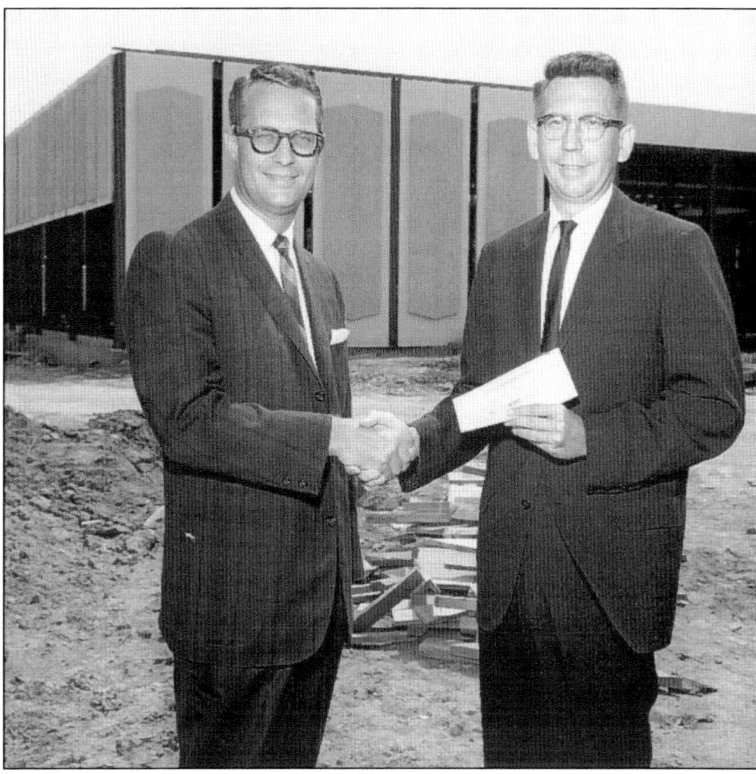

Cecil Beach (right) is shown receiving a check for $500 from Charles Cantrell, executive vice president of the East Gadsden Bank, toward the purchase of office furniture for the new library.

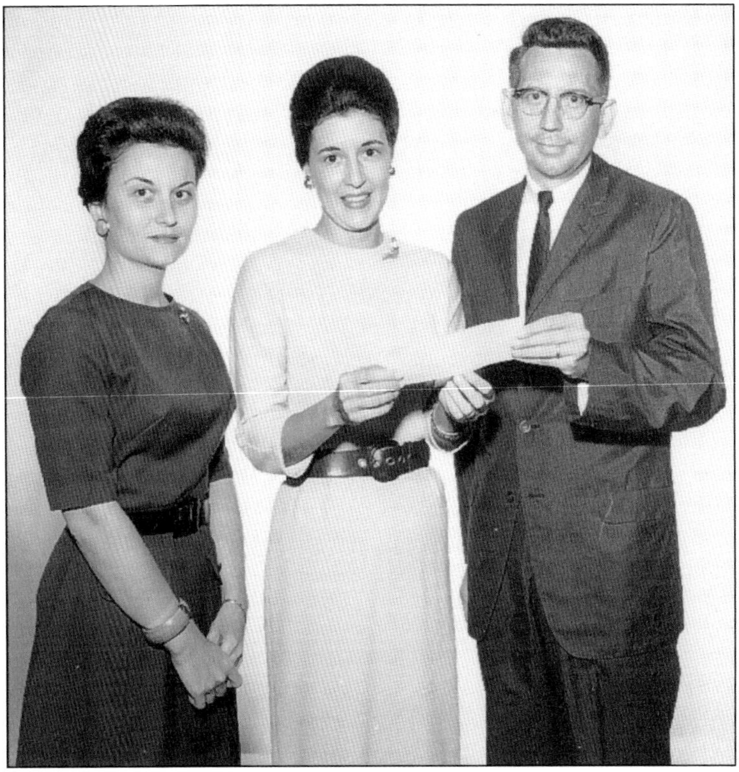

Gadsden Service Guild contributed $175 toward furnishings for the new library. Cecil Beach accepts the check from Mrs. Yates Dellinger (center), Service Guild president. With them is Mrs. Jack Torbert, Service Guild vice president.

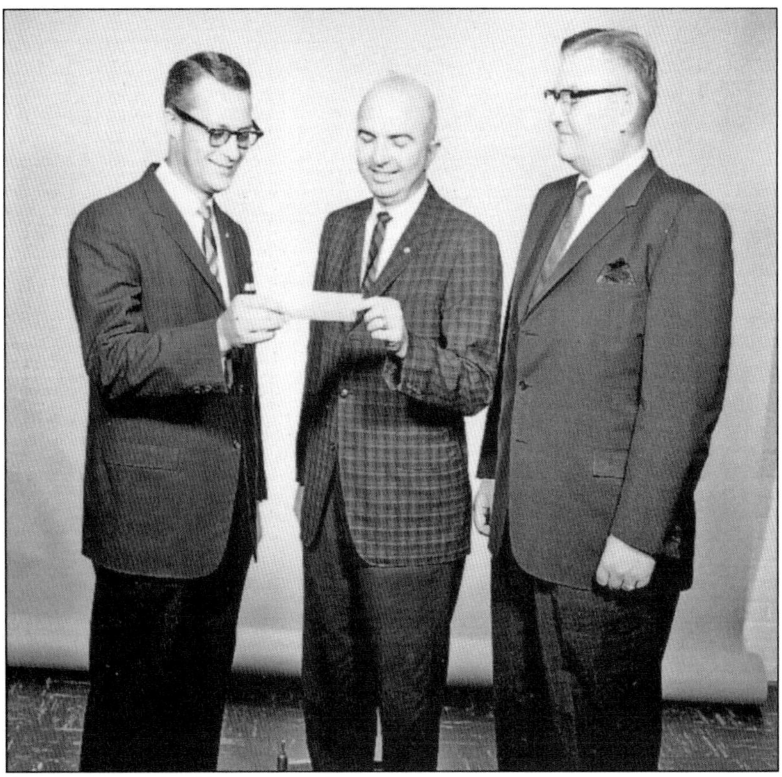

Charles Cantrell (left), president of Friends of the Library, accepts a check for $300 from the Gadsden Kiwanis Club for library furnishings. George Barnett, Kiwanis president, makes the presentation, as Kiwanian Glenwood Pierson looks on.

W. O. Briscoe (left), member of Friends of the Library committee on furnishings, receives a $300 check from the Alabama City Civitan Club, presented by club president E. C. Wheeler.

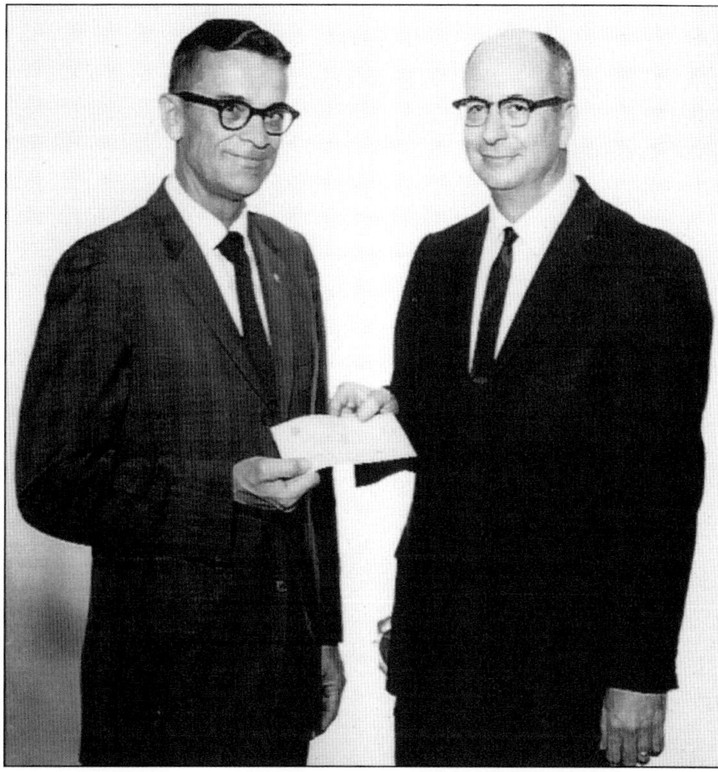

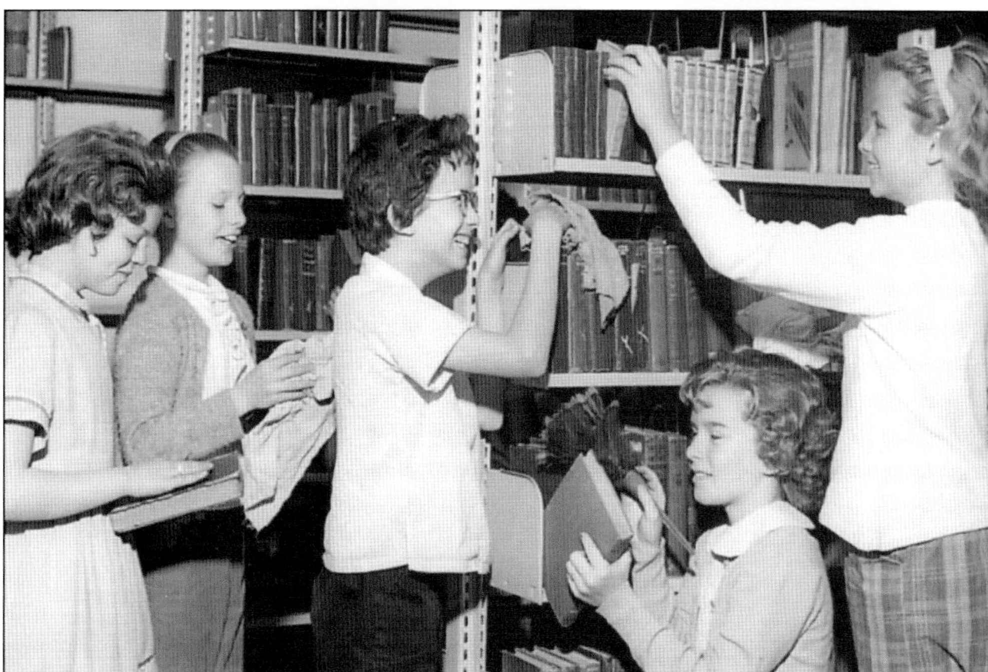

Girl Scout Troop 626 dusts shelves during preparations for the opening of the new library. From left to right, they are Laurinda Christian, Susan Gann, Jenny McClendon, Lannis Gazaway, and Betty Blythe.

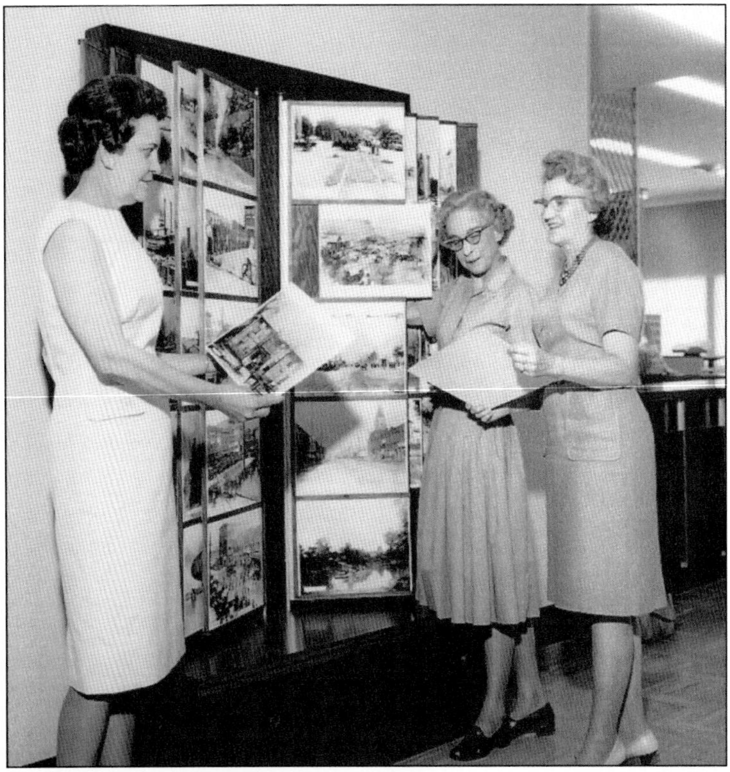

In April 1964, the Altrusa Club donated to the library a $350 custom-made multiplex cabinet, designed to display 100 large photographs. Working on the display are, from left to right, Ruth Hicks, Ramona Scarboro, and Iva Bugg. Old prints of Gadsden were collected, rephotographed, and restored by Scarboro. Due to the intensity of the response to the pictures, additional cabinets were purchased and remain a major attraction at the library.

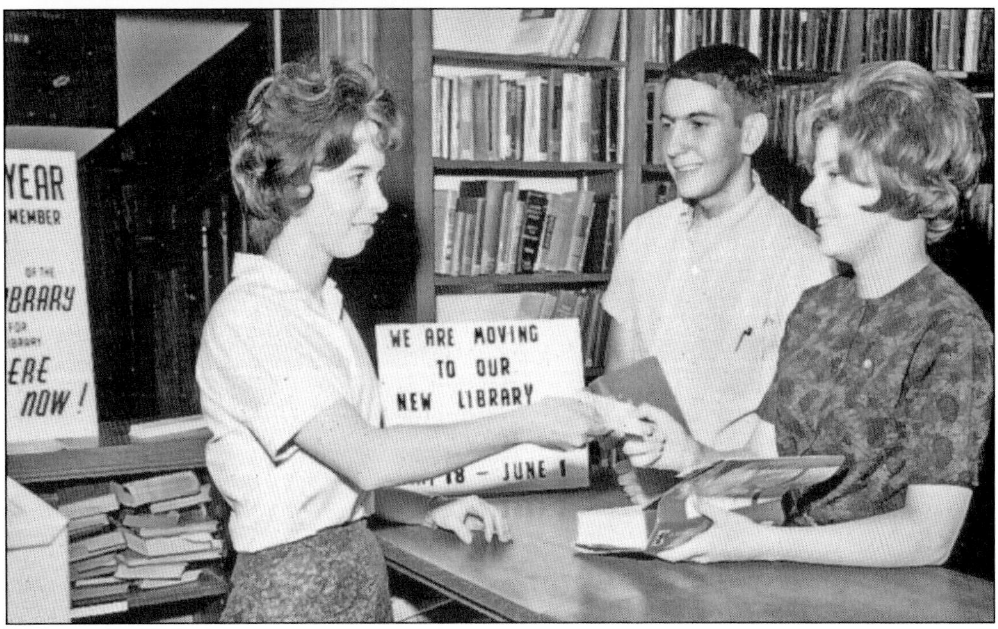

On May 16, 1964, the library on Forrest Avenue closed forever. *Gadsden Times* photographer Robert Moore took a picture of Gadsden High School students Dee Dee Ellis and Steve Means checking out the last books from Frieda Jones. Means would later become mayor of Gadsden and would be instrumental in procuring funds for the renovation of the College Street library in 2004. The old library was sold and demolished in 1967.

Volunteers helped move 50,000 books in alphabetical order two blocks from the old library on Forrest Avenue to the new building on College Street—in shopping carts! These Emma Sansom High School students, from left to right, are James Hill, Vernon Wise, and Ronnie Leftwich. Although not pictured here, Bobby Junkins, who later became the library director, recalls assisting in this task as a student volunteer.

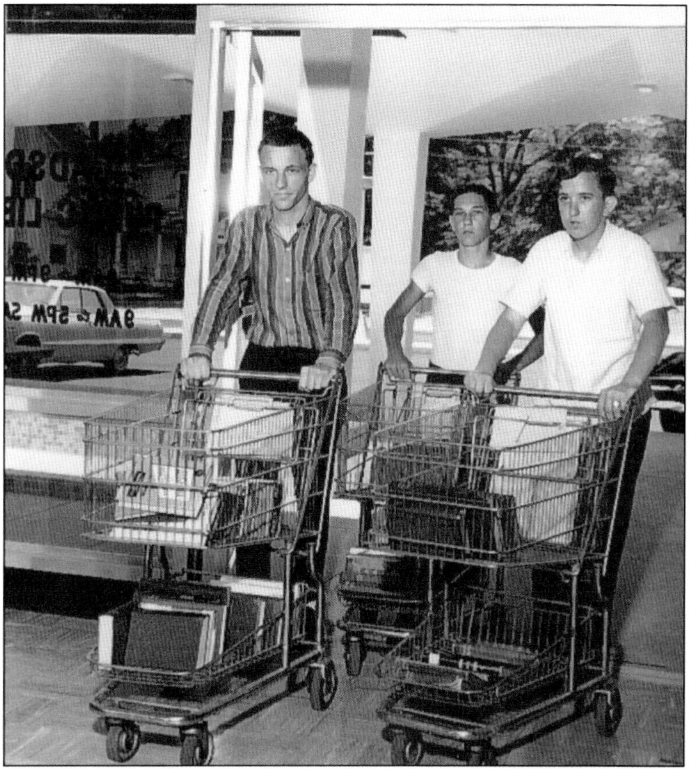

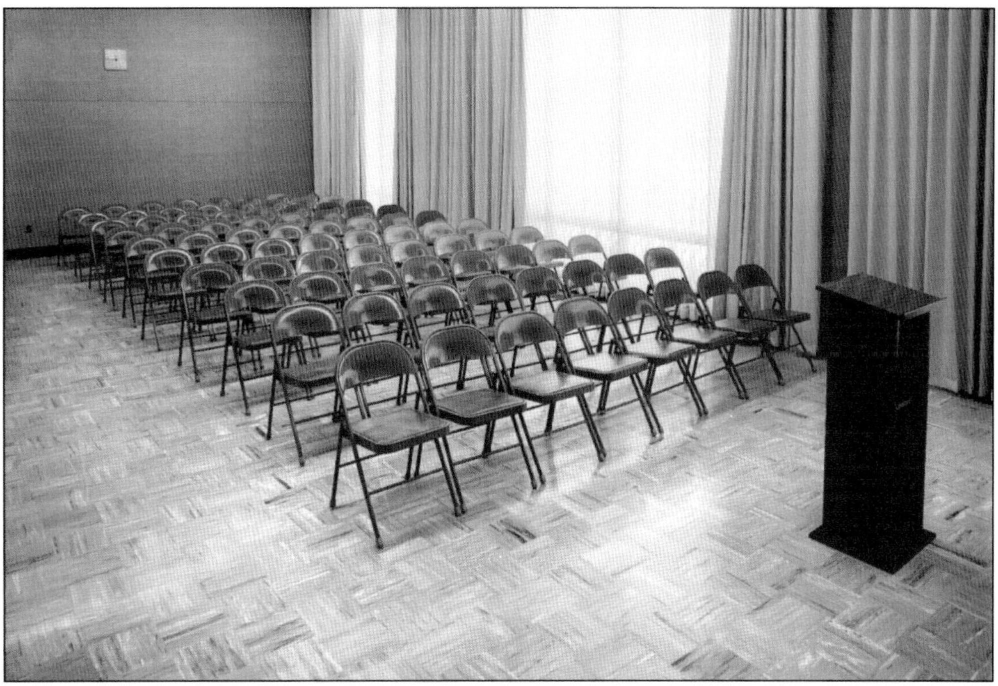

The lecture room, pictured here, was furnished and dedicated to Lena Martin by the Thursday Study Club. On June 1, 1964, Mrs. J. O. Finney Sr., who was chairman of the fund drive, wrote a check to the library for $1,750.

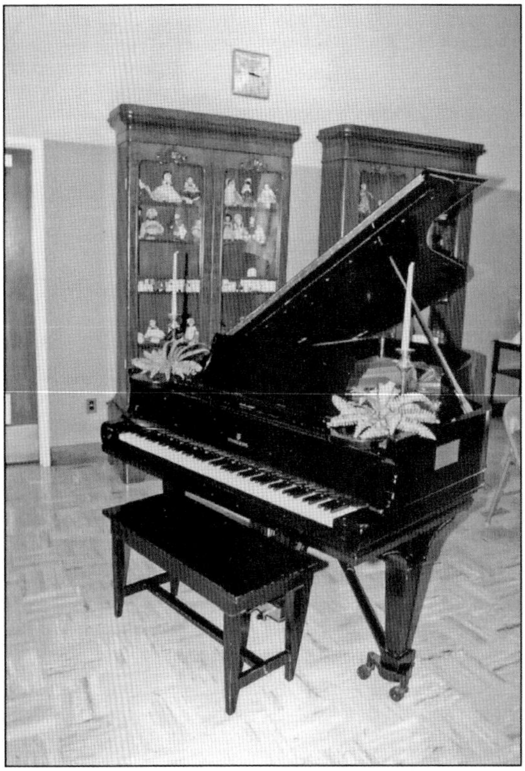

Civic leaders and the Friends of the Library raised a total of $1,700 to purchase a Steinway grand piano for the library from the Finney family. Scrupulously cared for by its musician owners, the magnificent instrument had been recently rebuilt and refinished. Considered one of Gadsden's finest grand pianos, many organizations recognized that it would be a cultural asset for Gadsden. It is still regularly used and tuned. Participating in the fund drive were the Altrusa Club, Gadsden Civic Theatre, Gadsden Music Club, Gadsden Woman's Club, and the Music Teachers Association.

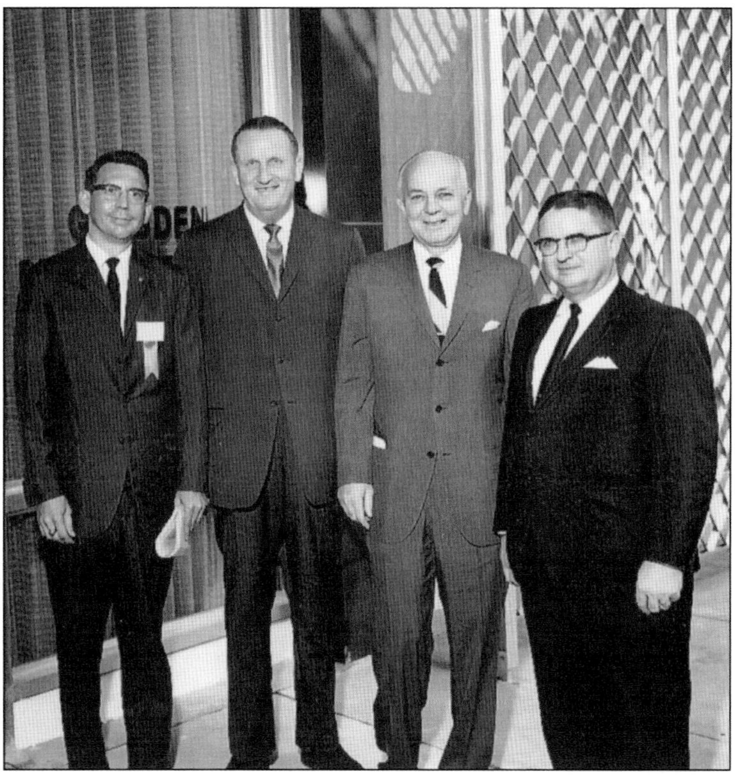

Dedication of the new library was held on June 28, 1964. Featured speakers were, from left to right, Cecil Beach, Lt. Gov. James Allen, Congressman Albert Rains, and Mayor Lesley Gilliland. Rains was instrumental in Gadsden Public Library being designated as a federal depository for government documents.

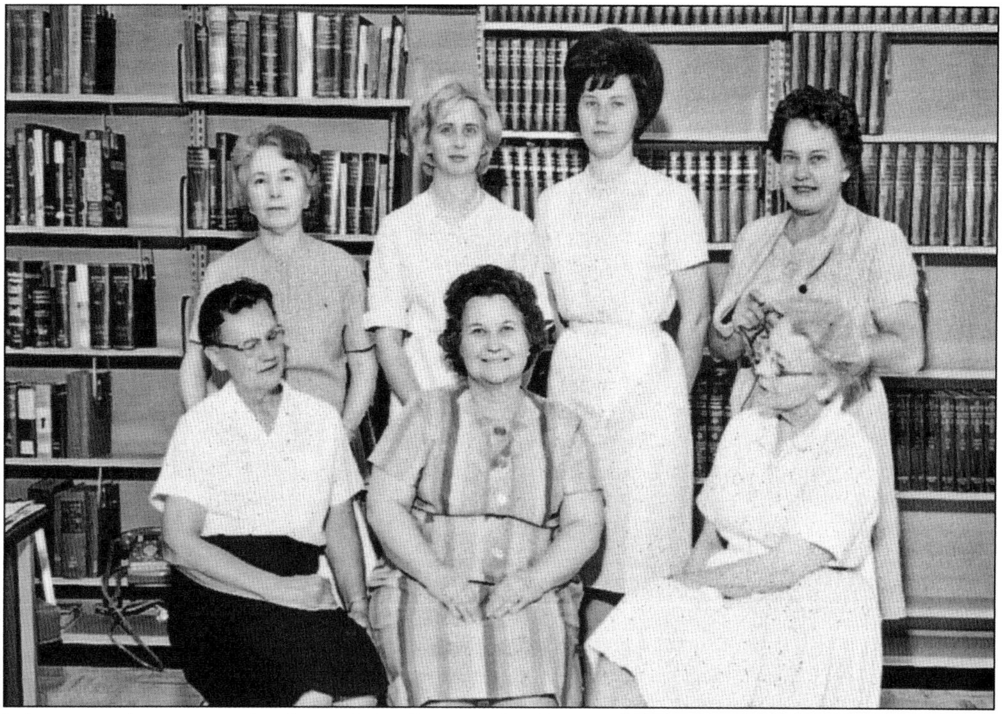

Library employees pose for these 1964 photographs. Pictured above from left to right are (seated) Mable Mosteller, Juanita White, and Bill Bentley; (standing) Miriam Childs, Joanna Evans, Jane Smith, and Gladys Brannon. Pictured below from left to right are (seated) Gaynelle Brewer, Laura Inzer, Freida Jones, Jane Matthews, and Audra Kerr; (standing) Louis Loveman, Alice Leach, Jimmy Junkins, Terry John Calhoun, and Monita Elliott.

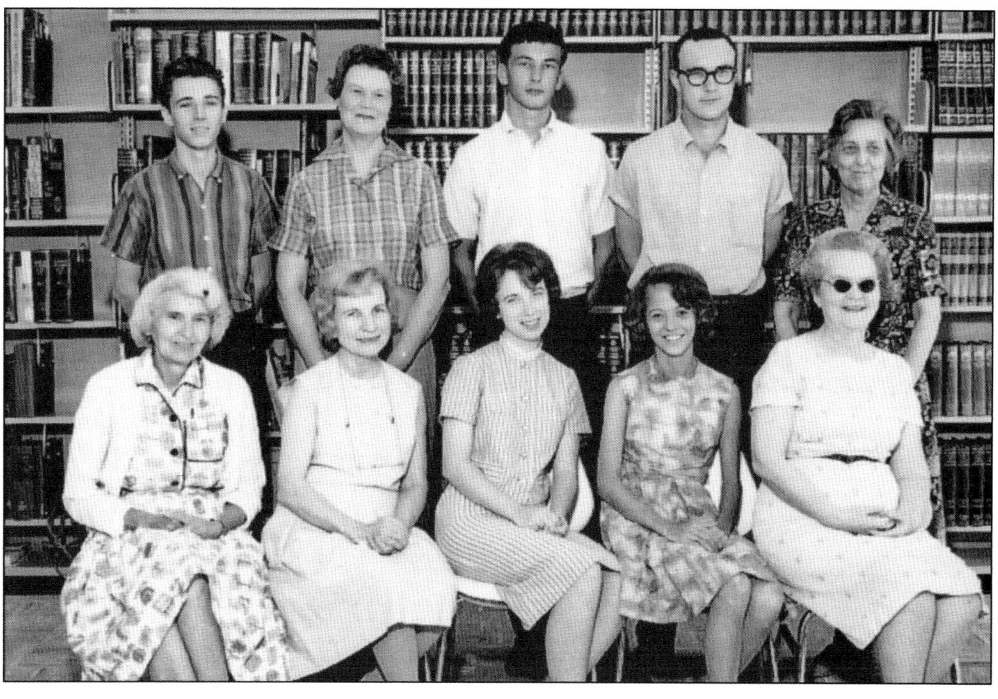

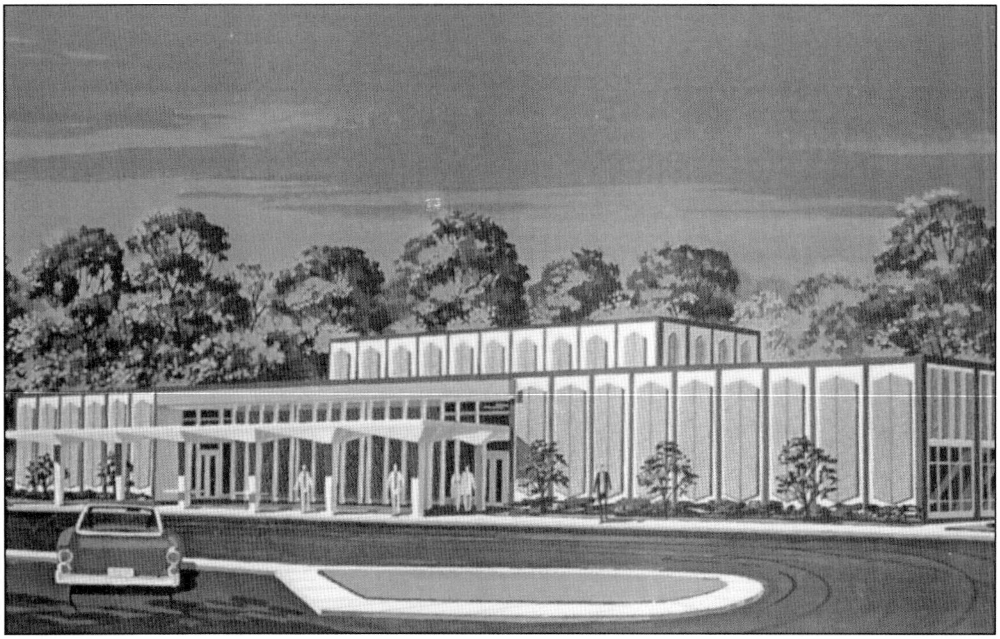

The library on College Street, shown in this postcard, opened on June 29, 1964. At the entrance was a shallow, rectangular, reflecting pool. It was drained and used as a planter after pranksters repeatedly filled the pool with soap. The new building had 40,000 square feet to house 200,000 volumes and was considered immense for its time.

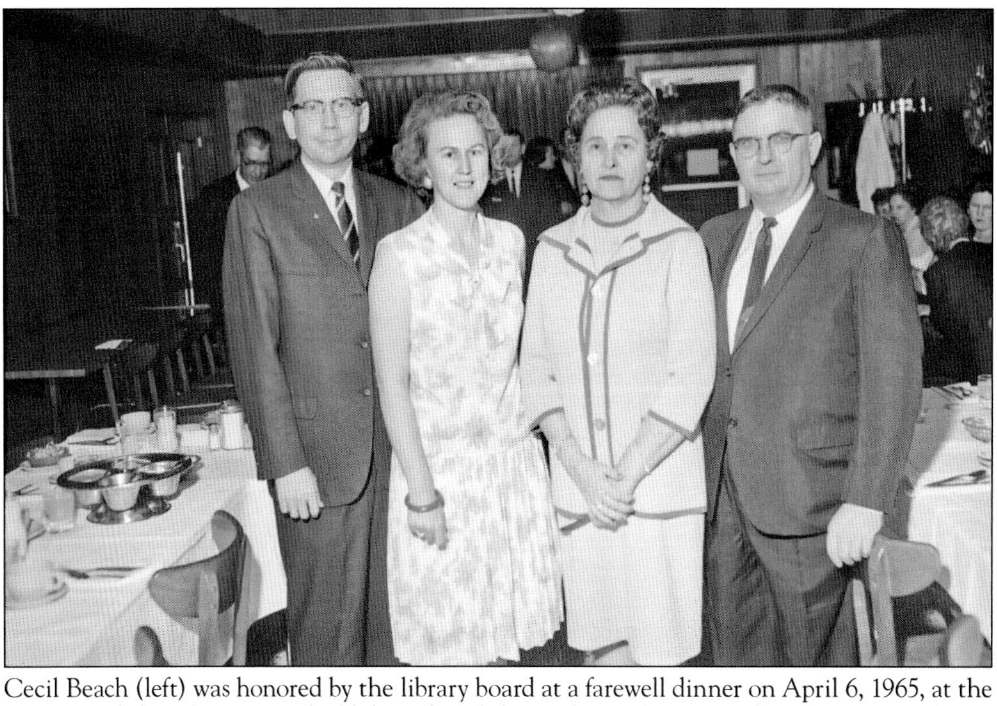

Cecil Beach (left) was honored by the library board at a farewell dinner on April 6, 1965, at the Mexican Chili Parlor. Pictured with him, from left to right, are Doris Beach, Mrs. A. C. Michaels, and Mayor Lesley Gilliland. Mrs. Michaels, board chairman, presented a watch to Beach as a token of the board's appreciation of his contribution to the community.

Four

Oscar Rymer 1965–1975

Oscar Rymer was hired in the fall of 1965. A substantial donation aided the collection's development, and two branch libraries were opened. National Library Week speakers were from academic fields and included a state library director and an encyclopedia editor. Nonfiction books outnumbered fiction books. During the late 1960s, insurance and retirement benefits were provided for library employees, and salaries were increased. The main library became so popular that security guards were hired for the night shift. It was Rymer who first reported hearing ghostly noises in the library when he worked there after hours to catch up on paperwork. He was accompanied by his miniature Labrador retriever, who seemed to hear the noises also and became agitated and upset. Rymer concluded a brief history of the library with this philosophical observation: "Before we look at the future we should identify the biggest enemy of the library yesterday and today. It is a false concept. It is a mighty myth, a myth that the public library is free. Like the ghosts in a mountain country graveyard who flee when the sun rises among the tombs and return to nightly haunts when darkness falls, these illusory ideas of a free library fade at the approach of truth and return when the winds of ignorance blow again. Library facilities today represent millions of dollars. They were bought with a price. They were not free. Only dedicated and enlightened citizens will have the vision to pay the price of providing the professional skill, planning, money, facilities, intellectual tools, and all other products to enable the library to continue to educate citizens from the cradle to the grave and to maintain its high standards as the only true university of the world."

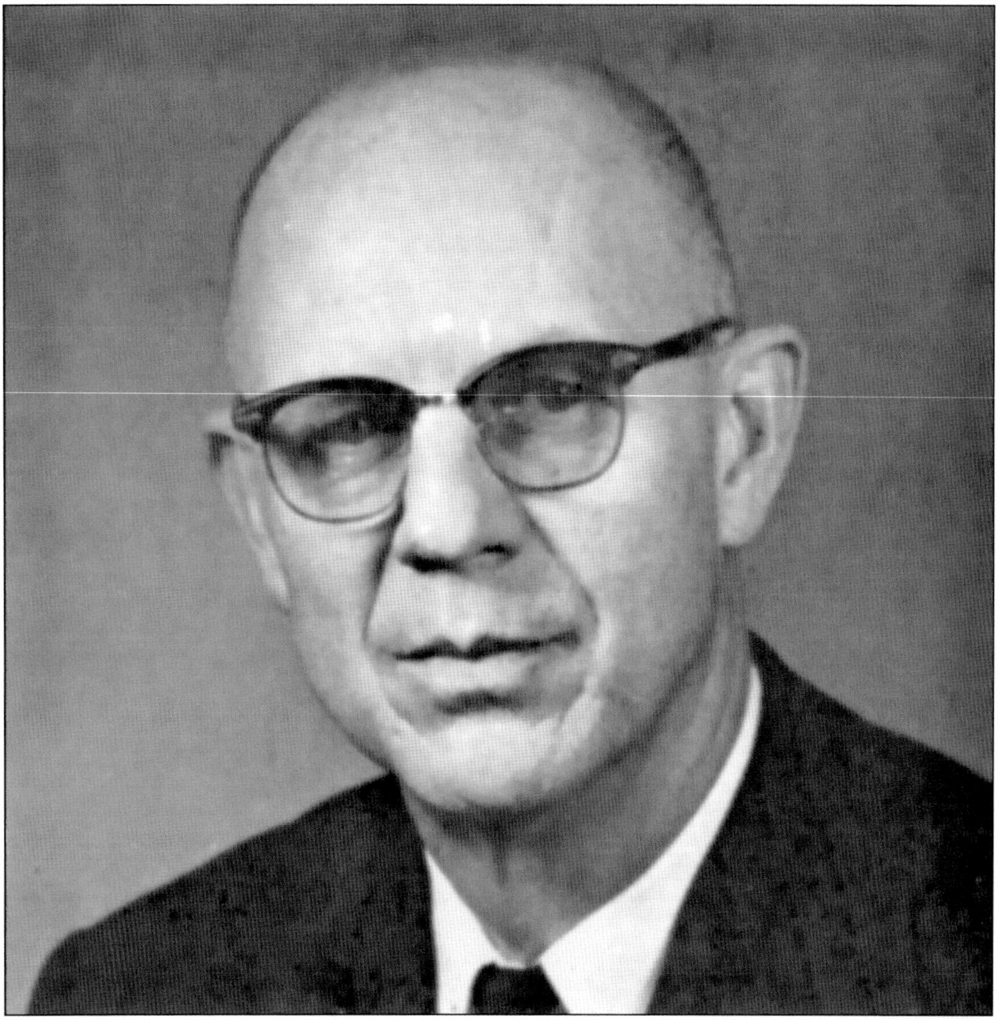

Oscar Rymer was born in a log house in 1910 in Virginia (later to become West Virginia). As a youngster, he worked for 5¢ an hour, 10 hours a day, doing farm work. Living near the river, he would sometimes yield to the lure of the calliope of the showboat *Silver Queen* and spend 25¢ to enjoy the floating theater. Realizing the value of education, he made it not only his vocation, but his hobby as well. No matter where he was stationed while in the U.S. Air Force, he always made a point to visit the local museums, libraries, art galleries, and other educational institutions. While in the service, Rymer visited more than 19 countries, including England, Scotland, India, Libya, and Egypt. Rymer wrote an article about Gadsden that appeared in the 1971 *Encyclopedia Americana*. Rymer was a retired U.S. Air Force colonel with a master's degree in library science from Florida State University.

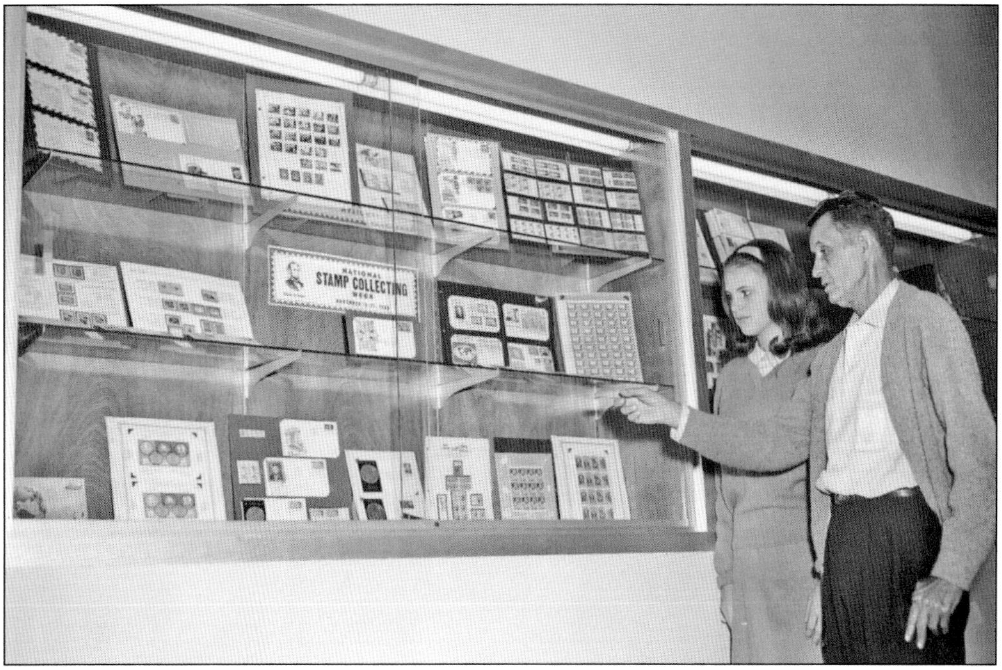

The Gadsden Stamp Society sponsored a stamp display at the library in conjunction with National Stamp Week in 1965. Chester Key, secretary of the society, views the display with Alicia Bryan.

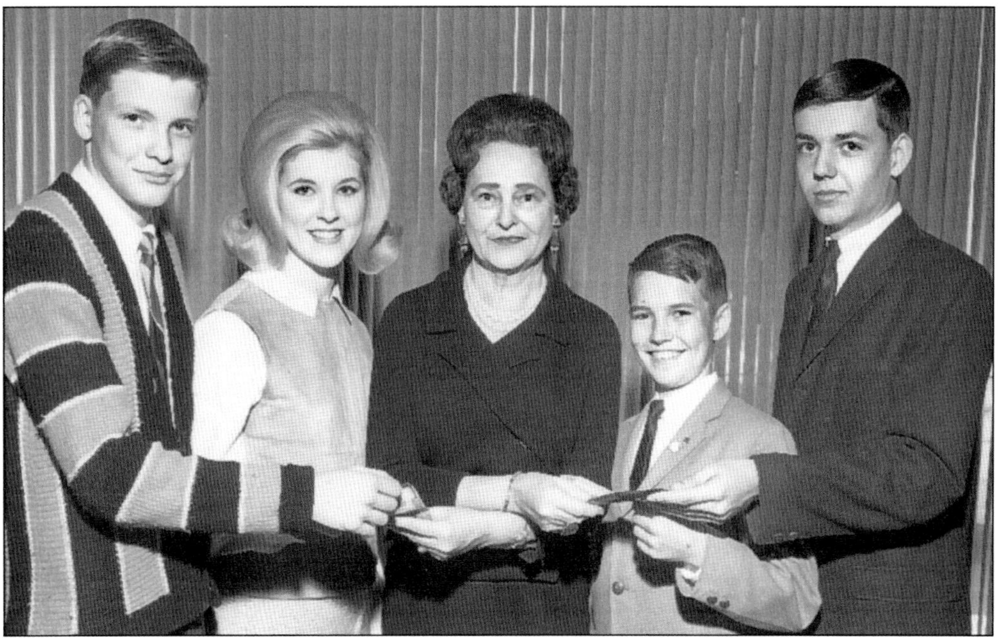

Friends of the Library president Mrs. A. C. Michaels (center) awards prizes to winners of the 1965 city-wide essay contest sponsored by Friends. From left to right, the students are Michael Sparks, Litchfield Junior High; Cathy Breeden, Gadsden High; Charles Hill, Litchfield Junior High; and Ricky Ryan, Gadsden High. Winning essays were chosen from more than 1,000 entries by junior and senior high school students.

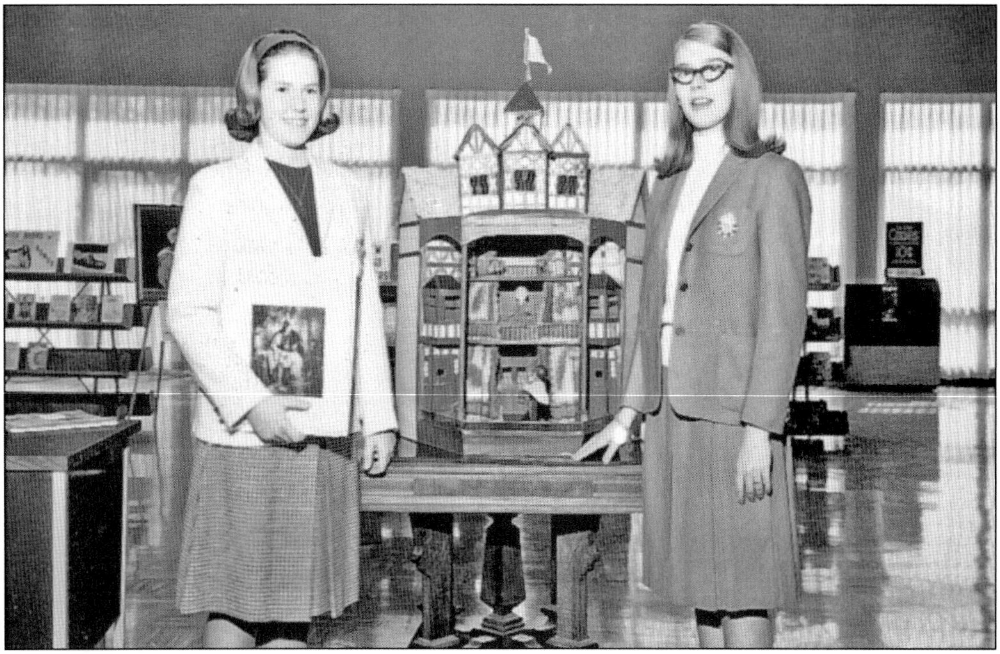

On display at the library in February 1966 is a scale model of the Globe Theatre. Nancy Sturkie (right) made the model from cardboard for her ninth-grade English project. Also on display is a notebook compiled by classmate Christie Adams on the life and works of Shakespeare. Both girls were students of Eleanor Kerns at Disque Junior High School.

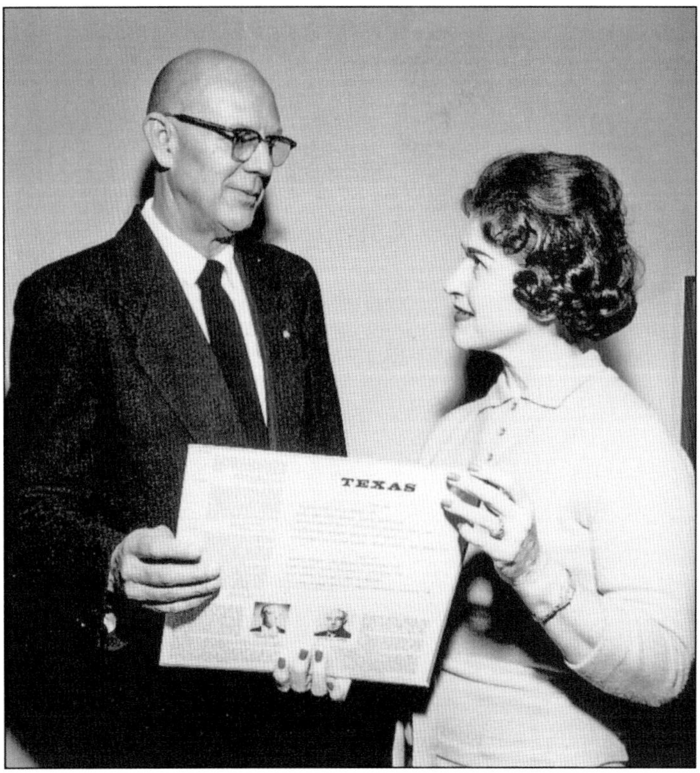

Mrs. R. C. Davis Jr., on behalf of the Gadsden Music Club, is shown presenting a recording of *Texas* to Oscar Rymer on March 2, 1966. The album was a recording of works by David W. Guion, performed by the Houston Summer Symphony and conducted by Ezra Rachlin. Guion was highly regarded for his ability to capture the spirit of Texas in music with such tunes as "Buffalo Bayou Song," "Prairie Dusk," and "High Steppin'," which were included on the album. Other songs he composed include "Home On the Range," "Turkey In the Straw," and "Arkansas Traveler."

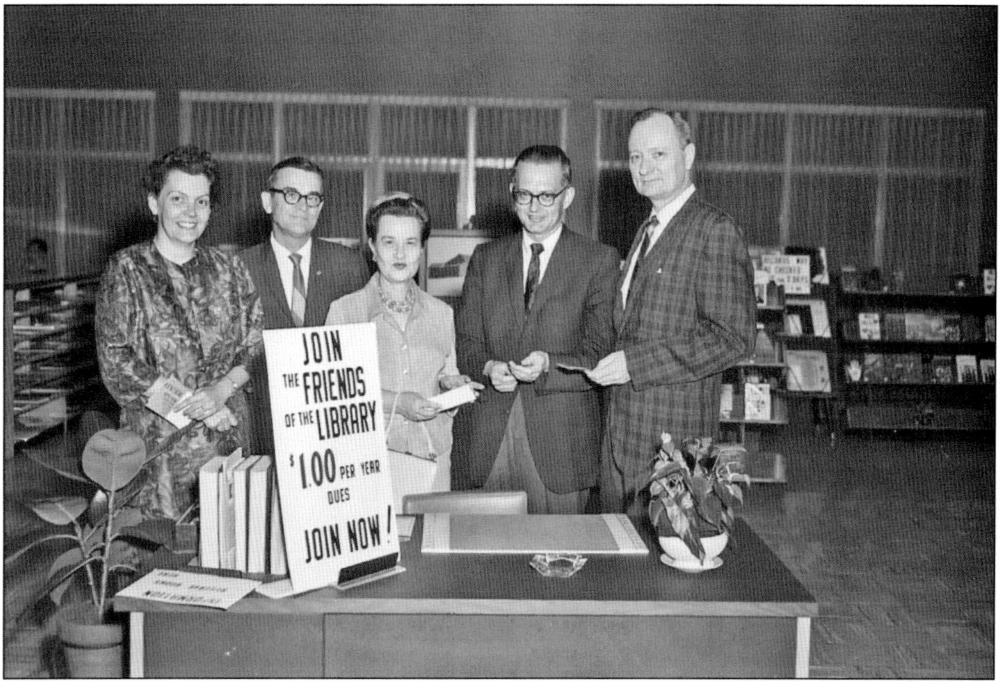

Friends of the Library officers, shown from left to right making preparations for the 1966 membership drive, are Luverna Waid, drive chairman; W. O. Briscoe, president; Mrs. Chester Stringer, publicity; Dr. M. D. Smith, second vice president, and Dr. William J. Tally, first vice president.

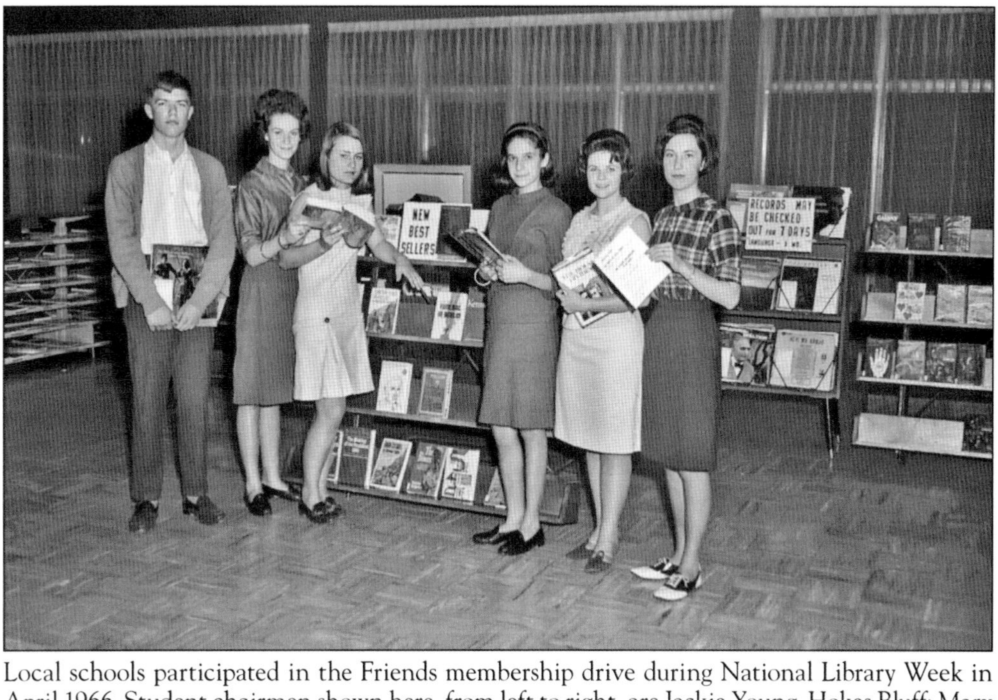

Local schools participated in the Friends membership drive during National Library Week in April 1966. Student chairmen shown here, from left to right, are Jackie Young, Hokes Bluff; Mary Lee Hardin, Gadsden High; Reynolds Smith, Gadsden High; Elizabeth Hardin, Disque; Martha Dawson, Southside; and Kay Hawkins, Etowah High.

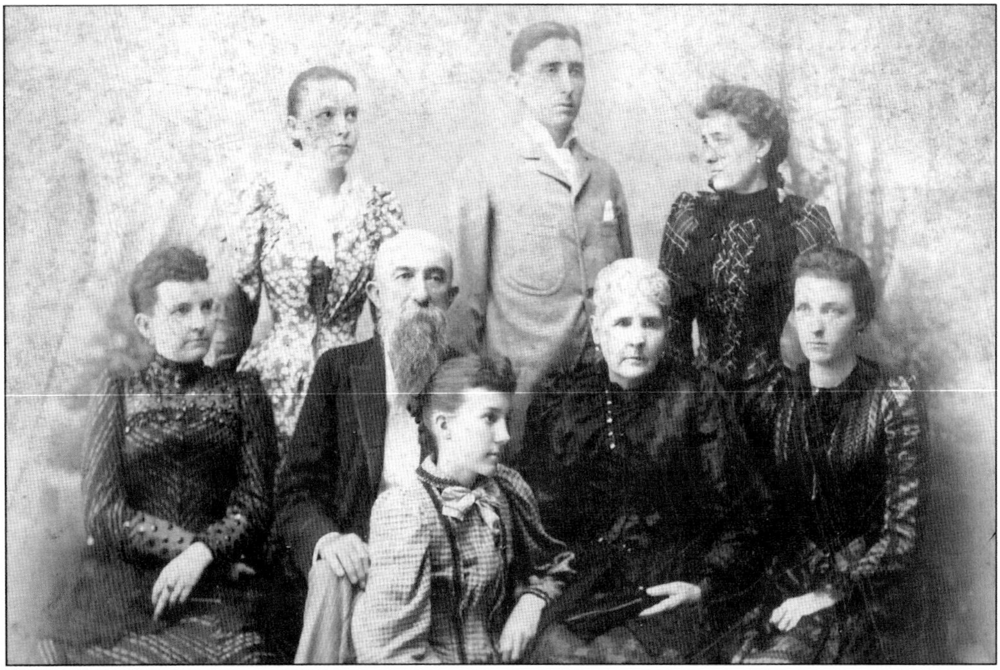

The $50,000 Kyle Library Fund was established in 1966, following the sale of land donated to the City of Gadsden by R. B. Kyle. Shown in this 1887 portrait, Kyle family members are, from left to right, (front center) Florrie Kyle; (seated) Nena K. Elliott, Col. Robert Benjamin Kyle, Mrs. R. B. Kyle, and Bessie Kyle; (standing) Robbie Kyle, T. S. Kyle, and Edith K. Thompson. Colonel Kyle was Gadsden's mayor in 1867. Florrie was a charter member of the Thursday Study Club.

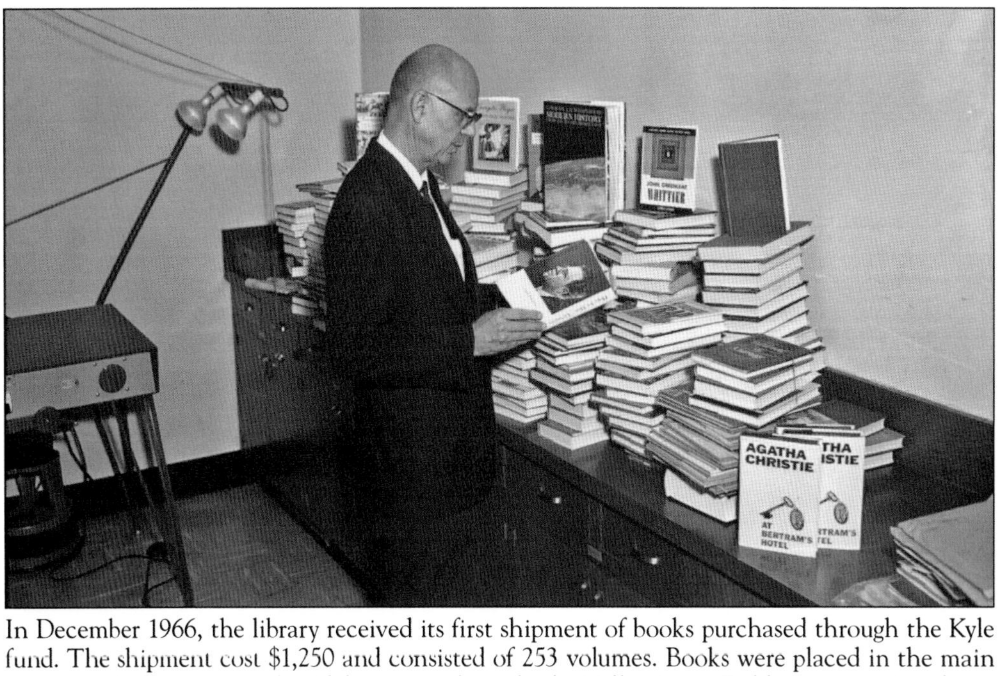

In December 1966, the library received its first shipment of books purchased through the Kyle fund. The shipment cost $1,250 and consisted of 253 volumes. Books were placed in the main library on College Street, the Alabama City branch, the Valley Street Field House on Tuscaloosa Avenue, the soon-to-open East Gadsden branch, and the bookmobile.

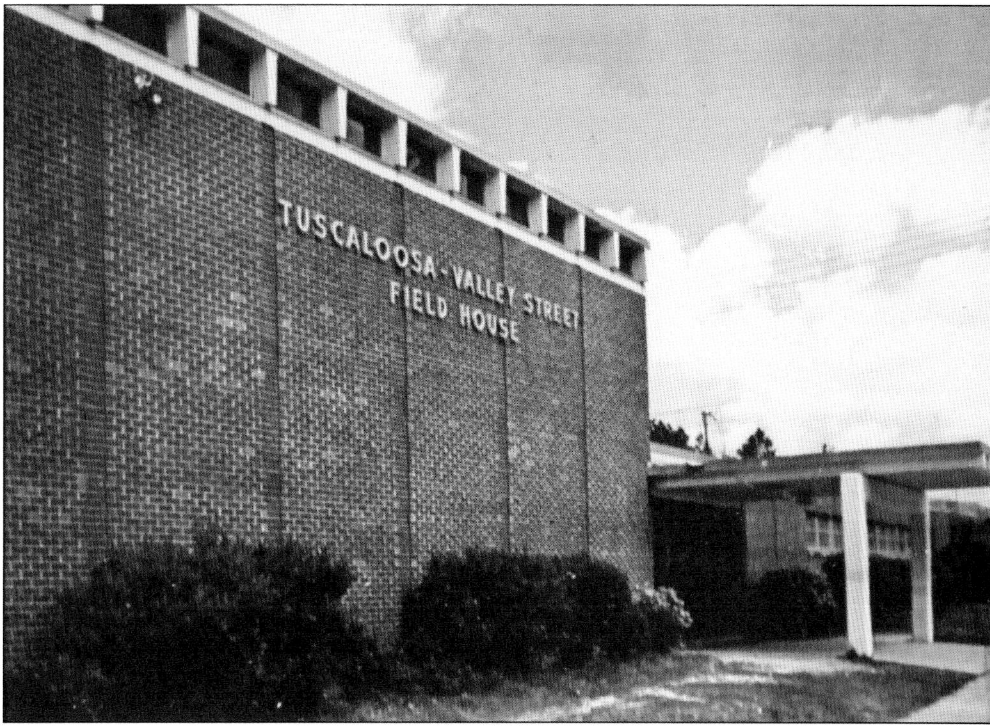

During Oscar Rymer's administration, the library expanded its services by adding two branches. The Tuscaloosa Valley Street Branch opened on March 27, 1966. The East Gadsden Branch, located in the newly constructed community center on Wilson Avenue, opened on October 16, 1967. Books purchased through the Kyle fund were part of their collections.

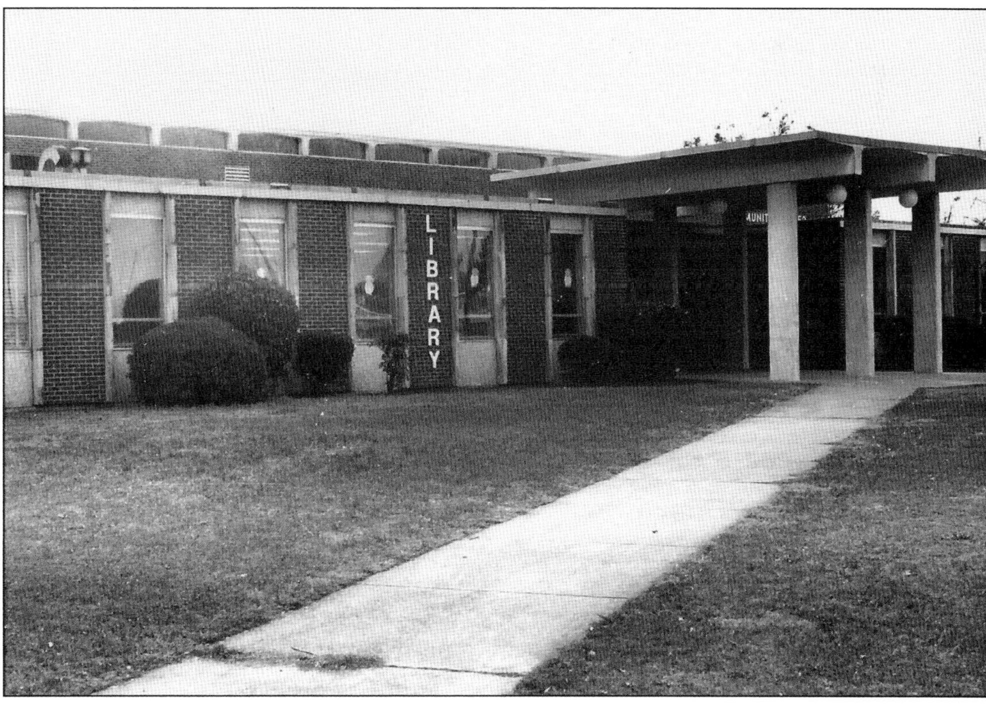

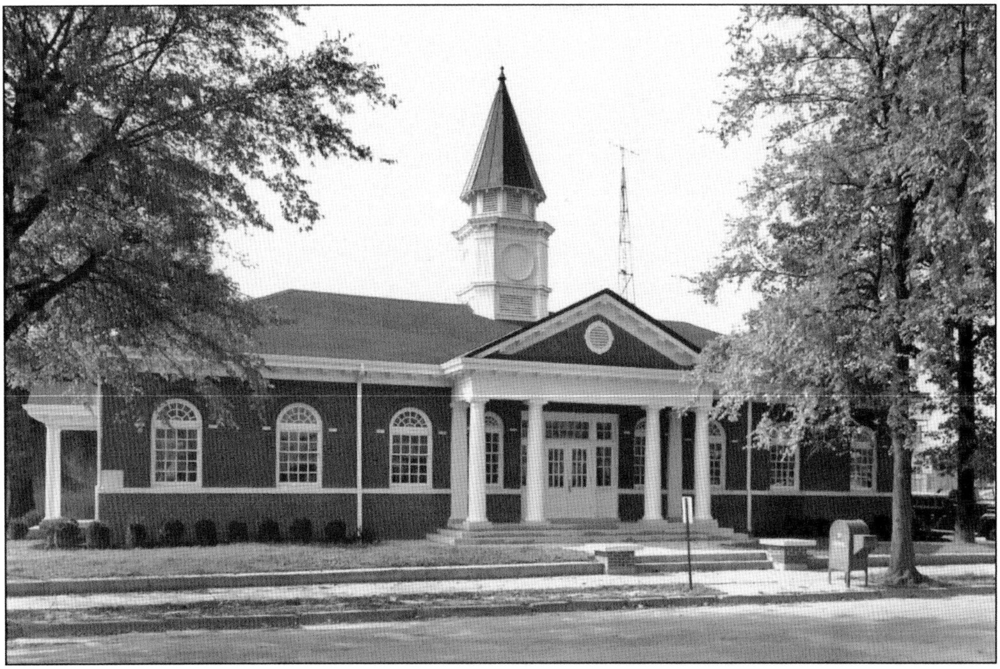

The Alabama City branch, which opened in 1938, was remodeled in 1966. Until 1965, the Alabama City Post Office shared the building with the library. When a new post office was built, the library was able to expand and remodel. Installation of air-conditioning was included in the $70,000 renovation. To fill the increased space, new books were purchased through the Kyle fund.

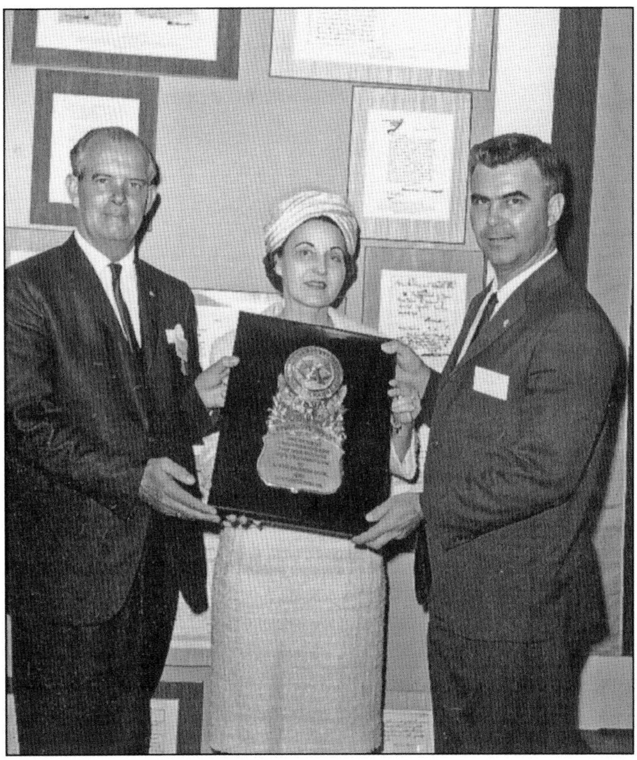

The Gadsden Exchange Club donated a collection of copies of historical documents in 1966. The collection, known as the Freedom Shrine, included the Gettysburg Address, "Star-Spangled Banner," and the Declaration of Independence, as well as many other documents significant to America's history. Marguerite Loveman (center), chairman of the library board, receives a plaque for the display from C. C. "Jack" Lee (left) and Lavelle Grant. Lee was chairman of the Freedom Shrine for Alabama, and Grant was president of the Gadsden Exchange Club.

Oscar Rymer (right) was proud to bring Dr. Louis Shores to Gadsden for a free lecture in 1967 to celebrate National Library Week. Shores was editor-in-chief of *Collier's Encyclopedia* and dean of the library school at Florida State University. Rymer was a student of Dr. Shores at Florida State, and Shores wrote a glowing letter of recommendation for Rymer.

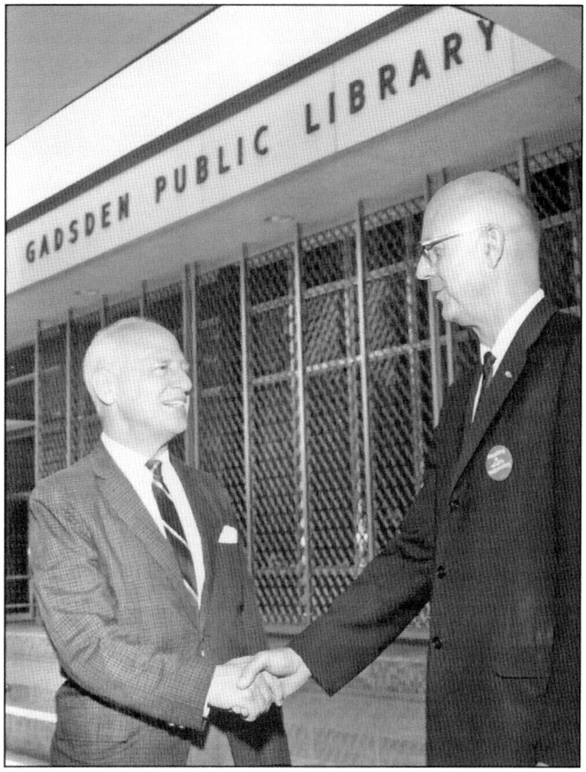

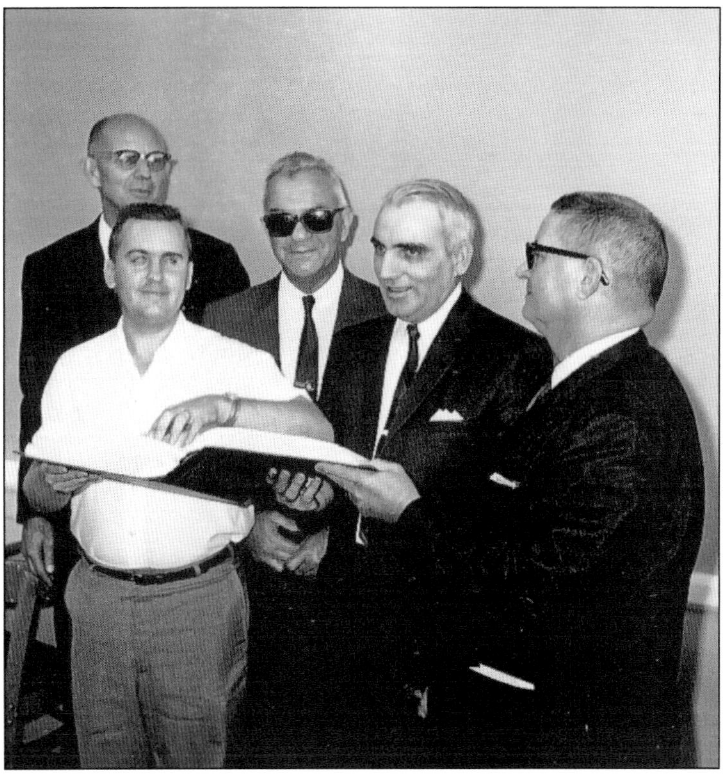

The Gadsden Chapter of the Alabama Federation of the Blind donated a 185-volume set of the *World Book Encyclopedia* in braille. In this September 25, 1968, photograph, Gerald Baker runs his fingers over the characters. From left to right, Col. Oscar Rymer, library director; Calvin Sexton, chapter vice president; Lester McGlaughn, chapter president, and Mayor Lesley Gilliland look on. The set cost $900, with the funds being raised through the White Cane drive. Placed in the reference department, the books occupied 57 feet of shelf space.

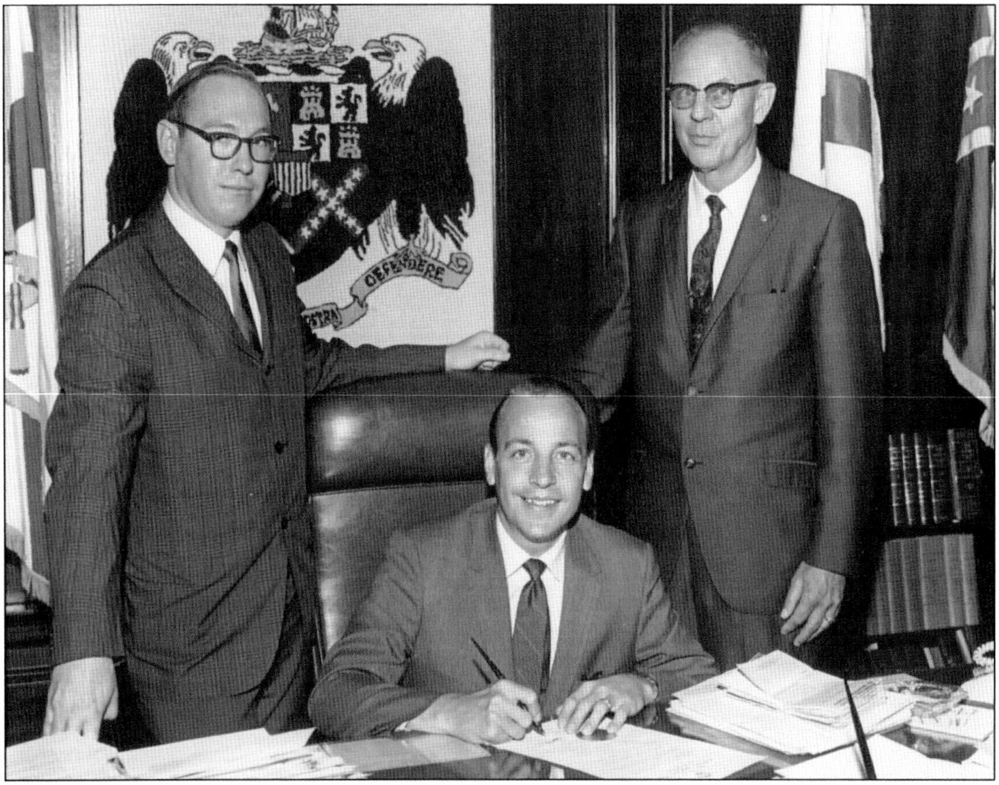

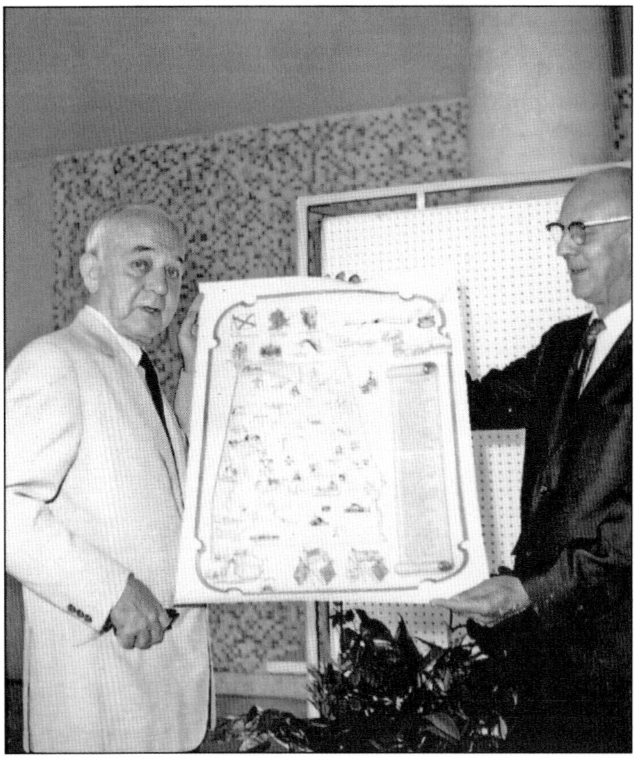

Gov. Albert P. Brewer signs the proclamation of National Library Week in Alabama. Observing from left to right are Gillis Doughtie, information specialist of the Alabama Public Library Service, and Oscar Rymer, executive director of National Library Week 1969 for the Alabama Library Association.

Oscar Rymer (right) is shown presenting Albert Rains with a Literary Map of Alabama from the Alabama Library Association for his outstanding work as state chairman of the 1969 National Library Week observance. Rains received the award at the June 10 meeting of the Gadsden City Commission. Mayor Lesley Gilliland praised Rains for his many years of support for Gadsden Public Library.

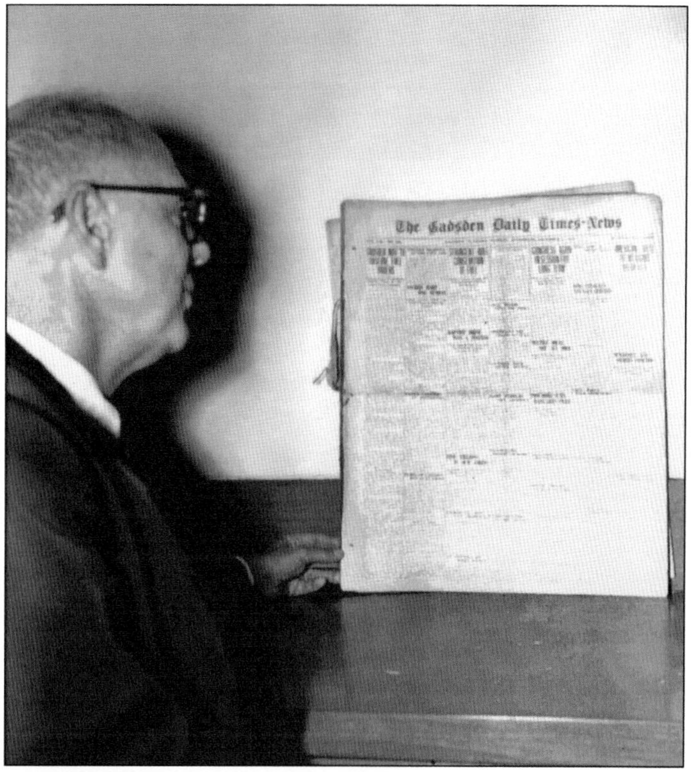

Oscar Rymer is shown looking at a 1919 copy of the *Gadsden Daily Times-News*, forerunner of the *Gadsden Times.* The newspaper ran an article on October 18, 1970, about the usefulness of the library in view of the growing popularity of television. Library statistics showed that Gadsden was a city that continued to appreciate its library—approximately 20,000 books were borrowed each month. The library's collection included items that looked into the past as well as into the future.

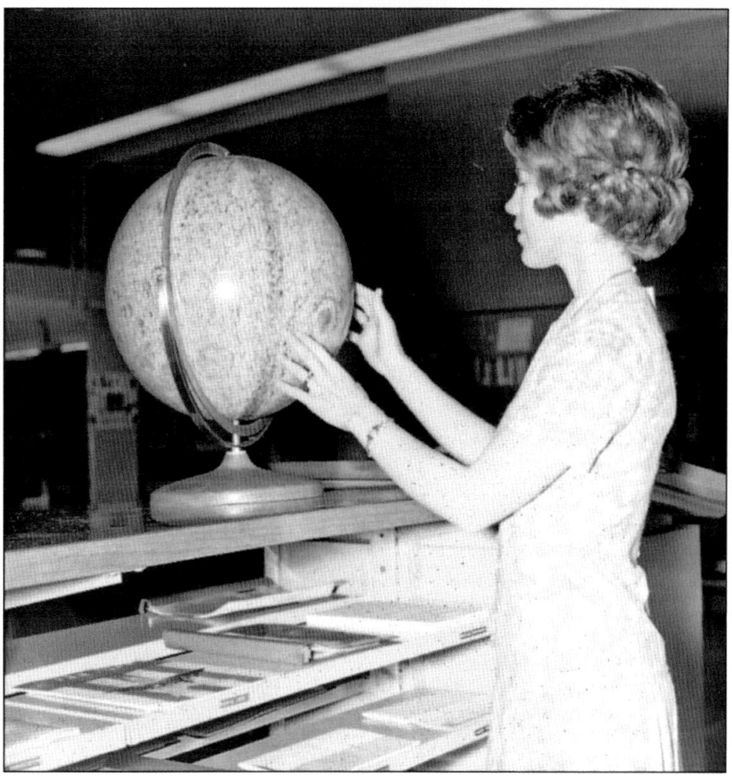

Not only did the library collection strive to preserve history, it also did its best to remain current as well. In the same article mentioned above, this photograph of Phyllis Massenburg, assistant reference librarian, appeared. The newspaper caption read that she "looks at the recently acquired lunar globe and dips 'into the future.'"

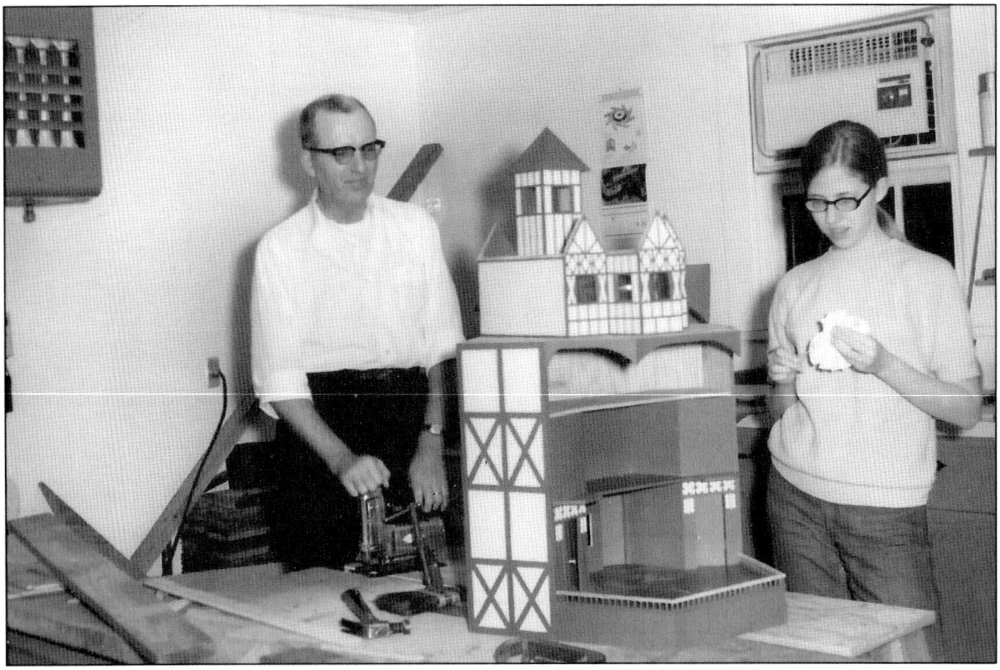

Jamie Jones, a ninth-grade student at Disque Junior High School, made a wood model of the Globe Theatre as an English class project in 1970 in the workshop of her father, James Jones. Jones donated the model to the library, and it is still on display.

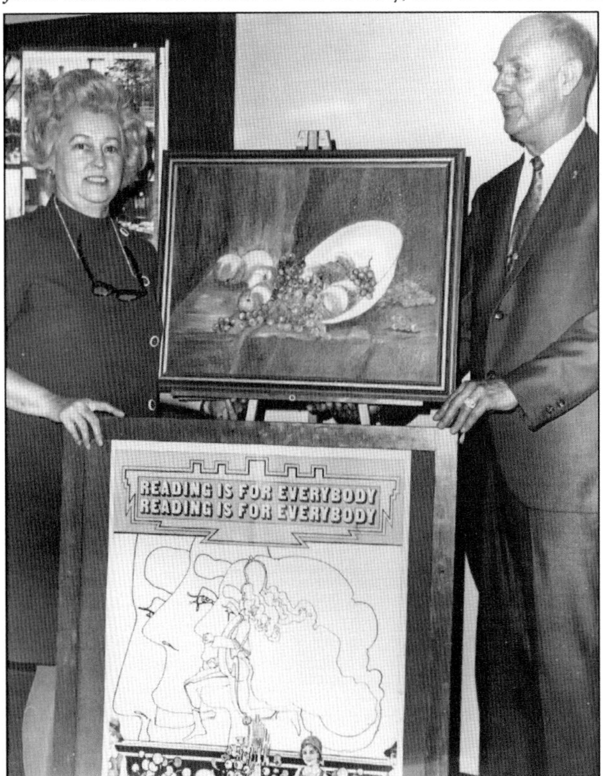

The 1970 National Library Week celebration included a display of works by local artists. Library employee Seattle Edmondson is shown presenting one of her oil paintings to Oscar Rymer for display. Another of Edmondson's paintings, *Fruit with White Bowl*, won first prize in the Museum Collection Jury Show that year.

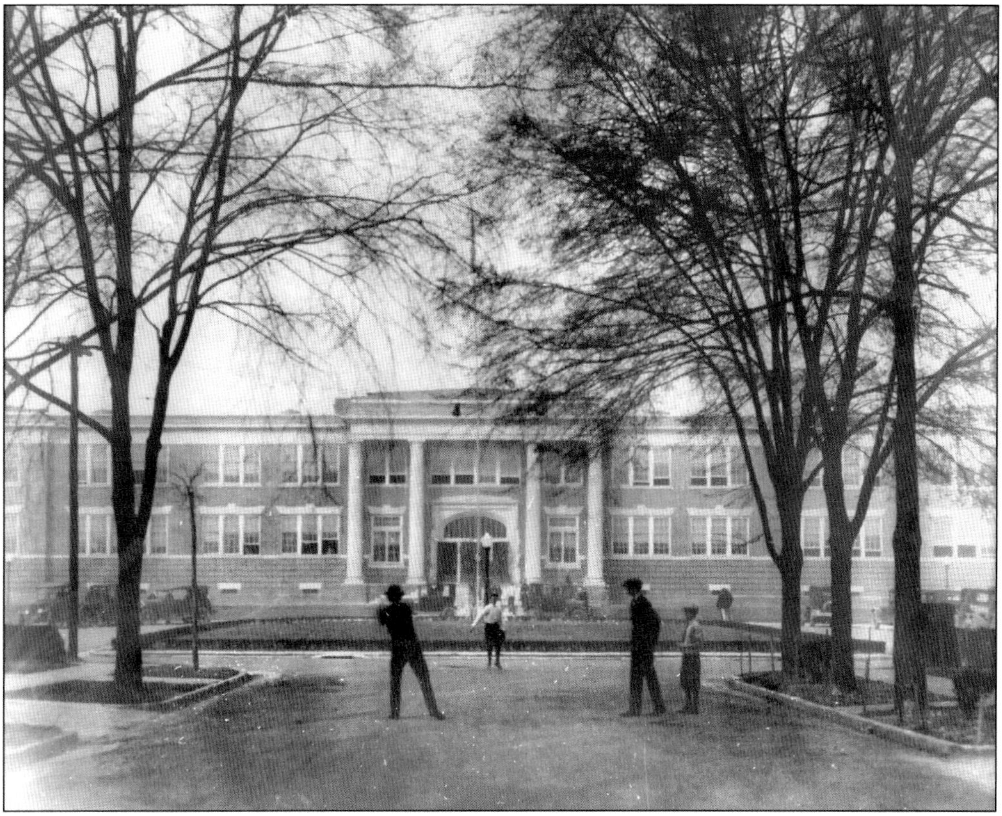

Gadsden High School, on Twelfth Street, was built in 1923. In November 1972, a destructive fire gutted the school. Firemen from Gadsden and surrounding areas battled the blaze throughout the night to prevent its spread to adjacent buildings.

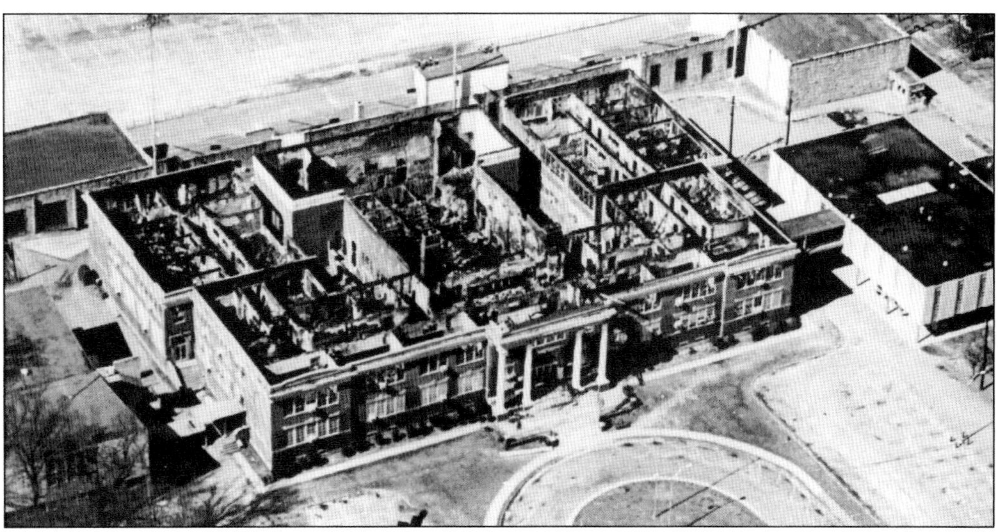

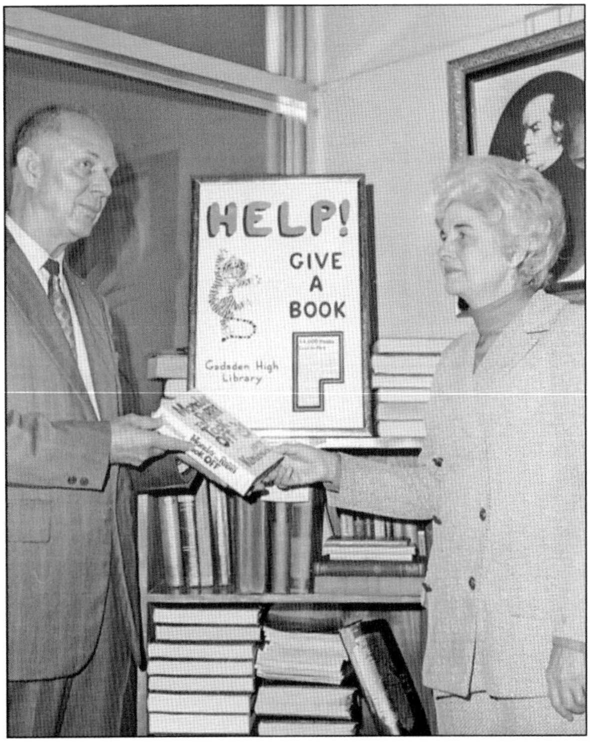

The Gadsden High School library lost 14,000 volumes in the 1972 fire. Always concerned with education, Oscar Rymer set up a stand at the main library to collect books from the public in an effort to replenish the school library. Rymer and Elizabeth Pruett, Gadsden High School librarian, inspect donated books.

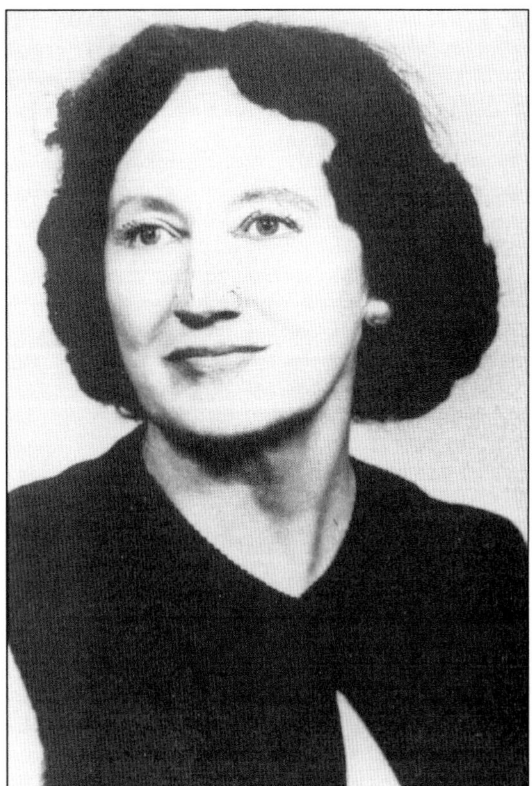

An autograph party was held at the library on April 1, 1973, in honor of Gadsden author Mary Elizabeth Counselman. Her most famous work, *Three Marked Pennies*, written when she was only 15, became a classic of American literature. A television adaptation was aired in 1960. Counselman wrote short stories and poetry in the horror genre. Her work was often compared to that of Edgar Allan Poe.

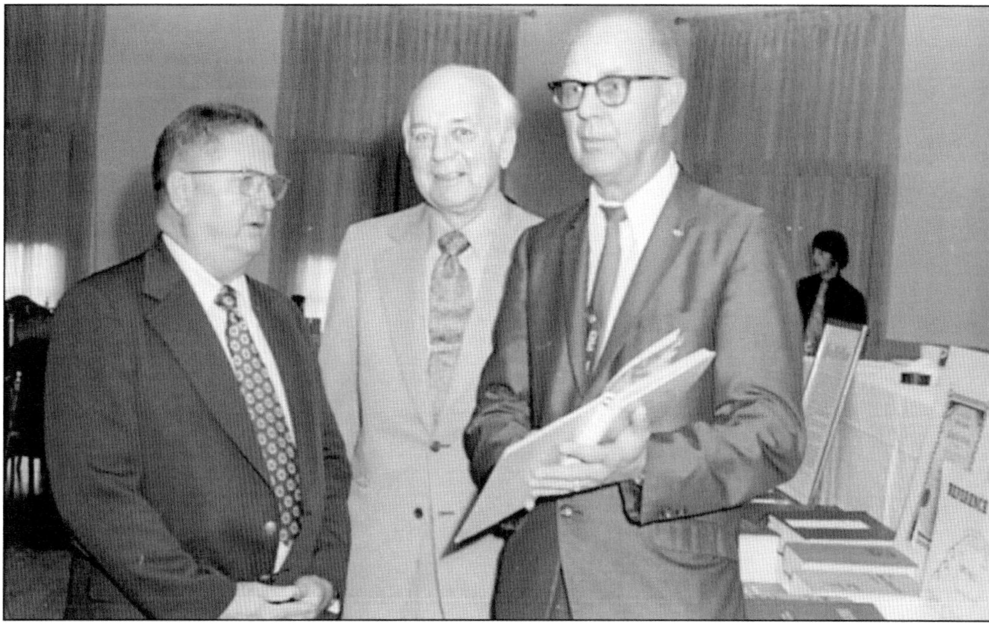

"Gadsden Public Library" was the theme of the chamber of commerce breakfast meeting in June 1973. The program emphasized the role of the library in the community. Former congressman and library board member Albert Rains presided over the meeting. In his presentation, he said, "Libraries are essential to free men in a free society." Pictured from left to right are Mayor Lesley Gilliland, Rains, and Oscar Rymer.

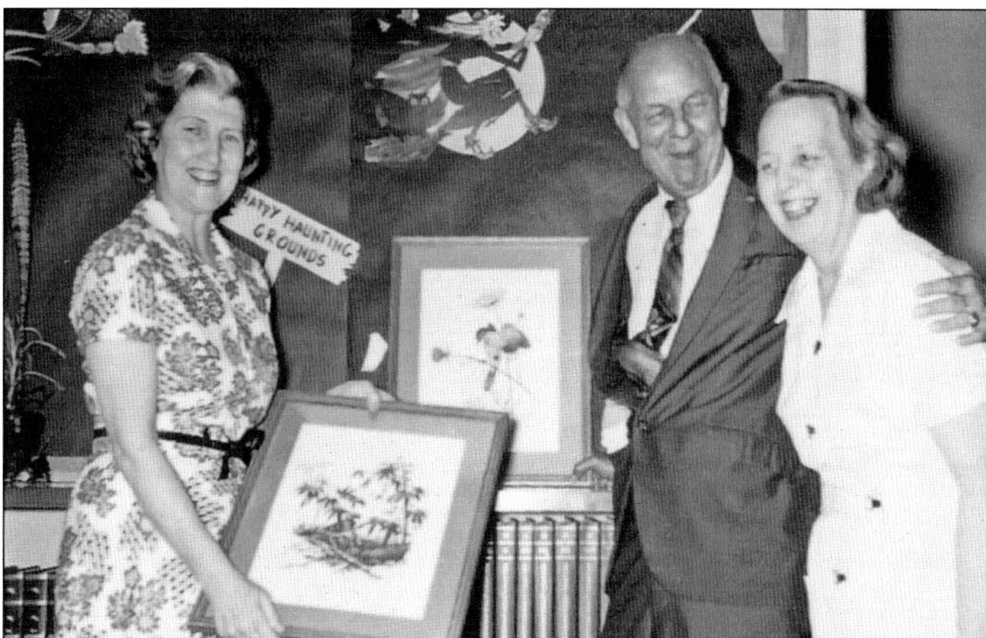

Oscar Rymer enjoys a candid moment with Margaret Nanos (left) and Margaret McGuire in this June 22, 1973, photograph. Nanos and artist Irene Wilson (not pictured) donated a series of wildlife prints to the children's department, which was headed by McGuire. The prints were of artwork by Ray Harm of Frame House Gallery and were valued at $300.

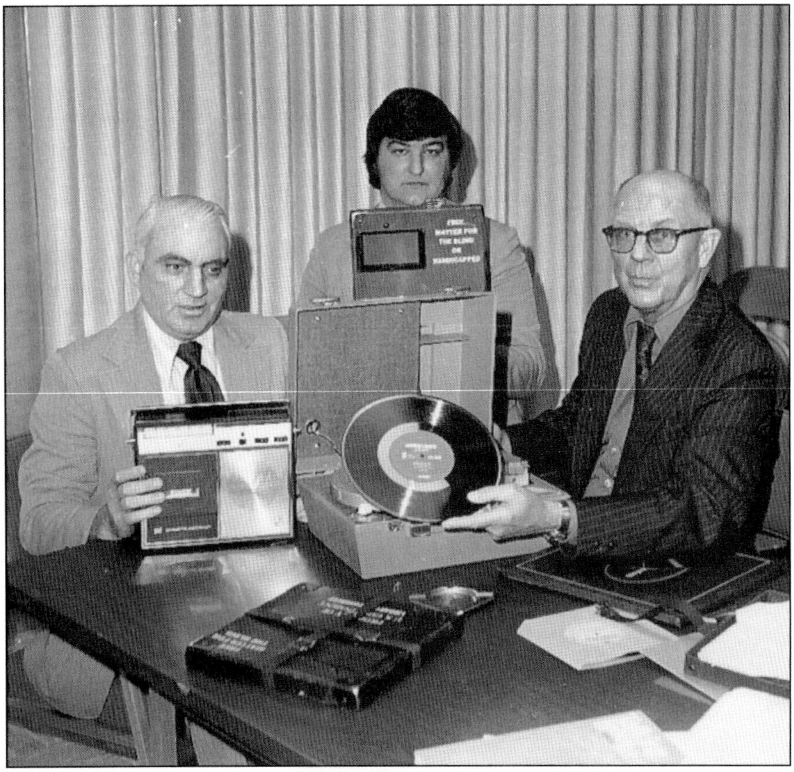

Talking books for the blind and physically handicapped were a new service made available at the library in February 1974. Lester McGlaughn (left), president of the Gadsden chapter of the Alabama Federation of the Blind, is shown with Bobby Junkins (center) and Oscar Rymer.

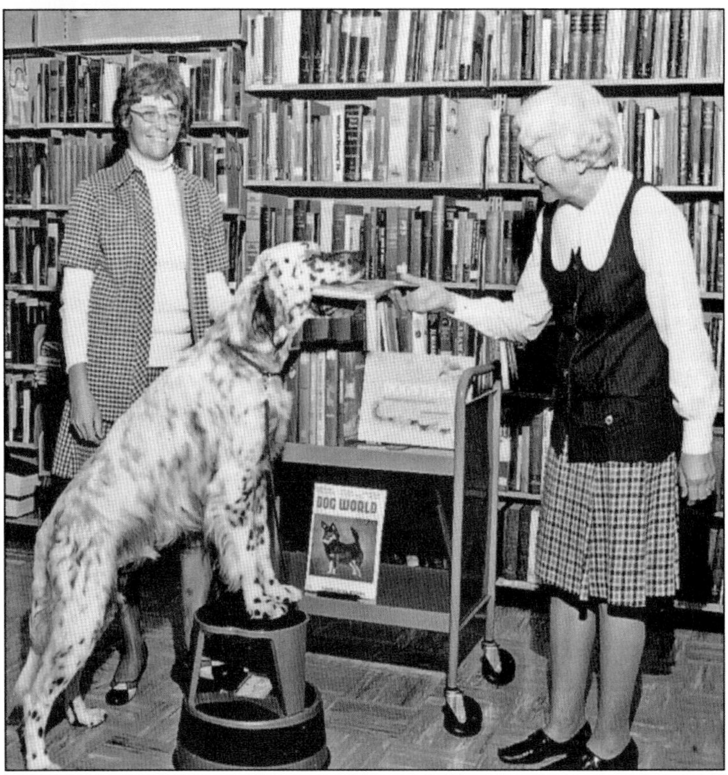

In October 1974, Gadsden Obedience Training Club donated five books, all on dogs, valued at $100. Presenting one of the books to reference librarian Margaret Rouse is Banner, a two-year-old, blue, Belton English setter. Looking on is Mrs. Jerome Gamblin, owner of Banner. Rouse was the reference librarian for 20 years until her retirement in 1985. Her decision to become a librarian was influenced by her childhood experiences, when the library and "Miss Lena" stood for the answer to any need or question.

Five

Bobby Junkins 1975–1988

In 1973, Bobby Junkins was hired as the assistant library director. Two years later, in 1975, Oscar Rymer retired, and Junkins was appointed the director of Gadsden Public Library. Ten years prior, Junkins was the first person hired by Rymer. Junkins, who was attending Gadsden State Junior College in its first class, worked three years as a part-time library page. Although the library had hosted a variety of programs and speakers in the past, they were usually of a more academic nature. Junkins began to bring in speakers that were authors of popular fiction in response to the changing desires of the public. Many activities that would have delighted the Bachelor Girls of 1897 were instituted during the Junkins years. Book review clubs and reading programs grew in popularity. Under Junkins's administration, the library added two wings, purchased personal computers, networked with other libraries, brought back the bookmobile service, and increased genealogy holdings. Area newspapers were microfilmed, oral histories were taped, and old pictures were copied for preservation. Junkins, also a state representative, was library director until 1988, when he was elected the probate judge of Etowah County.

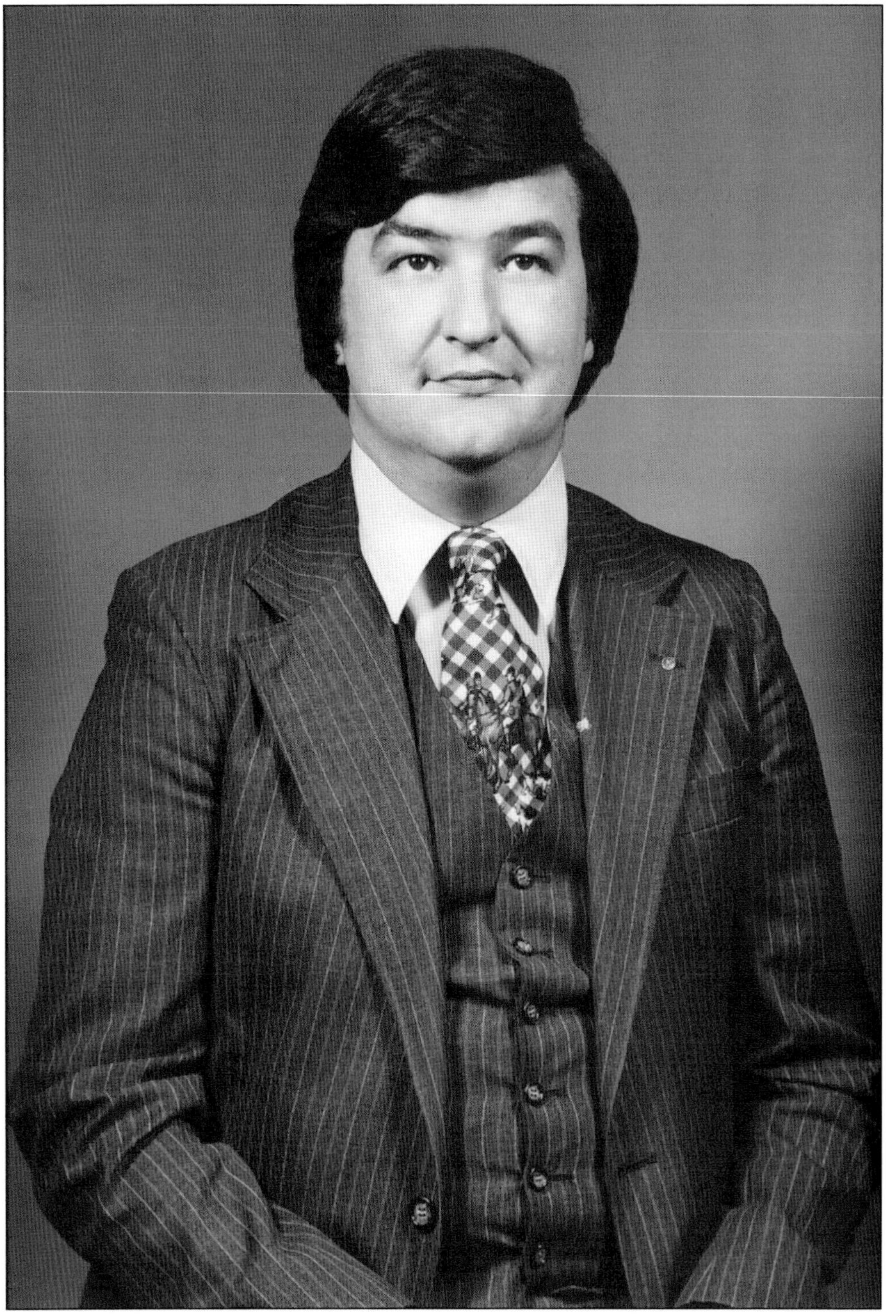

Bobby Junkins had a master's degree in education from Jacksonville State University, where he majored in library science and instructional media. At the age of 28, Junkins was one of the youngest directors in the South. If that was not distinction enough, he was also one of the biggest, standing 6 feet, 6 inches tall and weighing 240 pounds. Junkins was the 1976 president of the Public Library Division of the Alabama Library Association, where he worked to improve the formula for the distribution of library funding by the state. Active in numerous civic organizations, Junkins was recognized as one of Alabama's Four Outstanding Young Men in 1979. He was appointed by Gov. James Folsom to serve on the executive board of the Alabama Public Library Service.

The Coosa Valley Jaycees donated a tree to the library to brighten the 1975 holiday season in the children's department. Members pictured are, from left to right, (kneeling) Byron Cothran, state director, and Jimmy Collett; (standing) Steve Ervin and Larry Grimes.

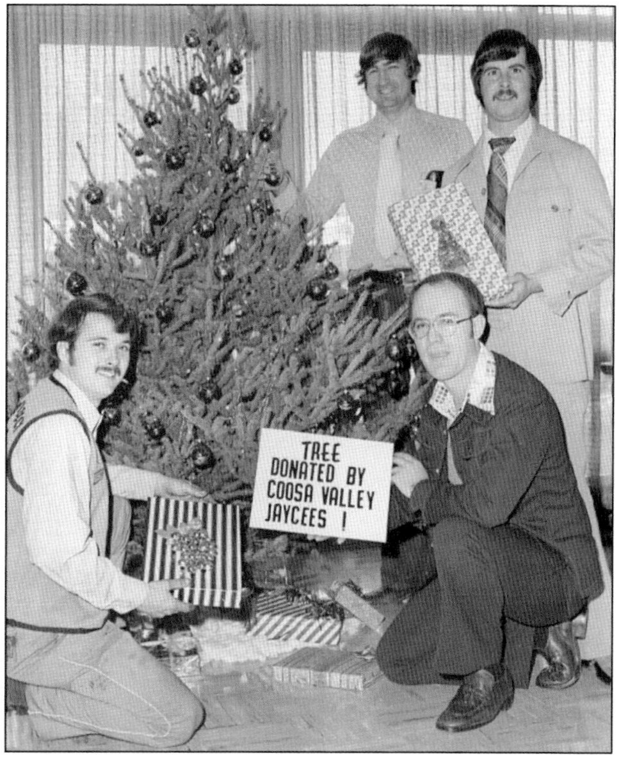

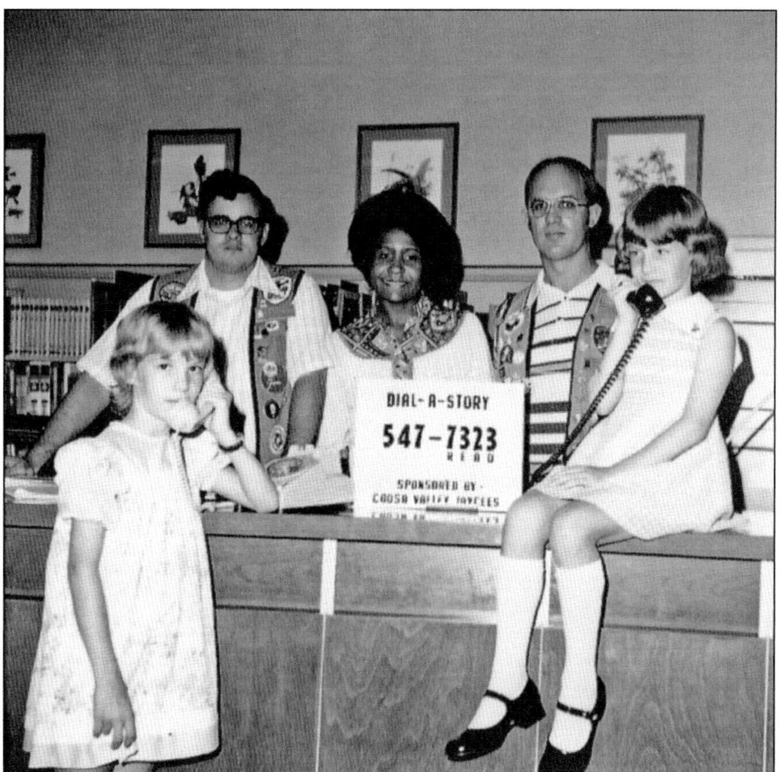

Paula Collett and her sister Kim (seated on counter) listen to a taped story over the telephone. Standing from left to right are Pat Sosebee; Lillie Jones, library clerk; and Jimmy Collett. Sosebee and Collett were members of the Coosa Valley Jaycees, who sponsored the equipment and telephone service for Dial-A-Story. The Jaycees won a state award for this 1976 project, which received 7,500 to 8,000 calls per month.

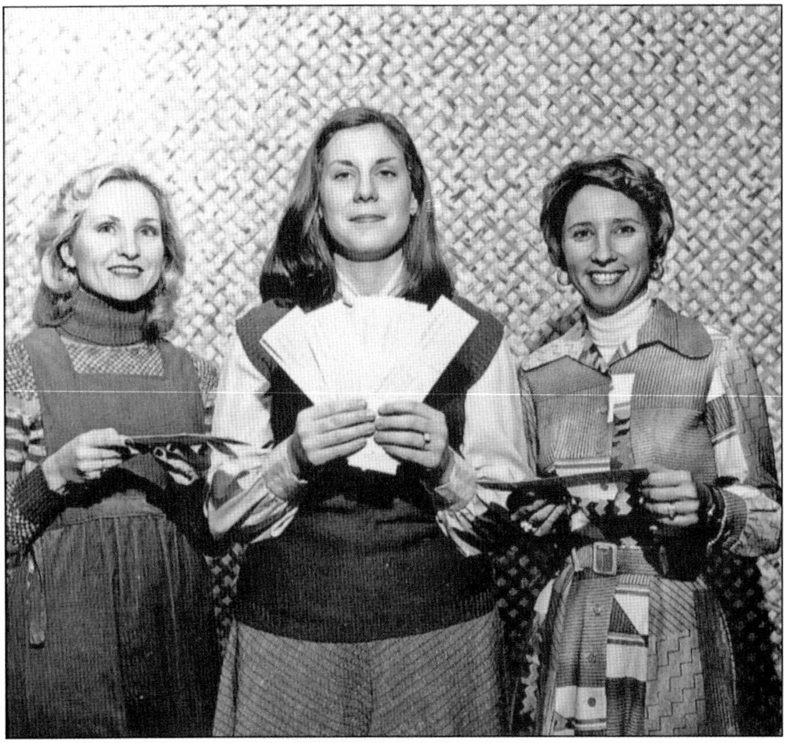

Shown finalizing plans for the 1976 Friends of the Library membership drive, from left to right, are Mrs. Jim Goodwyn, Mrs. Bill Drinkard, and Mrs. Sanford Shew, chairman.

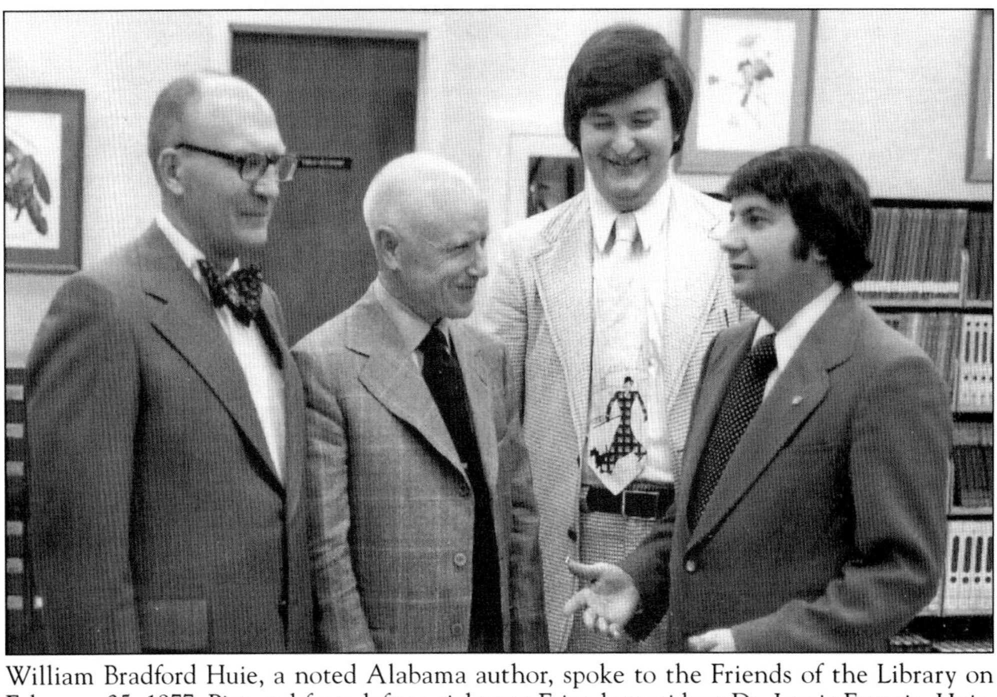

William Bradford Huie, a noted Alabama author, spoke to the Friends of the Library on February 25, 1977. Pictured from left to right are Friends president Dr. Lewis Francis, Huie, Bobby Junkins, and Mayor Steve Means. Huie was considered one of America's most controversial authors at that time. Huie's 21 books sold more than 28 million copies, and seven books were made into movies.

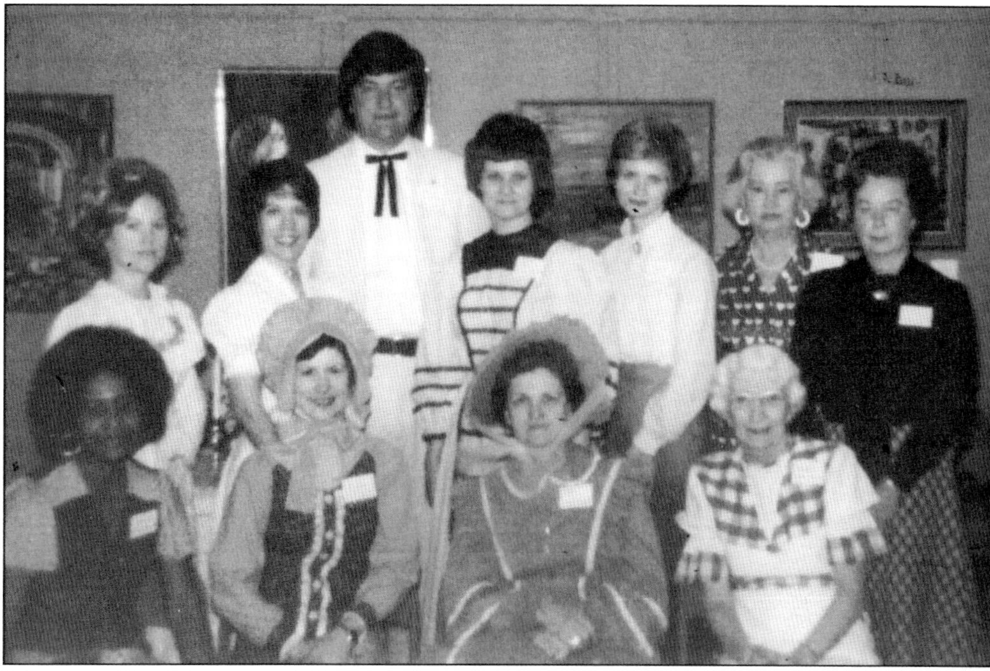

Library staff members wore 1890s period clothing for a reception honoring the Thursday Study Club during National Library Week in April 1977. From left to right are (seated) Lillie Mae Jones, Wanda Bush, Margaret Jones, and Margaret Rouse; (standing) Anita Brooks, Phyllis Massenburg, Bobby Junkins, Yvonne Burgess, Linda Vaughn, Seattle Edmondson, and Billie Bailey.

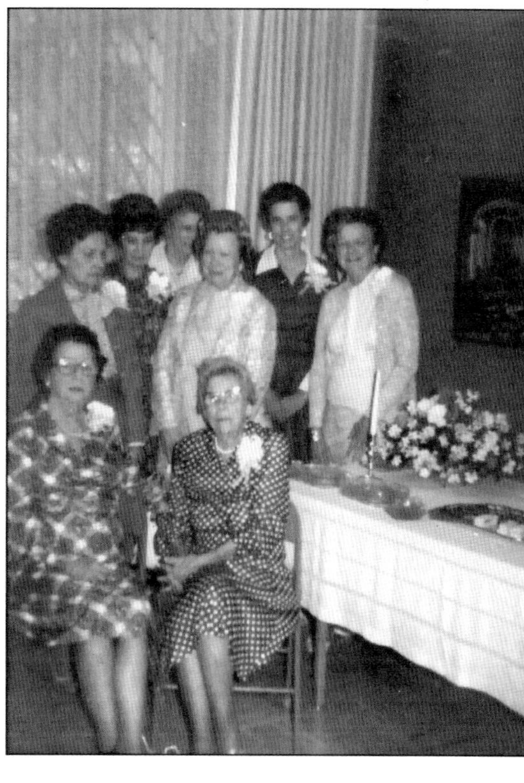

Thursday Study Club members attended a 1977 reception in their honor at the library. From left to right are (seated) Mrs. Alston Paden Green and Mrs. Morgan McCall; (standing) Mrs. Willis A. Harris, Mrs. James L. Hoffman, Annie Sue Bass, Mrs. William F. Byrd, Mrs. James D. Pruett, and Mrs. J. D. Bush.

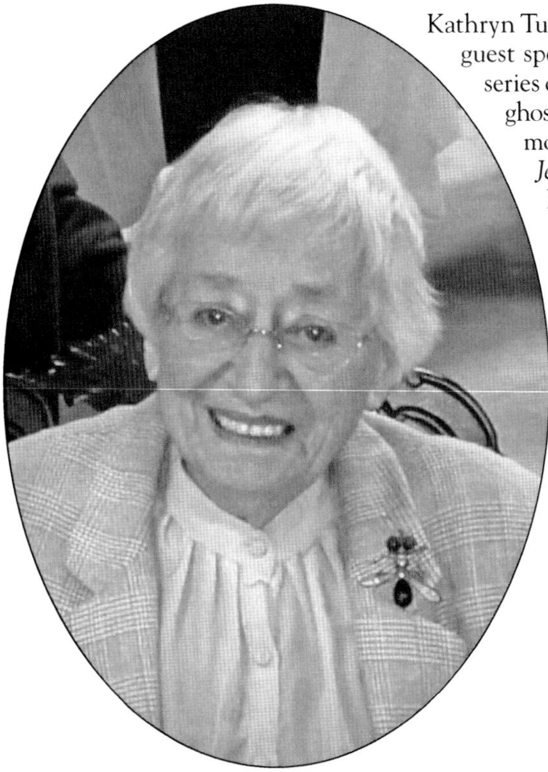

Kathryn Tucker Windham of Selma, Alabama, was the guest speaker at the Friends of the Library author series on January 19, 1978. The author of books on ghosts, recipes, and Alabama history, Windham's most popular book is *13 Alabama Ghosts and Jeffrey*. (Photograph used by permission from Rebecca Mitchell.)

In the late 1970s, the library promoted its extensive genealogical resources with this billboard in downtown Gadsden.

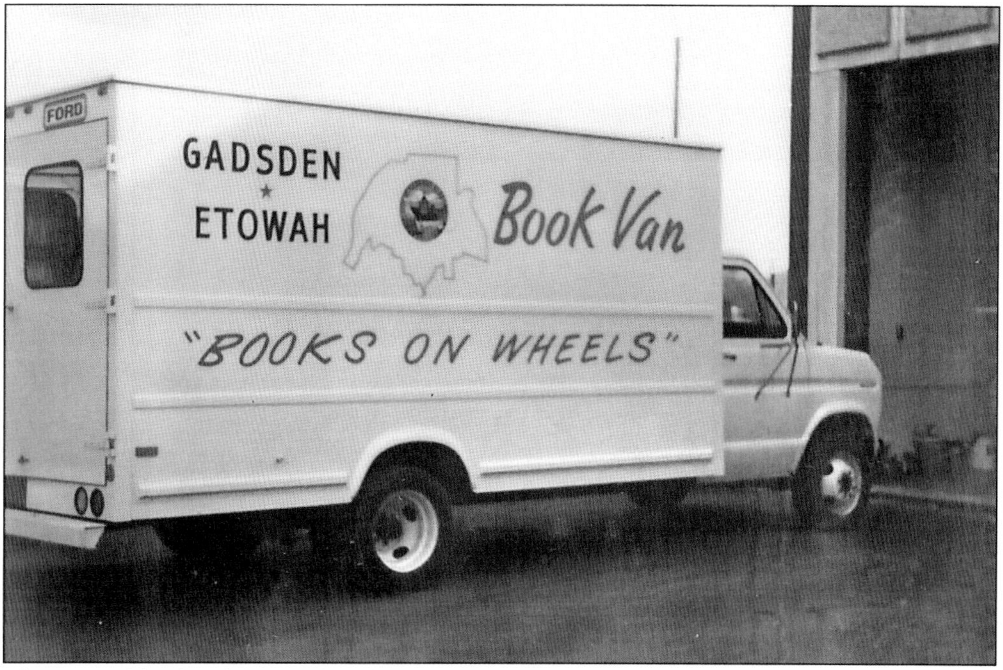

The original bookmobile, purchased in 1959, was sold in 1975. A new one was purchased in 1978 as a joint effort of the city, county, and state to reach areas not served by libraries. Bookmobile driver Ernestine Battles (below, left) is pictured delivering books to residents of the Gadsden Nursing Home in August 1978. Seated (from left to right) are Reeda Bradford and Nell Smith, with activities director Doris Bradford standing at right. The bookmobile made 55 stops throughout the county, and readers eagerly awaited its arrival. Battles retired in April 2002 after 23 years at the library.

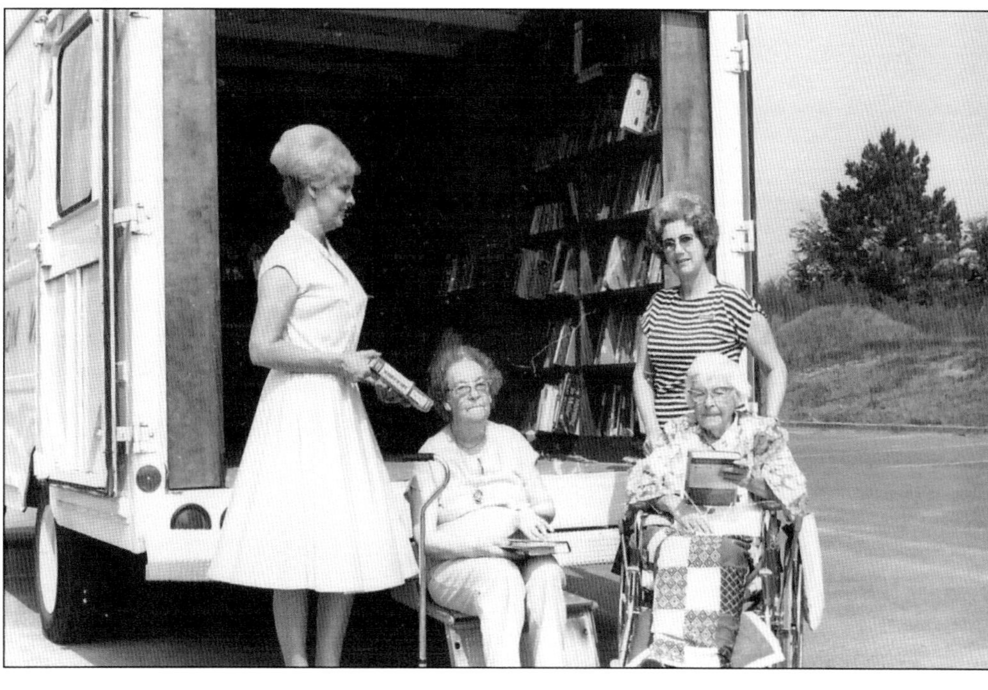

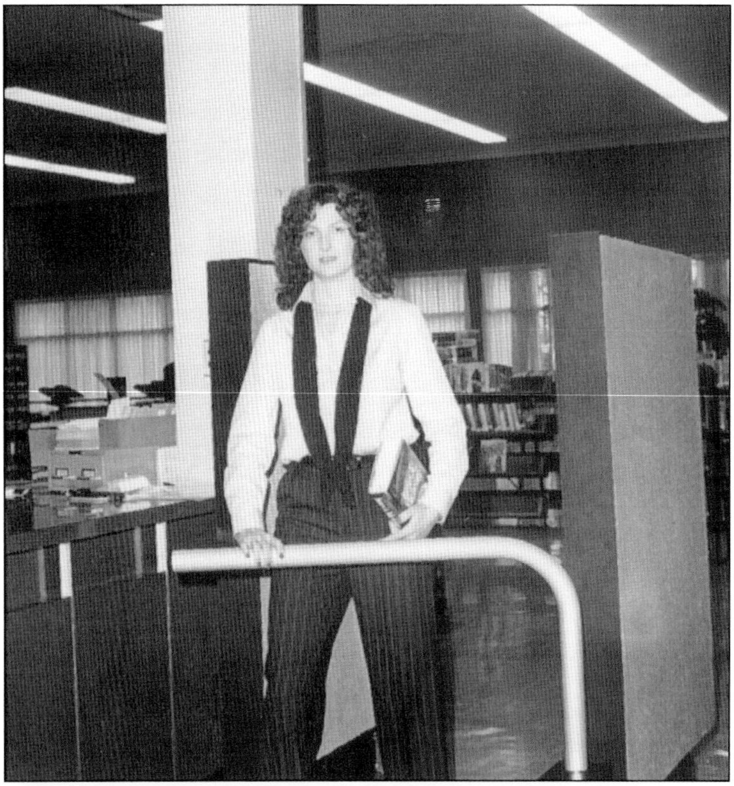

Circulation supervisor Paula Morris demonstrates the book detection system installed at the main library in 1979.

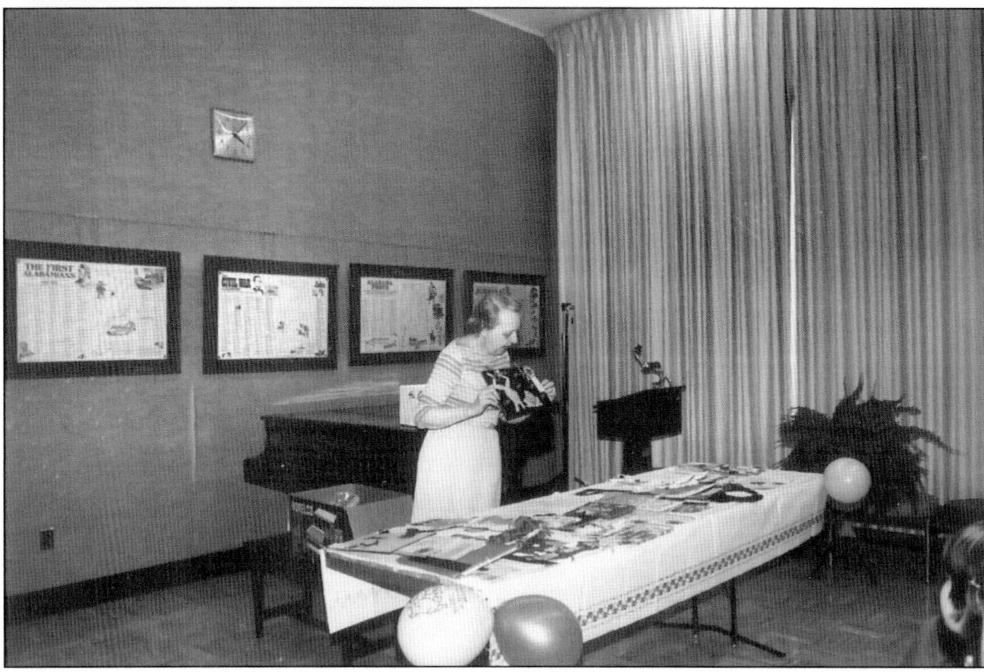

Children's librarian Margaret McGuire displays winning entries in the Create-A-Book competition, first held in 1979. McGuire retired in 1993, and the annual contest was named in her honor. More than 300 entries were typically submitted, and large crowds were in attendance on awards day.

Alabama journalist and novelist Paul Hemphill (right) presents a copy of his new novel *Long Gone* to Bobby Junkins. On the left is Charles Cantrell, president of the library board. Hemphill spoke to the Friends of the Library on September 4, 1979. The author of 15 books, Hemphill focused much of his writing career on the blue-collar South.

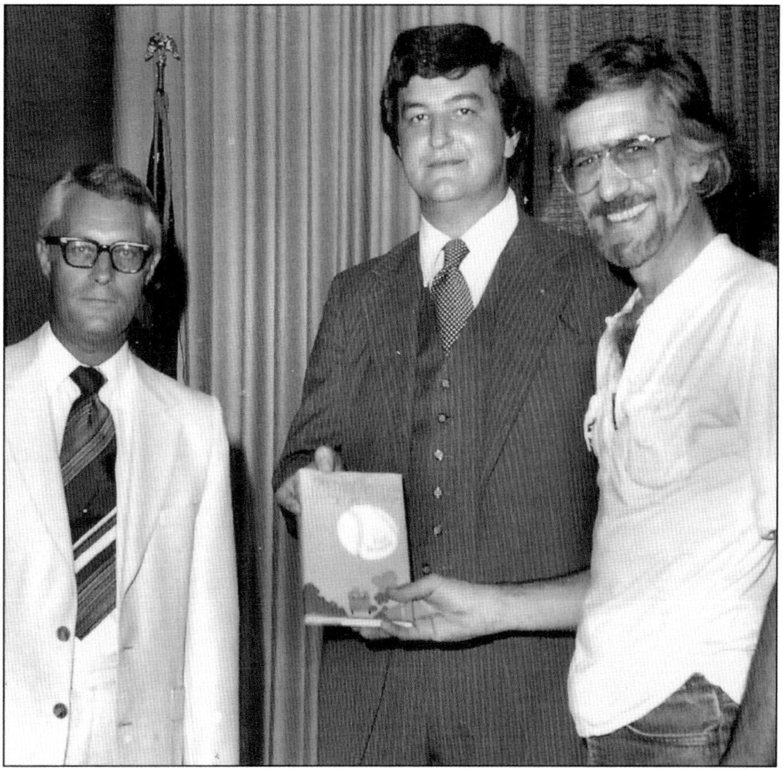

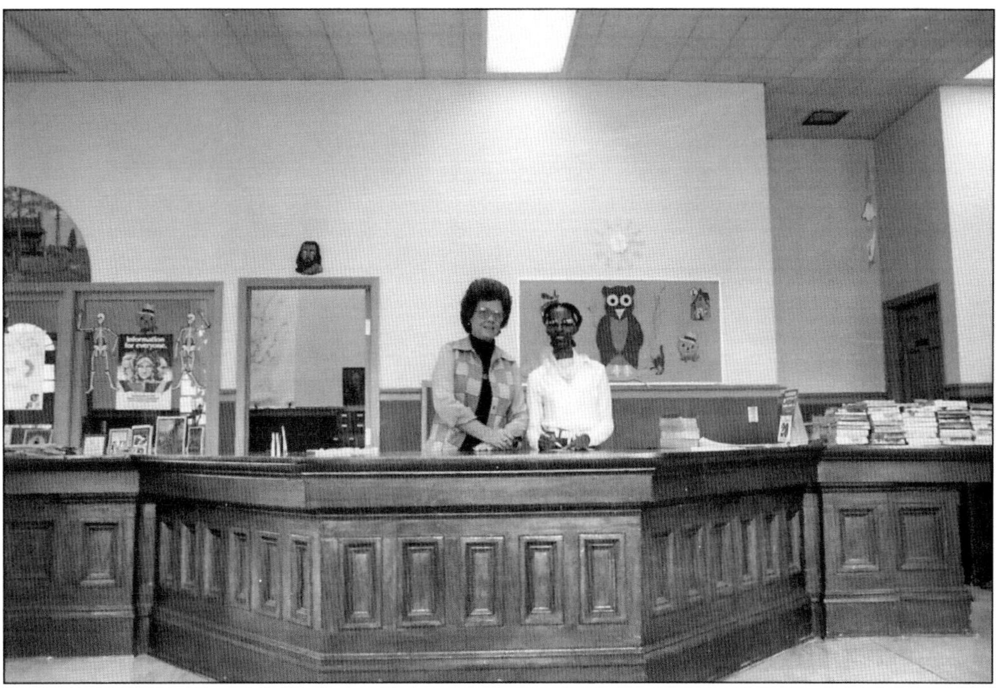

At the Alabama City Library in 1980, Virginia Bishop (left) and Debra Thomas stand behind the checkout desk that was originally used in the old Carnegie Library on Forrest Avenue. Bill Allison, a retired policeman, restored the desk, moved it in sections, and set it up here.

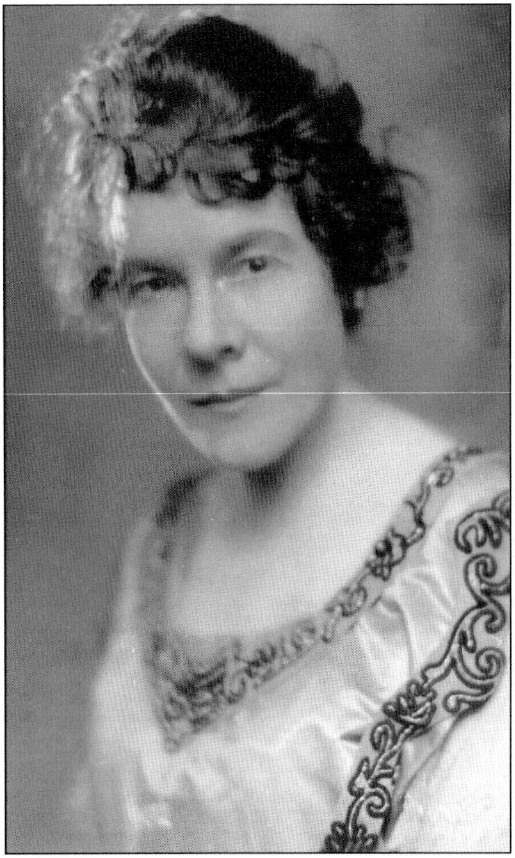

In recognizing American Music Month in February 1981, the Gadsden Music Club paid tribute to Annie Mathilde Bilbro with a display at the library. One of Alabama's most celebrated musicians, Bilbro was a charter member of the Thursday Study Club. Sometime between 1890 and 1900, Bilbro opened a studio in Gadsden. There the people of Gadsden had access to her exceptional methods of teaching piano. Known primarily as a composer of children's music, Bilbro's unique methods are said to have revolutionized the teaching of children's piano literature.

In 1981, a branch library was included as part of the newly opened Carver complex on the site of the old Carver High School (CHS). This wall mural of the school, painted by famous artist and former CHS student John Sandridge, is a focal point in the library. Trophies, class pictures, and other memorabilia were restored by the library for display in the facility. CHS, located on Tuscaloosa Avenue, was known for its outstanding band, athletic programs, educators, and curriculum.

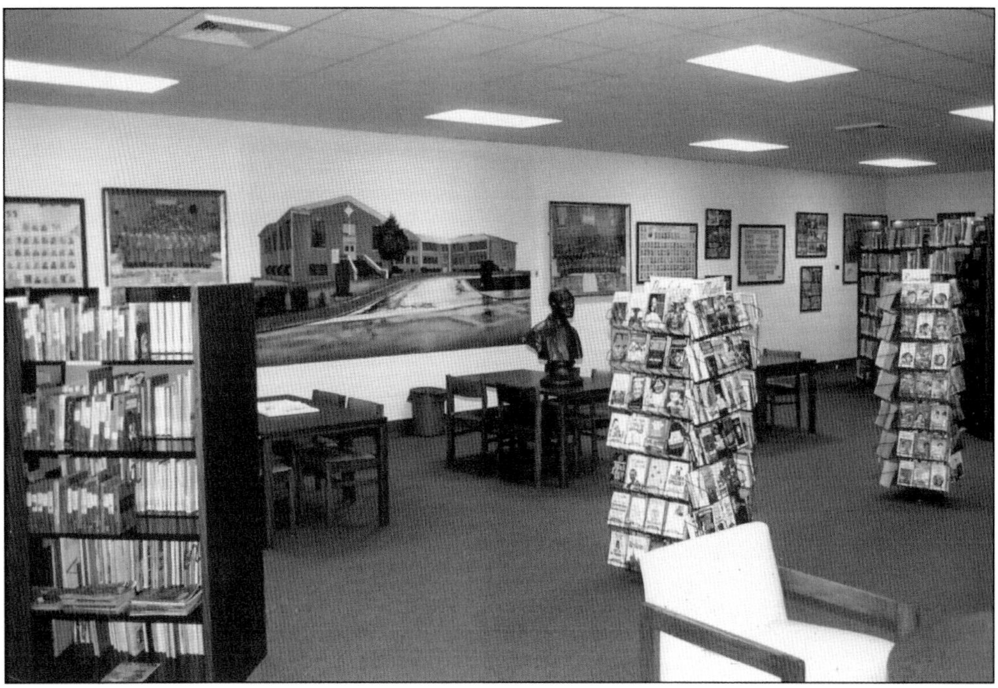

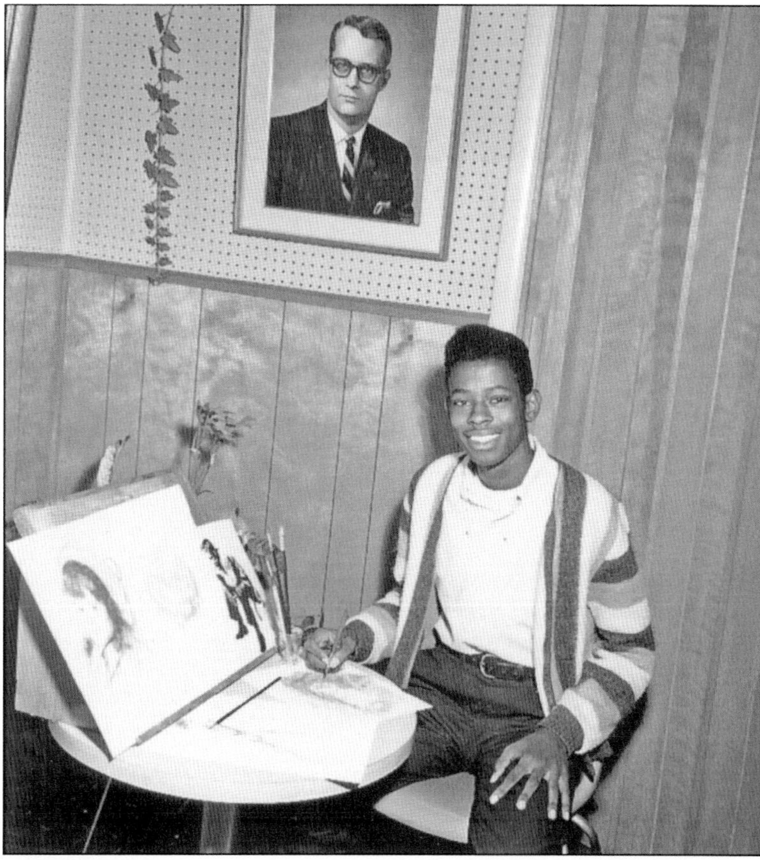

Shown here in the late 1960s, Gadsden author and artist John Sandridge had his first art exhibit at the main library. Sandridge was the first African American to be licensed by the Coca-Cola Company to create a series of paintings incorporating an African American theme. Pictured below is a library exhibit in the 1990s featuring Sandridge's Coca-Cola art and Luv Life Collectibles.

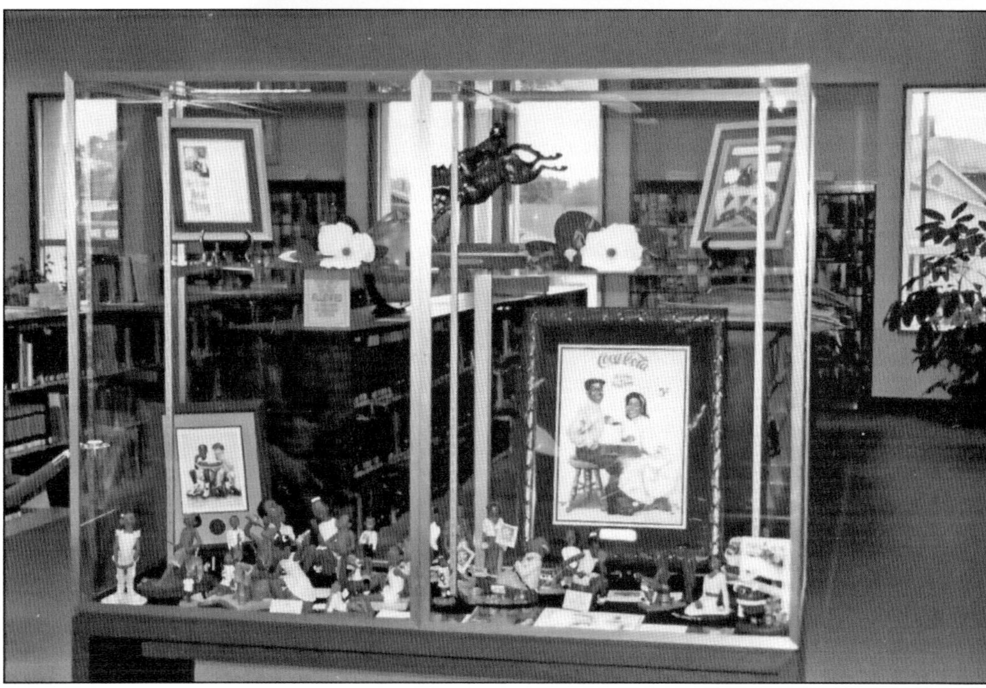

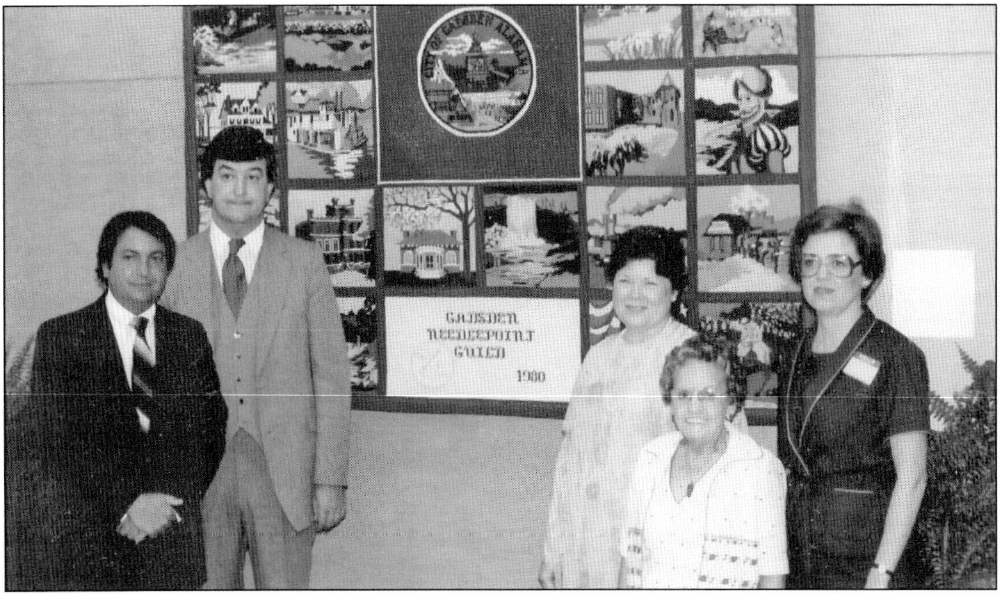

Mayor Steve Means (far left) is shown accepting the tapestry *Historic Gadsden in Needlepoint* from officers of the Gadsden Needlepoint Guild. The tapestry, along with a hardbound book of the patterns, was presented to the library on August 4, 1981. Shown at the presentation are, from left to right, Means; Bobby Junkins; Carol Wesley, chairman of the project; Viola Seckel, president; and Linda Simmons, secretary-treasurer and publicity chairman. The tapestry, which took two years of planning and work, is made up of 36 seven-inch squares and depicts historic local scenes, including the 1906 Carnegie Library.

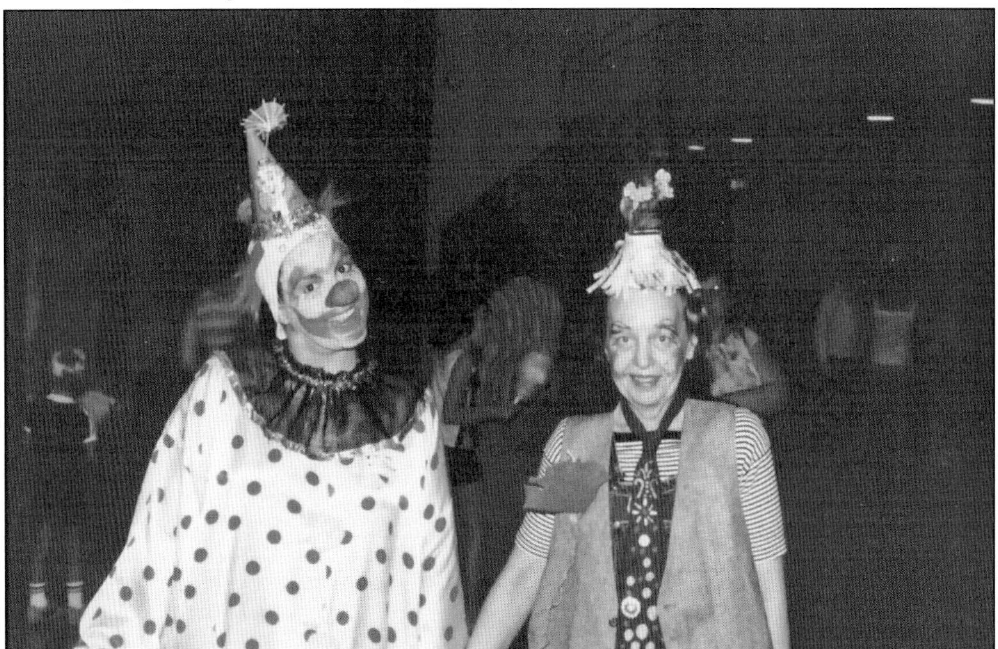

Staff members Diane Brown (left) and Margaret McGuire are dressed up for the August 1981 circus magic reading program.

The Gadsden Jayceettes and the Friends of the Library cosponsored the first annual book sale in December 1982, where more than 8,000 outdated and duplicate books were sold. Shown sorting books for the sale, from left to right, are Ginger Barkley, library clerk and Jayceette; Anita Brooks, acquisitions; and Randy Holland, reference assistant.

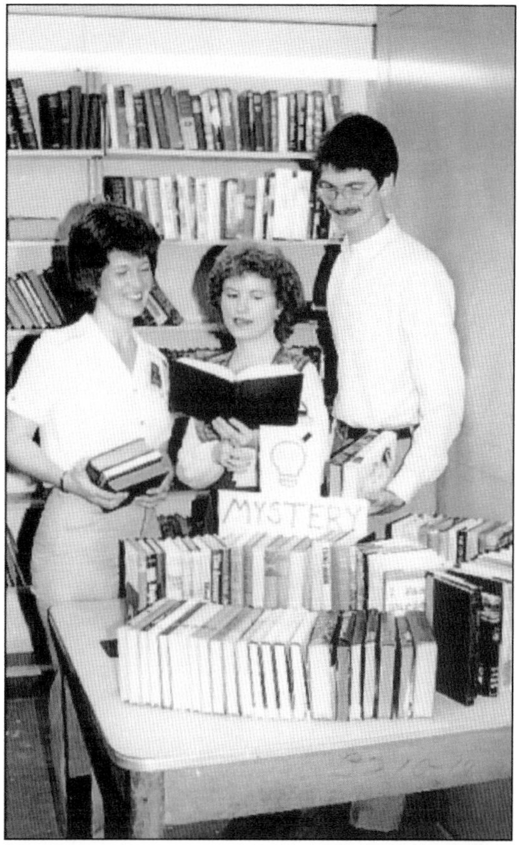

Bobby Junkins was elected to represent District 30 in the Alabama Legislature, where he served from 1982 to 1988. Members of the Etowah County Legislative delegation shown here are, from left to right, (first row) Joe Ford and June Bugg; (second row) William Drinkard and Junkins. While serving on the Ways and Means Committee, Junkins helped libraries tremendously, with state funding increasing significantly.

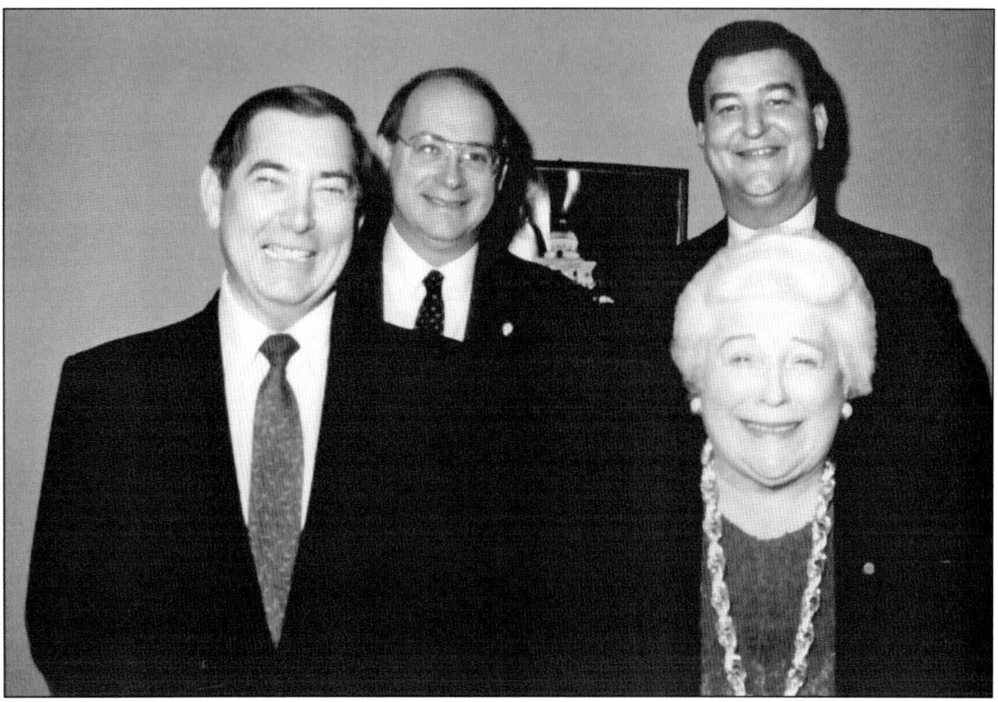

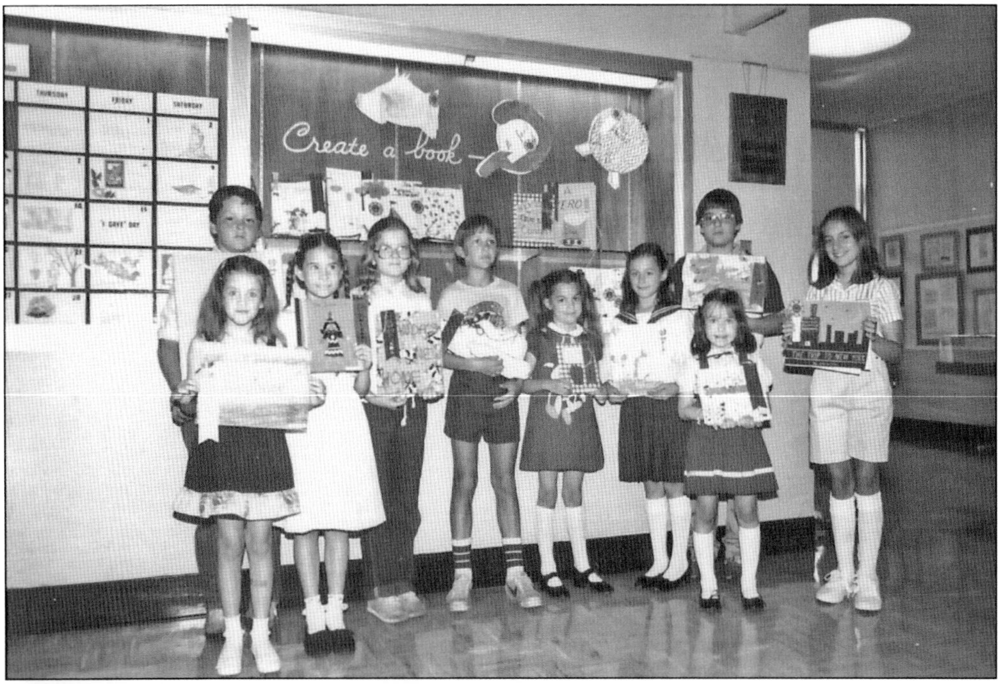

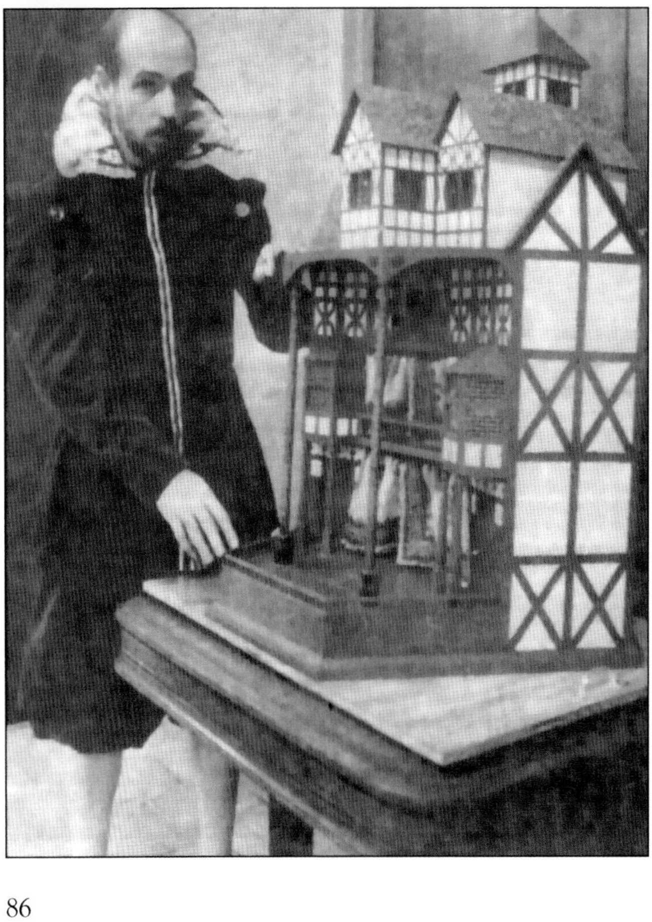

Winners of the 1983 Create-A-Book contest were, from left to right, Kim Jolley, Neal Burchfield, Amanda Snow, Leigh Behrens, Jimmy Baird, Jana Watson, Sally Inzer, Steven Smith, Rachel Johnson, and Catherine Inzer.

Louis Loveman, a library page, is shown in 16th-century costume as part of a Shakespeare seminar in July 1984. The replica of the Globe Theatre was built by Disque Junior High School student Jamie Jones as an English class project in 1970.

A genealogy wing was added to the library and named in honor of Congressman Albert Rains in recognition of his service to the library, the community, and the nation. Shown at the ribbon-cutting on September 8, 1985, are, from left to right, Mayor Steve Means, Allison Rains, Albert Rains, and Bobby Junkins. The new wing included the Alabama Room, which houses local and state history, works by state authors, and genealogy specific to Alabama.

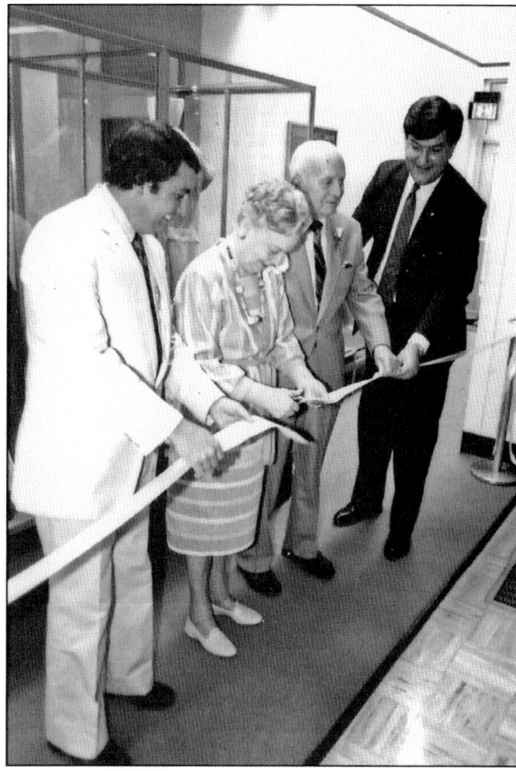

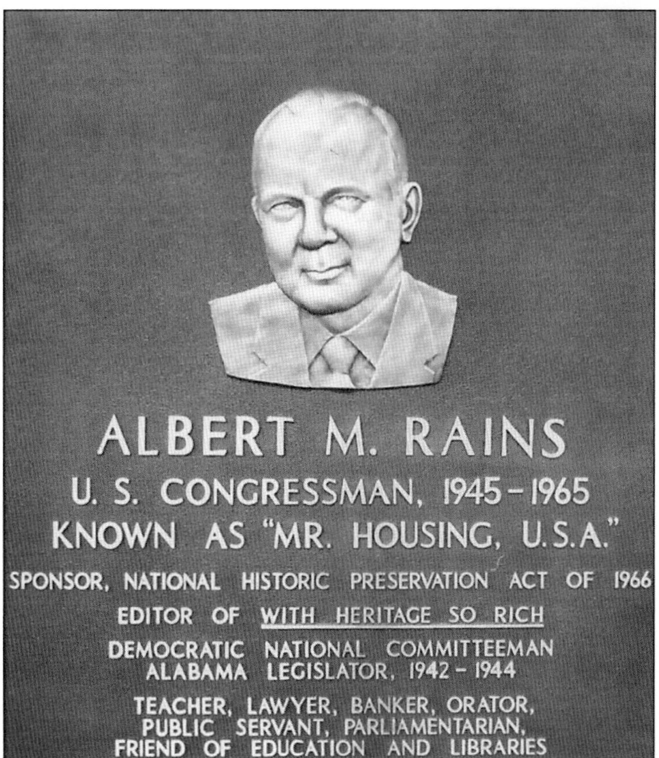

Albert Rains began practicing law in Gadsden in 1929. He was elected to the Alabama Legislature in 1940 and served until 1944, when he was elected to the U.S. House of Representatives. Rains represented the Fifth Congressional District until his retirement in 1965. The sponsor of much important legislation, Rains wrote many bills that provided housing for low-income families and was known as "Mr. Housing, U.S.A." Millions of Americans own homes because of his efforts. While chairman of a study group on historic preservation, Rains filed a report that became a best-selling book entitled *With Heritage So Rich*. As a result of this study, the Historic Preservation Act of 1966 was enacted by the U.S. Congress into law.

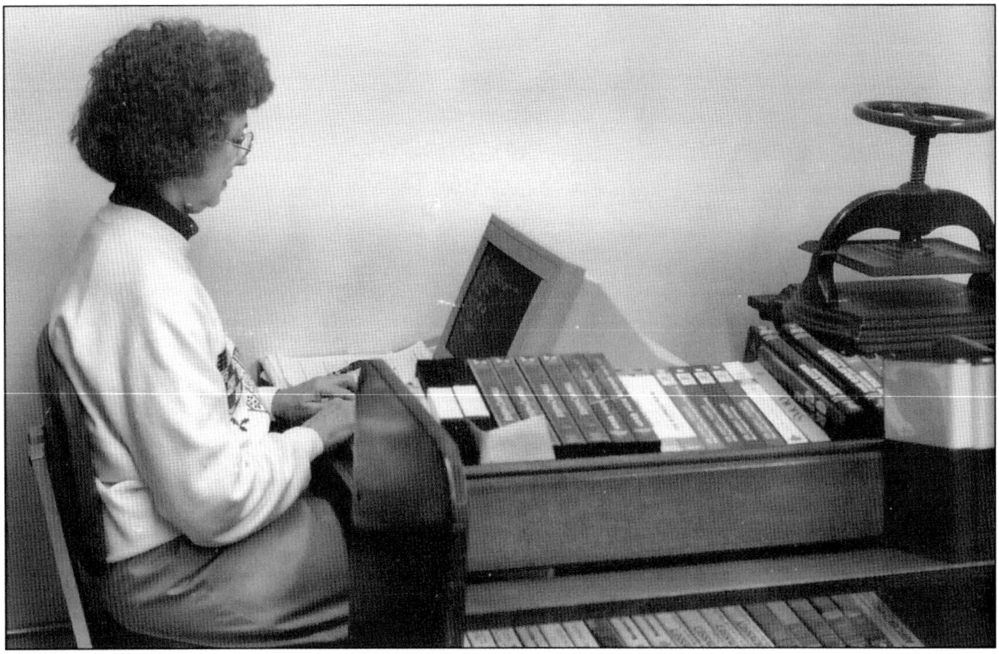

In 1984, the library staff began converting to an electronic, online system. As a founding member of a north Alabama library consortium, Gadsden Public Library was one of the first libraries in the state to offer computerized access. Library clerk Sybil Dean enters bibliographic information into the database.

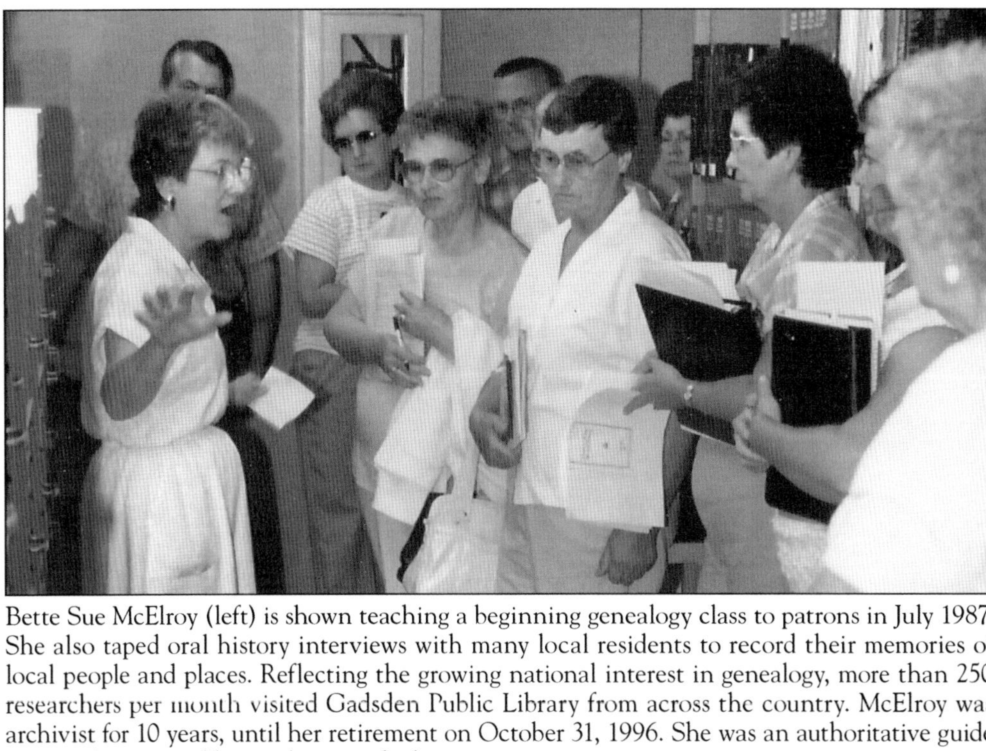

Bette Sue McElroy (left) is shown teaching a beginning genealogy class to patrons in July 1987. She also taped oral history interviews with many local residents to record their memories of local people and places. Reflecting the growing national interest in genealogy, more than 250 researchers per month visited Gadsden Public Library from across the country. McElroy was archivist for 10 years, until her retirement on October 31, 1996. She was an authoritative guide to genealogists, and her enthusiasm for history was contagious.

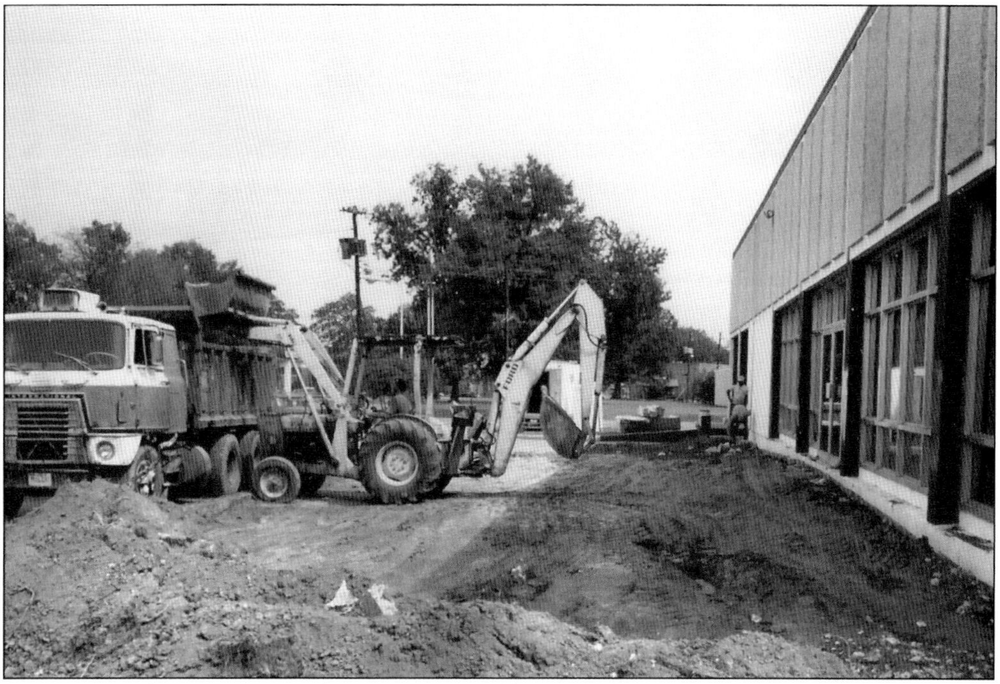

Construction began in September 1987 on an addition to the children's division. The expansion added 3,600 square feet, doubling its existing space. The Alabama Public Library Service allocated $200,000 for the project, and the remaining $73,000 was funded by the City of Gadsden.

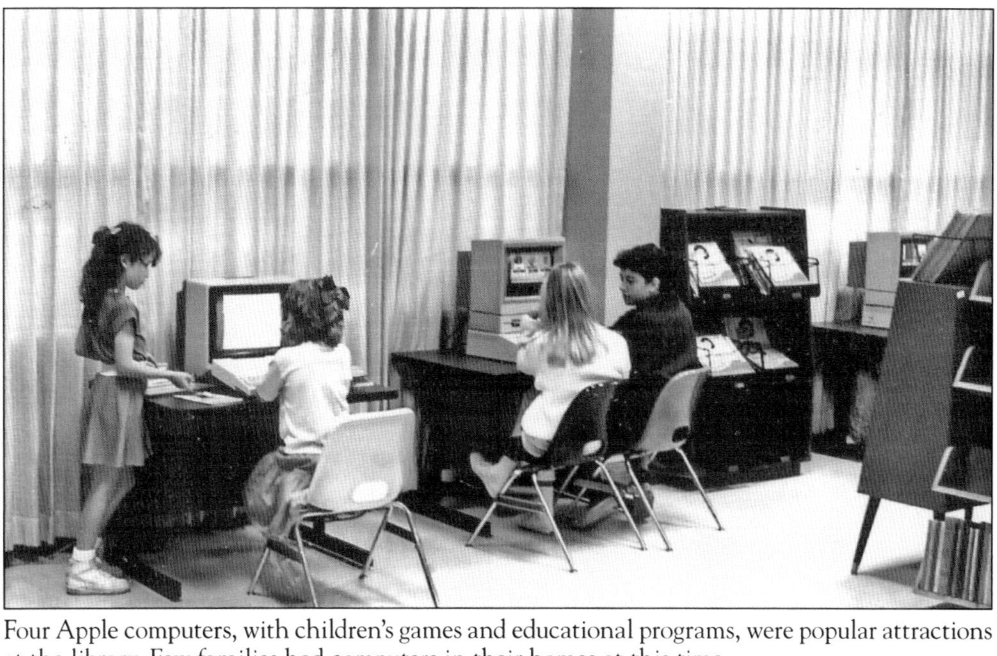

Four Apple computers, with children's games and educational programs, were popular attractions at the library. Few families had computers in their homes at this time.

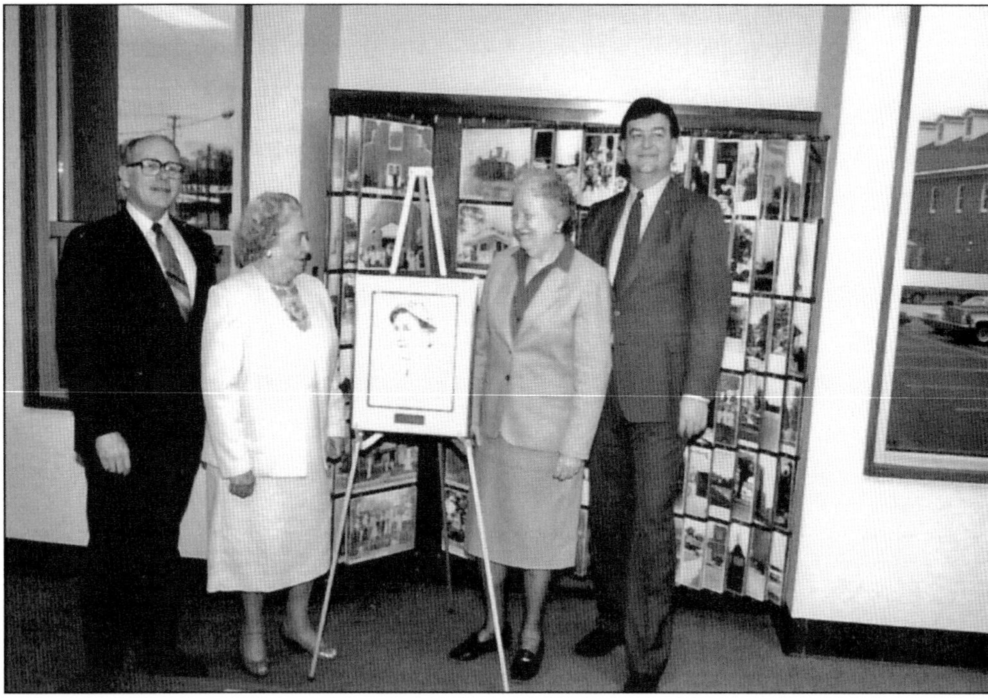

The Etowah Historical Society presented a portrait of founder Mary Harrison Lister to the library on October 8, 1987. From left to right are Elbert Watson, Margaret Lister McDonald, Hazel Oliver, and Bobby Junkins.

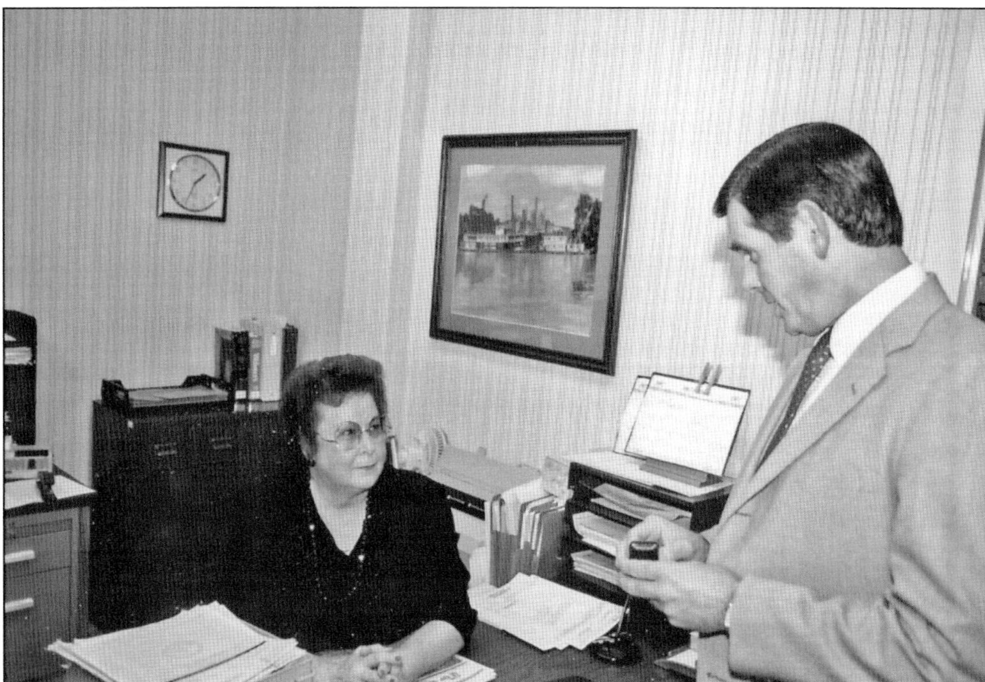

Mayor David Nolen presents a service pin to library business manager Billie Bailey, who retired on December 31, 1987. Bailey was hired by Oscar Rymer in 1966.

Six

Rebecca Buckner Mitchell 1988–2001

Rebecca Buckner Mitchell served as the library director from 1988 to 2001, a time when services were changing rapidly to meet the technological needs of the staff and community. Initially, the library's new automated system managed circulation transactions, acquisitions, and other staff functions. During 1993, online catalog access for the public was implemented. While some people missed the card catalog when it was removed in 1999, many younger, more computer-oriented patrons never learned to use it. With its extensive collection, Gadsden Public Library filled interlibrary loan requests from online users across the state. Collection development, inventory, and weeding outdated materials were priorities during Mitchell's administration. The Friends of the Library organization was active in the early 1990s under the direction of John McFarland and Jim McGuire. Each year, summer readers were rewarded by the library with certificates, refreshments, entertainment, and prizes. The Ancestor Swap Meet began in 1999 as a fund-raising project of the Northeast Alabama Genealogical Society. With the library as a cosponsor, it became a highly anticipated annual event for participants to share research and swap information. In 1998, Microsoft chairman Bill Gates awarded Gadsden Public Library a grant of $27,000 from the Gates Library Foundation for training, Internet access, software, and computers. Classes for the public on basic computer instruction were first offered by staff members in 1999 and became one of the library's most popular services. Under Mitchell's direction, the library forged ahead in the rapidly developing electronic world, with staff and patrons accessing the Internet through high-speed connections.

"We are out of space," Mitchell often said, beginning in interviews as early as 1995. Asbestos in the building limited wiring modifications; heating, cooling, and lighting systems were inadequate. The building no longer lent itself to changes for accommodating new technology, which was an integral part of its operation. In 2001, funding for the purchase of land across the street from the library was awarded through the Etowah County Library Committee's share of the county's one-percent sales tax. Future plans included development of the property for parking lot expansion. Then, in January 2002, Rebecca Buckner Mitchell took the director's position at the Alabama Public Library Service in Montgomery.

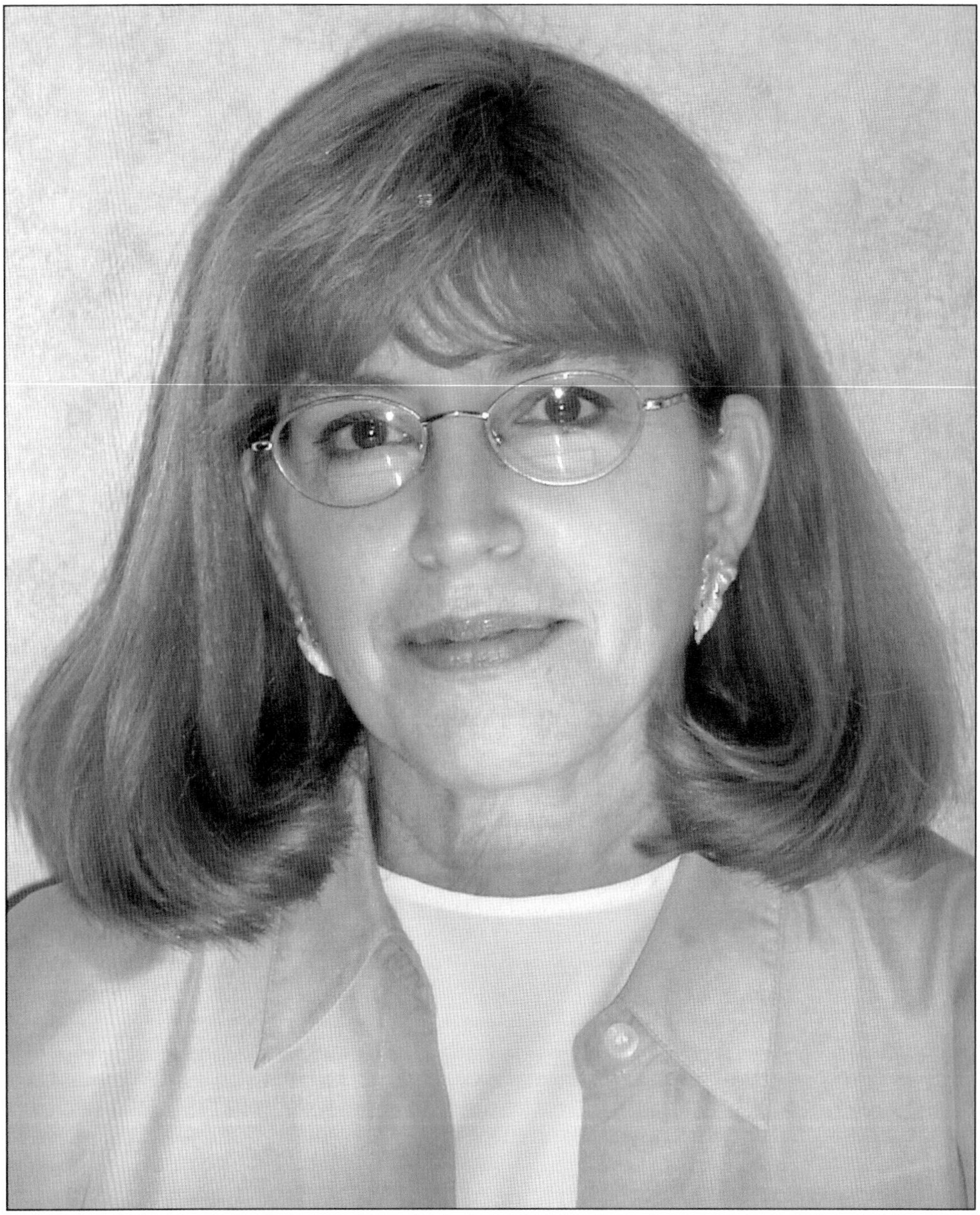

Rebecca Buckner Mitchell received her bachelor's degree from the University of Mississippi and graduated from the University of Alabama with a master's degree in library science. After serving as the director at Talladega Public Library for five years, Mitchell became the medical librarian at Gadsden's Baptist Memorial Hospital in 1982. In 1987, Mitchell became a bibliographic instructor for the Houston Cole Library at Jacksonville State University, where she taught for 18 months until accepting the Gadsden director's position.

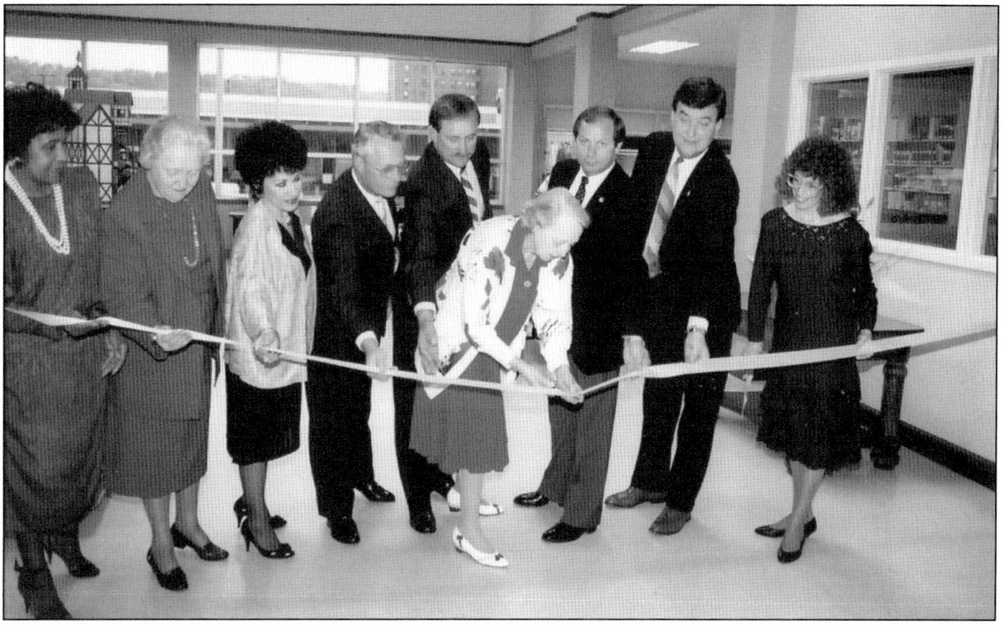

Dedication of the new children's wing was held on April 9, 1989, during National Library Week. Children's librarian Margaret McGuire (center) cuts the ribbon, while being assisted by, from left to right, Lillie Jones, Hazel Oliver, Janie Copeland, Charles Cantrell, Lewis Fuller, John Colvin, Bobby Junkins, and Rebecca Buckner Mitchell.

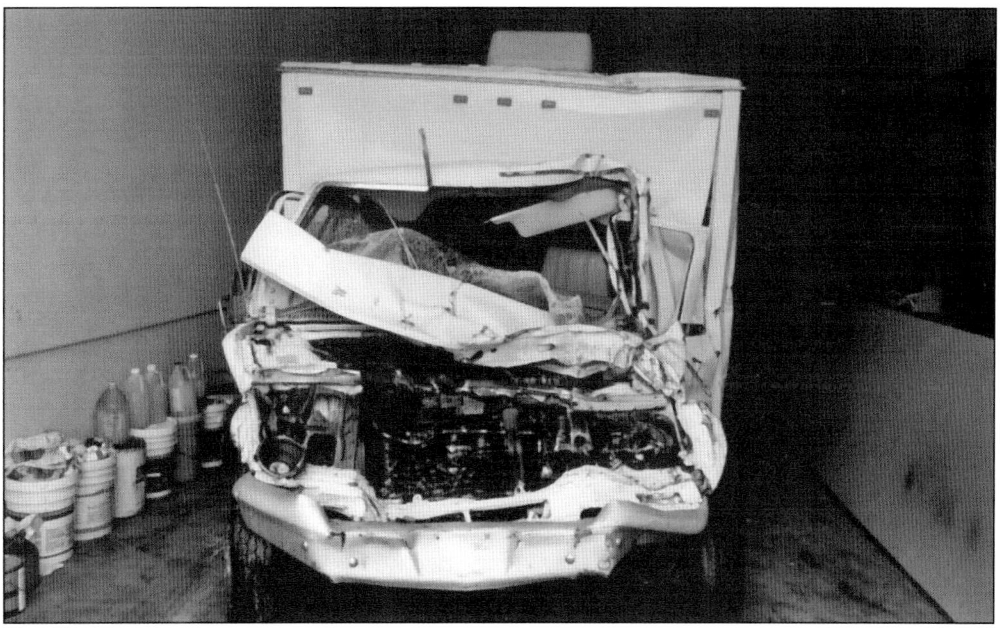

In November 1989, the bookmobile was involved in a wreck with a tractor-trailer truck. It could not be repaired, and 1,400 books were damaged by diesel fuel. The driver, Brenda Lankford, was hospitalized for two weeks. After two months of being out of service, a used bookmobile replaced the one that was wrecked. Bookmobile services were retired in 1992 because of the age of the vehicle and laws requiring the operator to have a certified driver's license. A books-by-mail program was established in 1993.

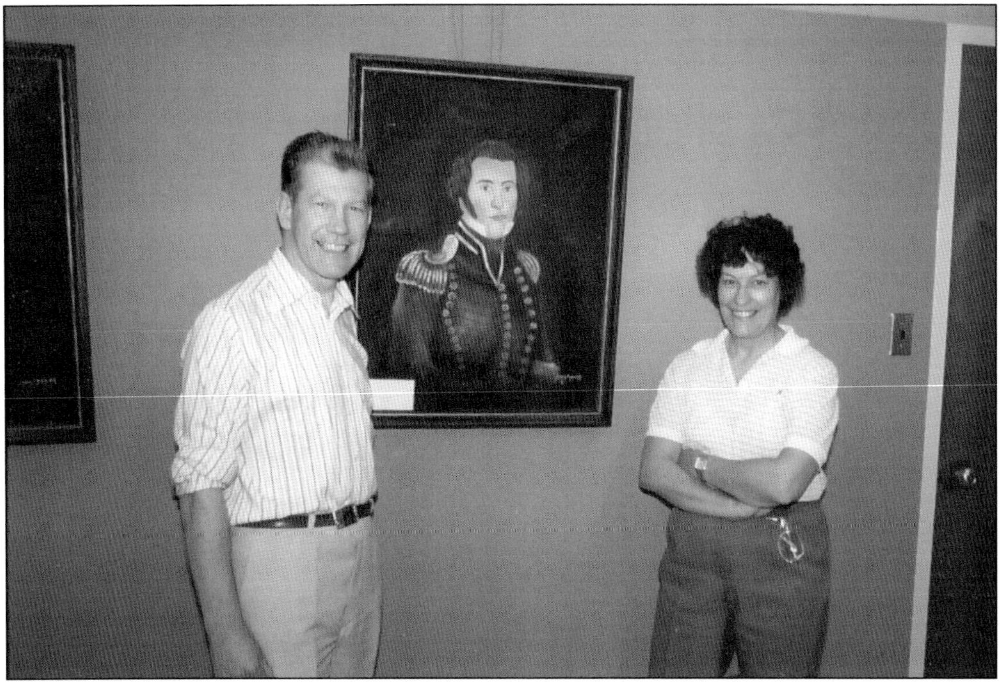

Mr. and Mrs. Edward John Gadsden from England are shown visiting the library in the late 1980s. The painting of James Gadsden that hangs in the background was painted by local artist Danny Crownover. Crownover became a historian in his own right, specializing in the history of the city of Gadsden.

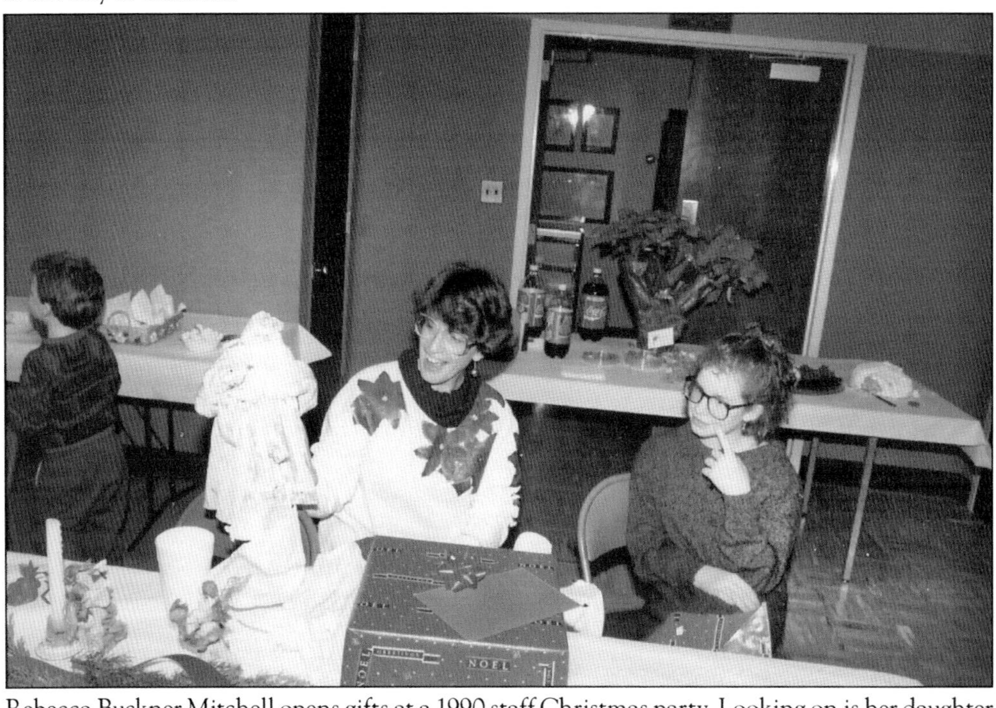

Rebecca Buckner Mitchell opens gifts at a 1990 staff Christmas party. Looking on is her daughter Amanda, age 12, who would become the library director in 2006.

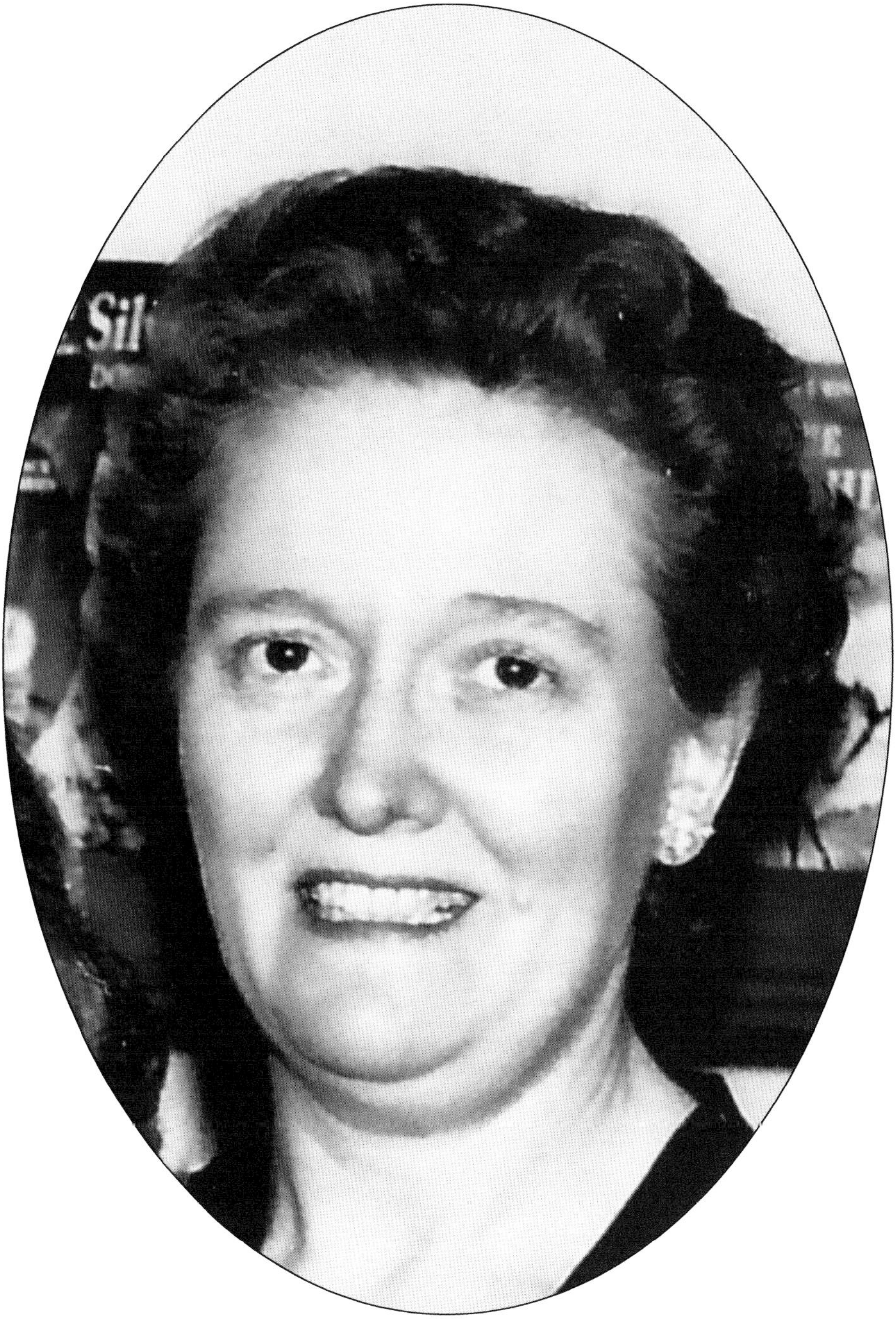

"Hazel Oliver: She's Known for Making the Wheels Go Round," read the headline of a *Gadsden Times* article by Deirdre Coakley on September 16, 1991. Oliver was a library volunteer as a teenager, when the library was located on Forrest Avenue. Pictured here in 1964, Oliver helped raise money to buy furniture and equipment for the library on College Street. Oliver was appointed to the library board in the early 1970s by Mayor Lesley Gilliland and, in 2006, is the longest-serving member. Also active in numerous civic affiliations, Oliver was a charter member of the Etowah Historical Society.

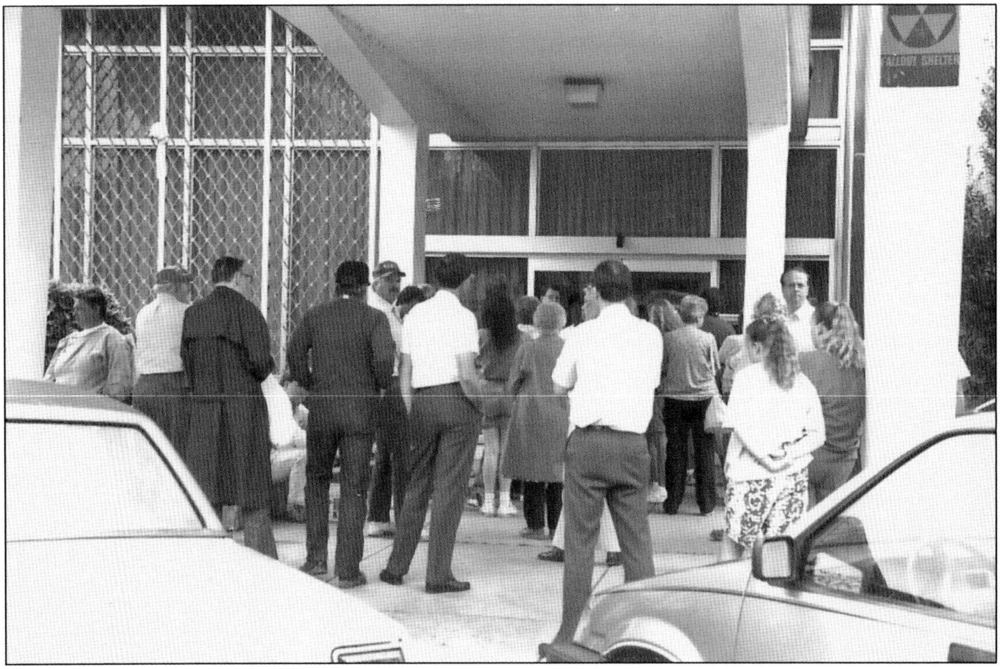

Crowds line up, waiting for the opening of the library's annual book sale. With many books priced at 10¢ and 25¢, these sales were enormously popular with book lovers shopping for a bargain.

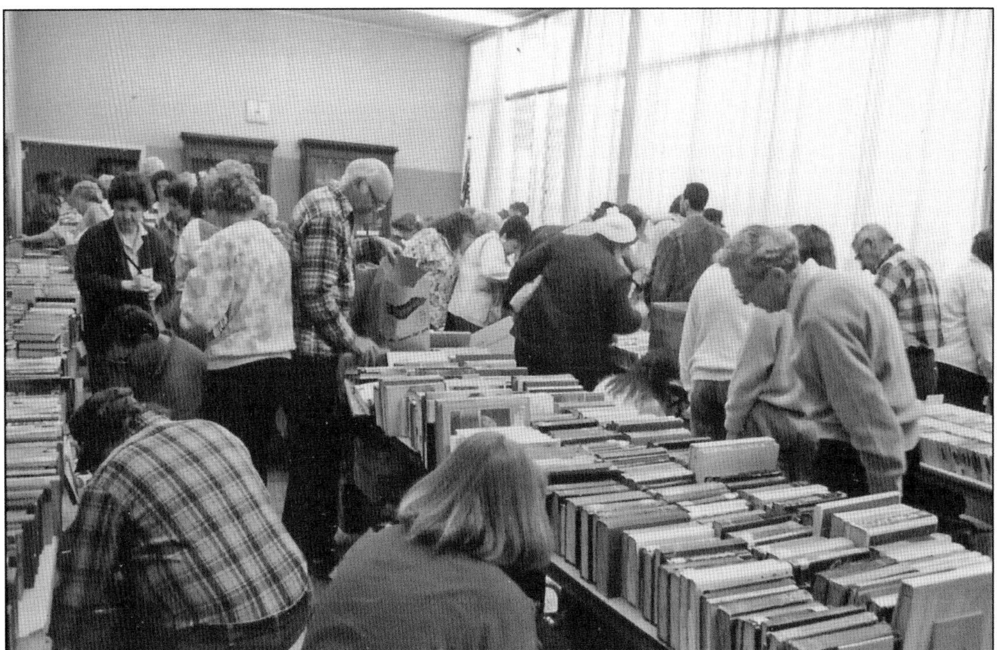

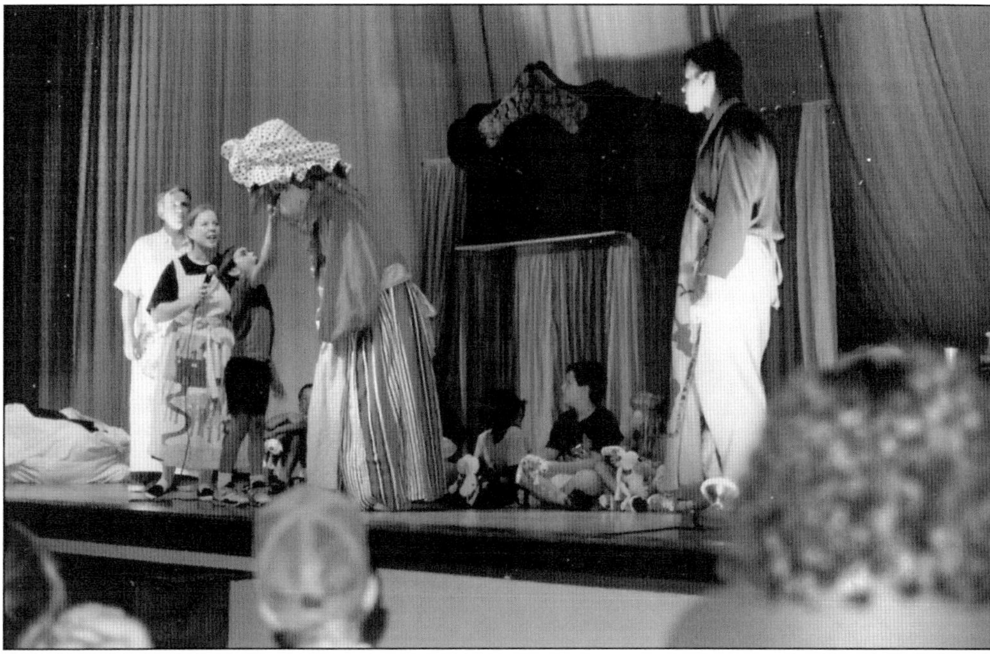

Puppeteers of Berea College in Kentucky entertained children at the Gadsden Convention Hall in July 1993. The troupe also presented free puppet-making workshops at the Center for Cultural Arts. Sponsors of the two-day Puppet Caravan were Gadsden Public Library, Alabama Power Company, and the Center for Cultural Arts.

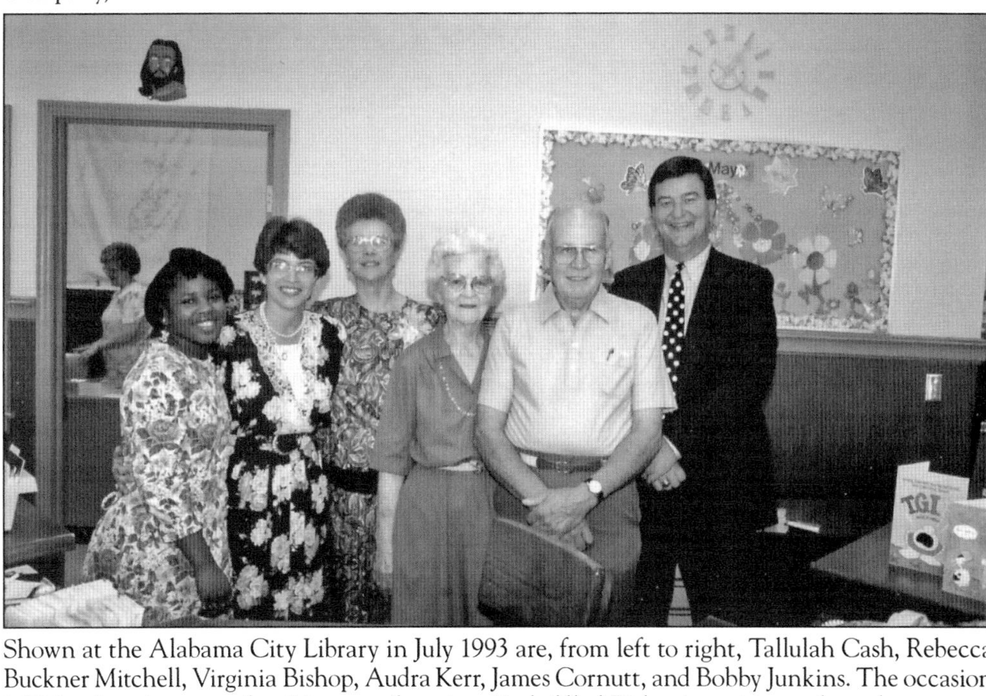

Shown at the Alabama City Library in July 1993 are, from left to right, Tallulah Cash, Rebecca Buckner Mitchell, Virginia Bishop, Audra Kerr, James Cornutt, and Bobby Junkins. The occasion is Bishop's retirement after 24 years of service. Cash filled Bishop's position as branch manager. Kerr worked at this library when it opened in 1938 until her retirement in 1975. Cornutt worked part-time at the Alabama City branch.

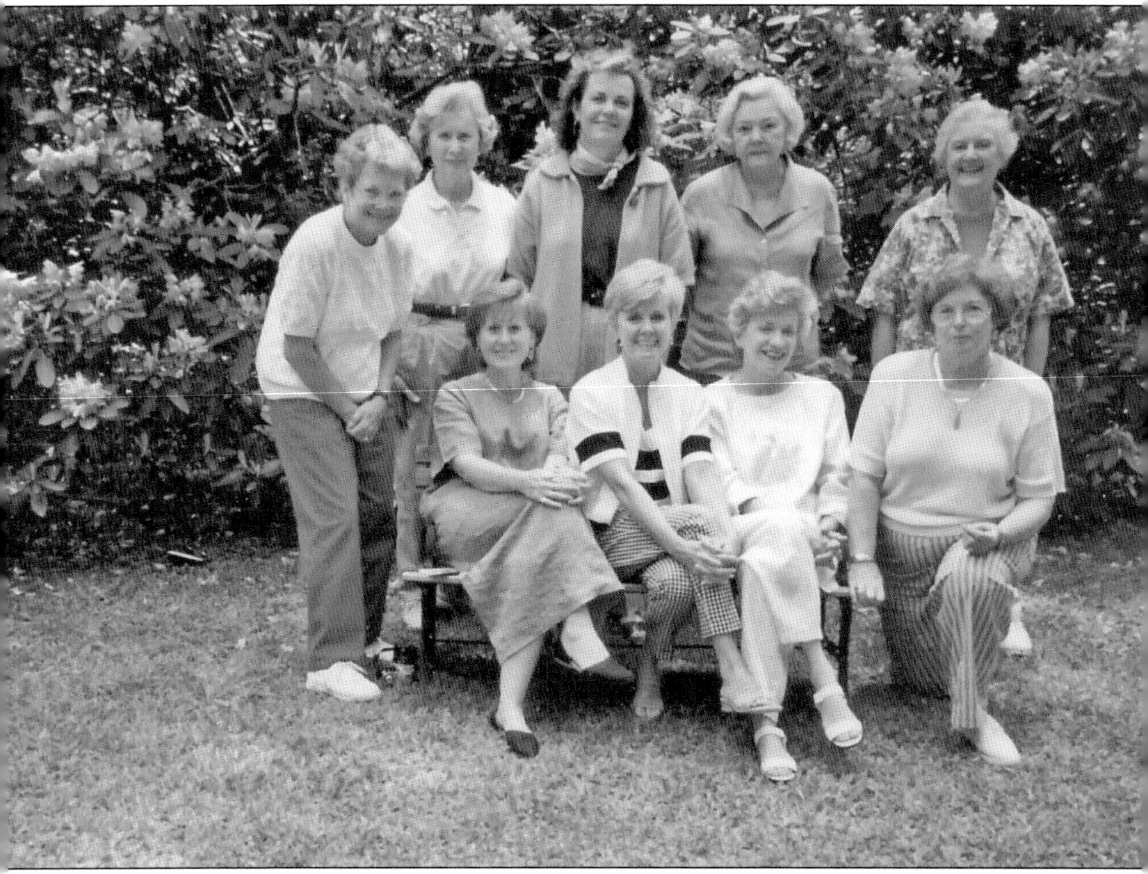

The Thursday Study Club observed its 100th anniversary on September 18, 1997, with a celebration in the library's Lena Martin Room. It honored the efforts of the young women who assembled a collection of books and opened a free public reading room. Former library director and probate judge Bobby Junkins talked about the impact of the library in a community. A handsome plaque commemorating the club was unveiled by Mayor Steve Means. Former and present members attended, and many gave reminiscences. Club members pictured here at the Mentone home of Dr. Scott and Jeanne Vance on May 15, 1997, are, from left to right, (seated) Mrs. Jeffrey (Celeste) Cedarholm, Mrs. Thomas (Judy) Dawson, Mrs. James (Susan) Little, and Mrs. Gordon (Iris) Isbell; (standing) Mrs. Robert (Bette Sue) McElroy, Mrs. James (Juanita) Hinton, Mrs. William (Mandy) Hartzog, Mrs. Scott (Jeanne) Vance, and Mrs. Charles (Betty) Thompson.

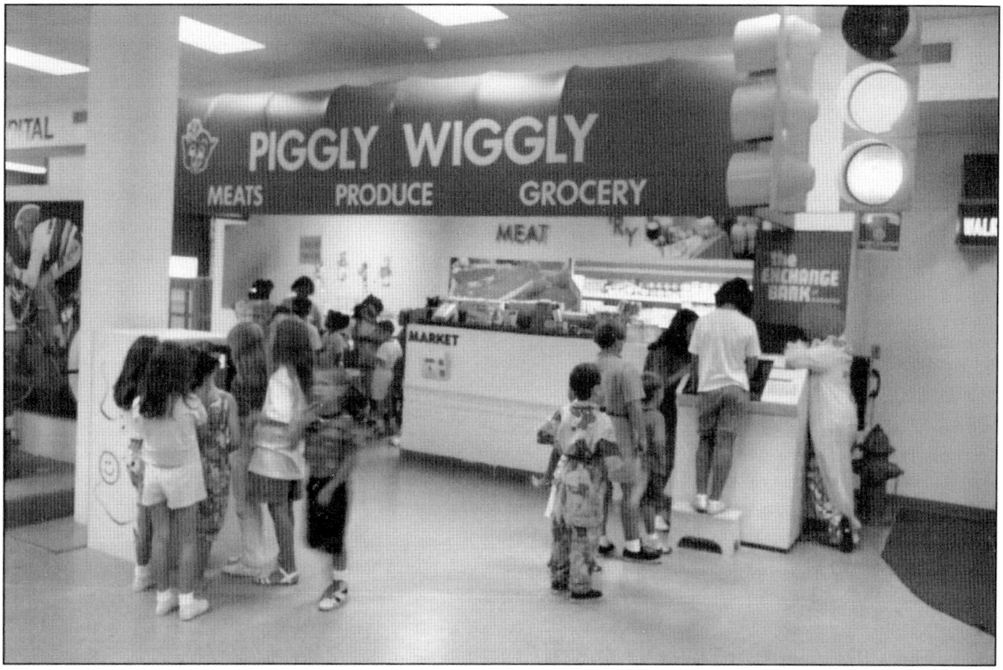

The 1991 summer reading program finale took place at Kids Town USA in the Cultural Arts Center's Imagination Place, where children experienced shopping for groceries and getting money from an automated teller machine. Magician Archie Wade (below) demonstrates a trick to unidentified volunteers during this 1997 children's summer reading program performance at the Gadsden Convention Hall.

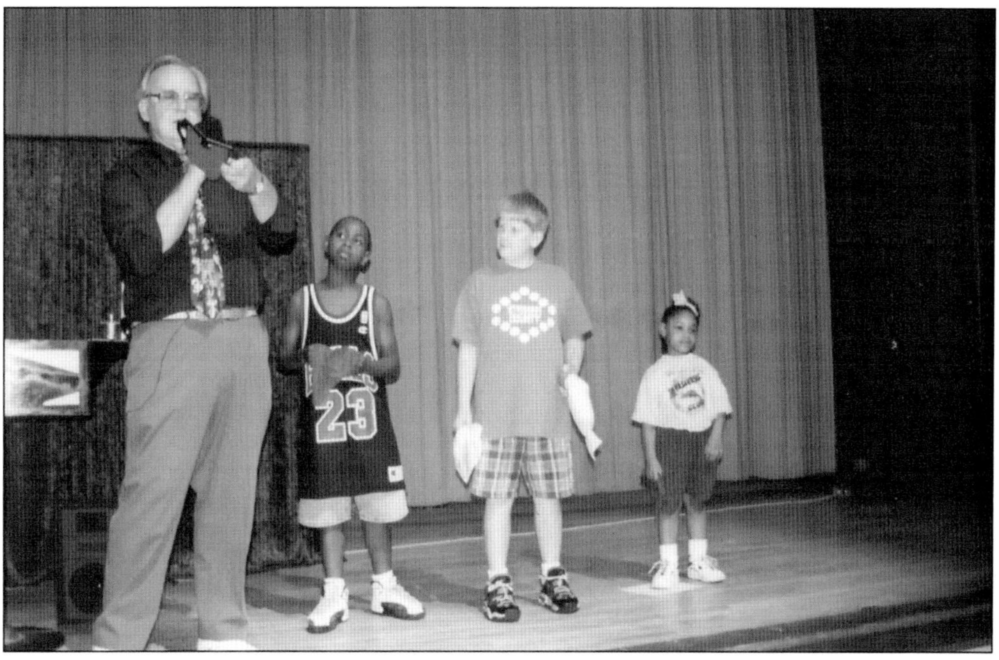

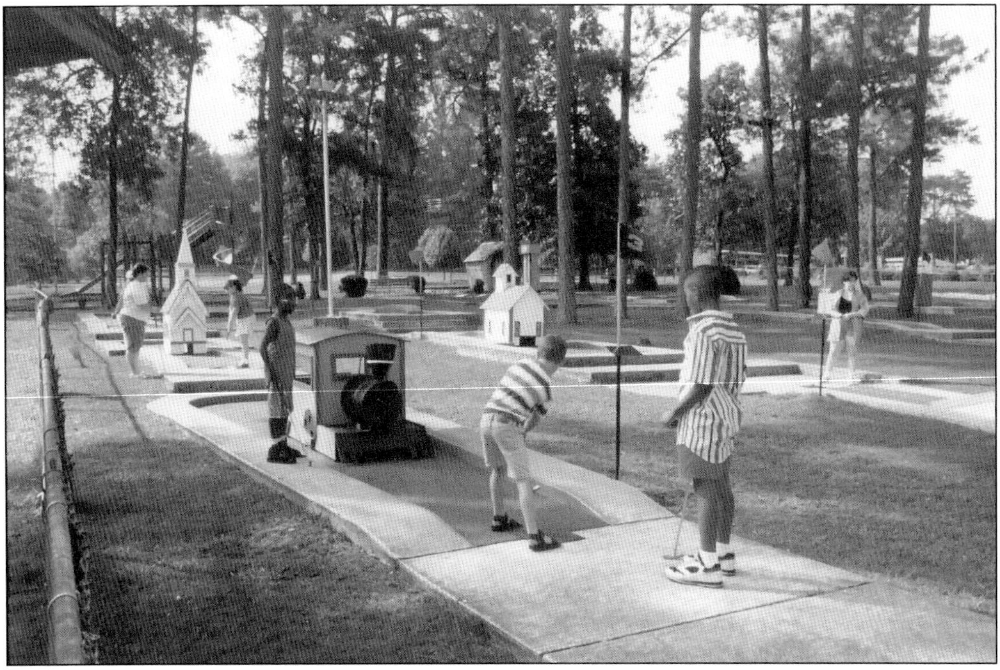

In 1995, the library treated children who completed the summer reading program to miniature golf, train rides, and other fun activities at Noccalula Falls Park.

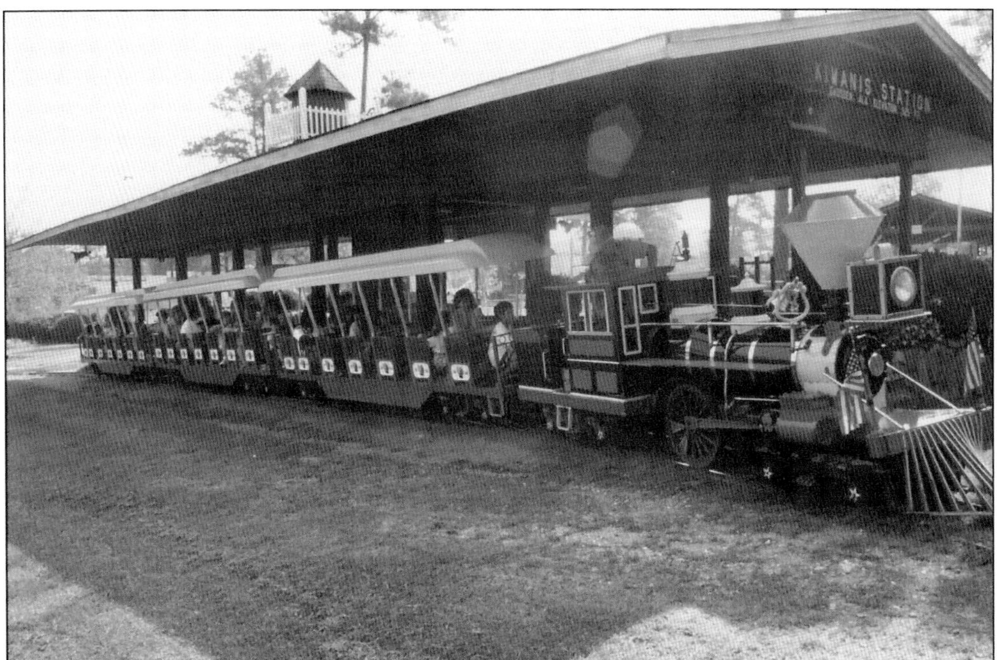

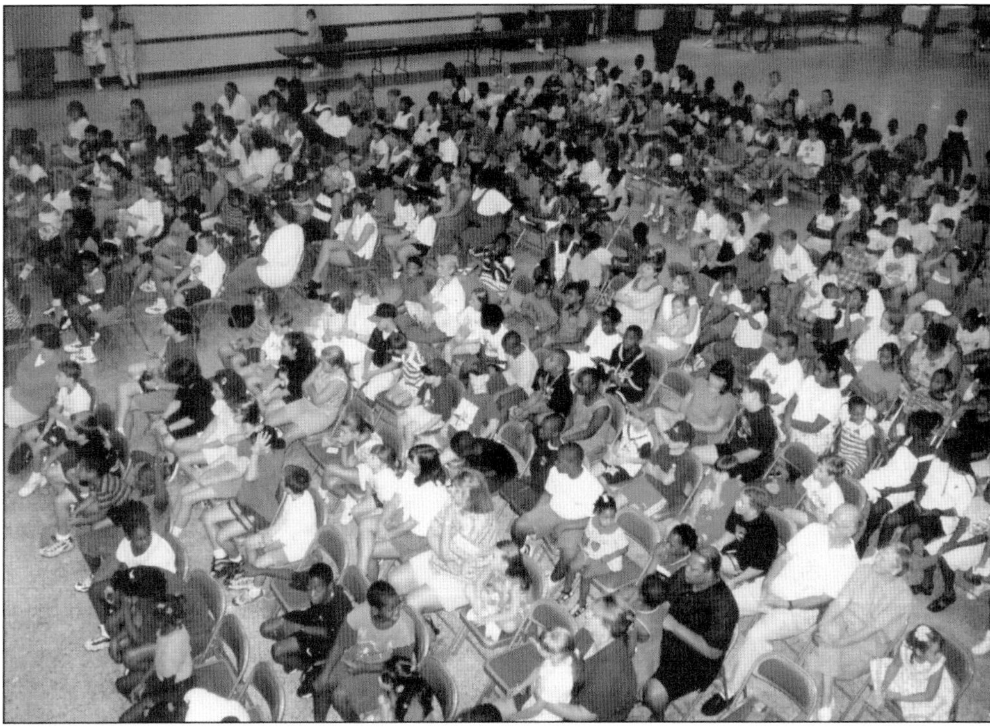

A large crowd participated in this 1998 summer reading finale program at the Gadsden Convention Hall, where they were entertained by band members, from left to right, Jared Lee, Michael Amberson, and Jeremy Jackson.

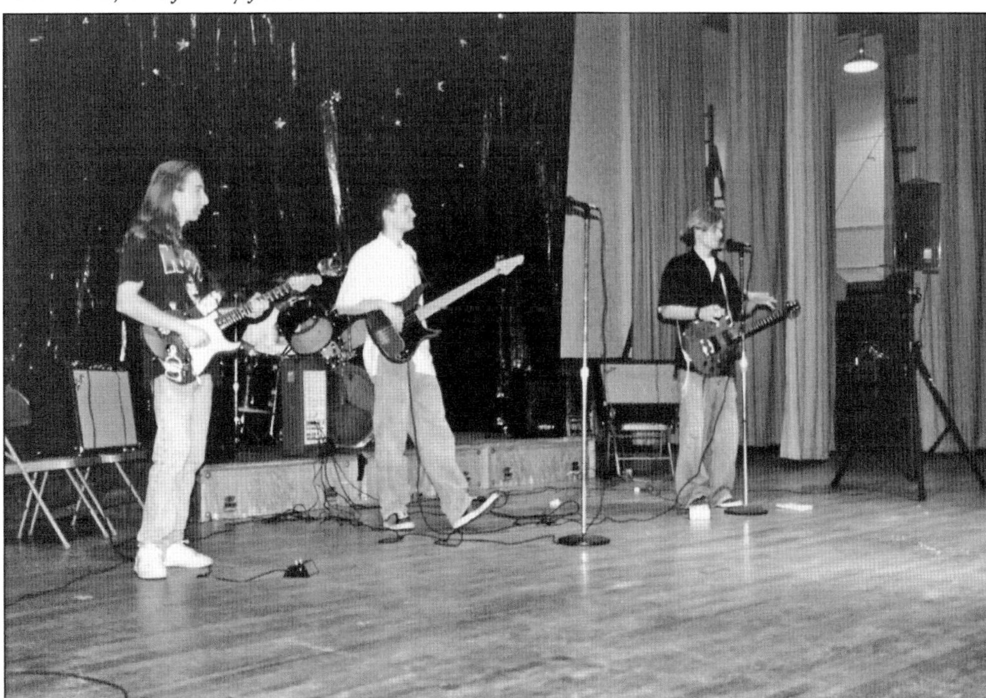

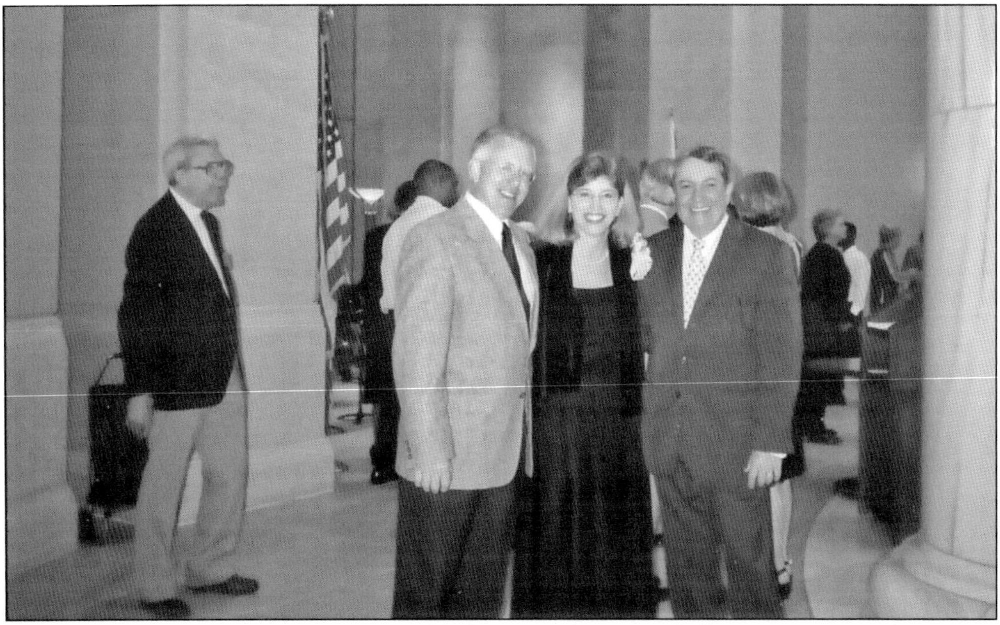

The Alabama Library Association elected Rebecca Buckner Mitchell as vice president/president-elect for 1999–2000, a testament to her leadership in promoting the welfare of libraries in the state. The Alabama Library Association president's reception was held in April 2001 at the Alabama Supreme Court Building in Montgomery. Pictured with Mitchell are her husband, Derick Mitchell (left), and Mayor Steve Means.

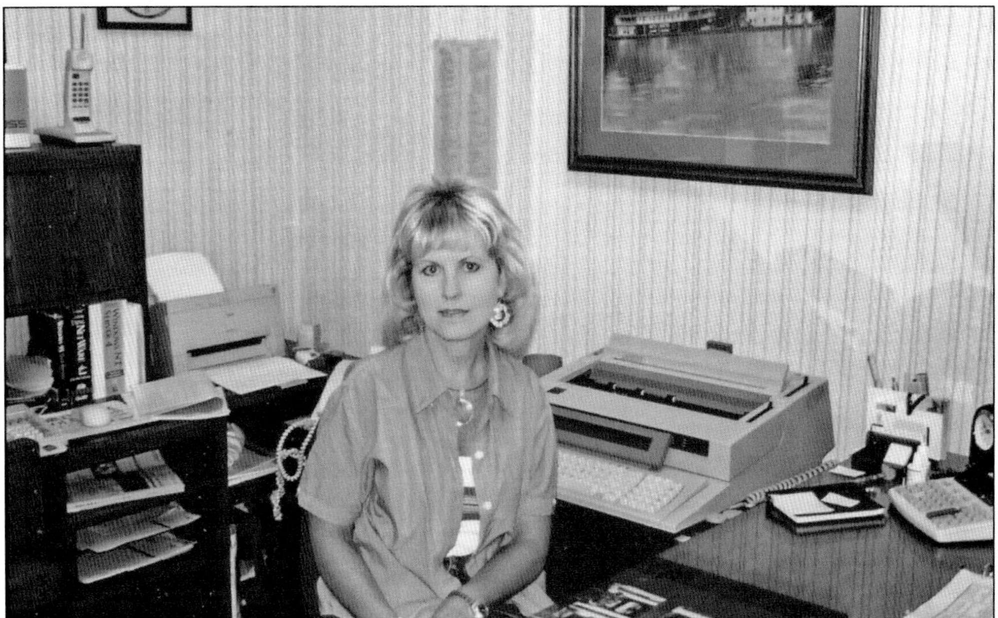

With Anita Brooks as interim director, the library continued its technological progress. Like Bobby Junkins, Brooks began her library career shelving books. While serving as library administrator, Brooks worked with five directors—Rymer, Junkins, Mitchell, Howington, and Jackson. She acted as the planner and coordinator for the 2004–2006 library renovation project.

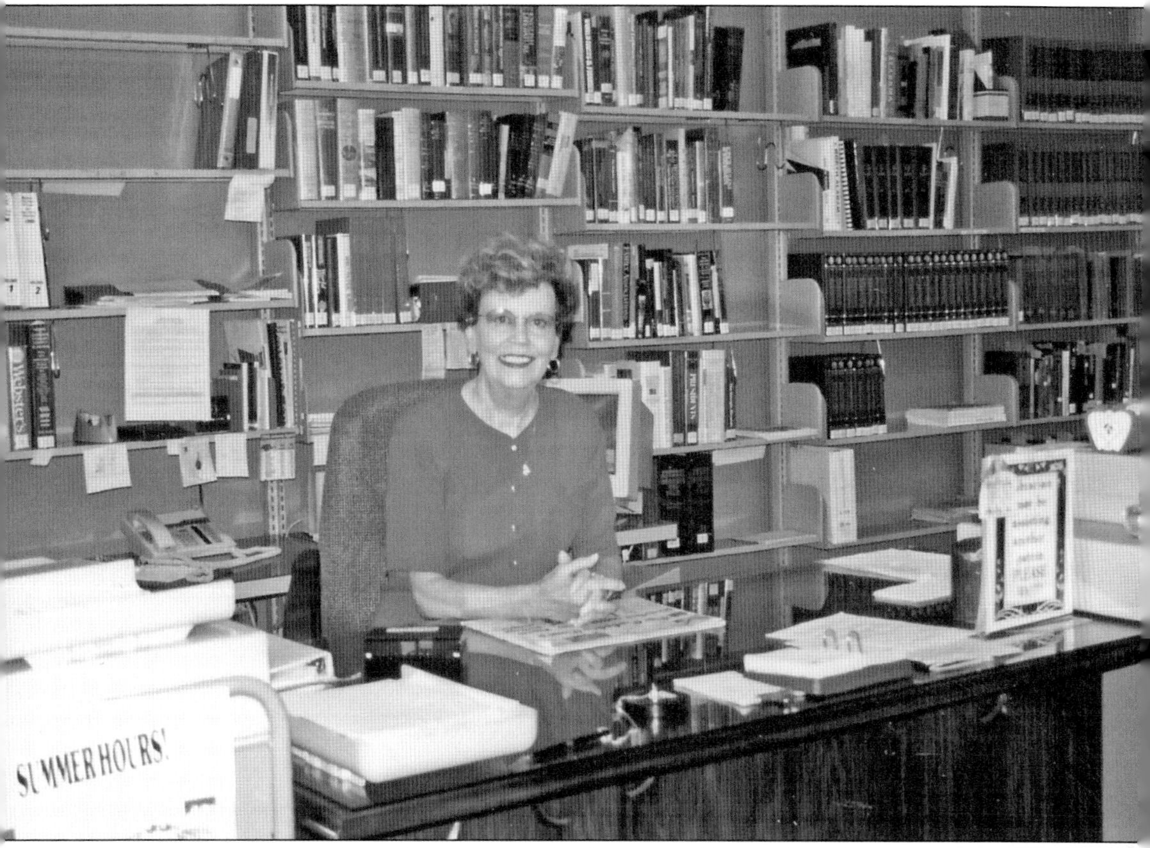

Gadsden native Barbara Owen Reed joined the library staff in 1982. When Margaret Rouse retired in 1985, Reed became the reference librarian. A good memory and a lifelong fascination with solving problems were two of the many qualities she brought to the job. As a child, Reed spent many hours at the library on Forrest Avenue when Lena Martin was the librarian. With a love for Nancy Drew mysteries, Reed's childhood ambition was to be an investigator for the FBI. Every day at the library presented new challenges to solve, as the reference department received more than 30,000 questions per year. After retiring in 2002, Reed continued to be active in the preservation of local history.

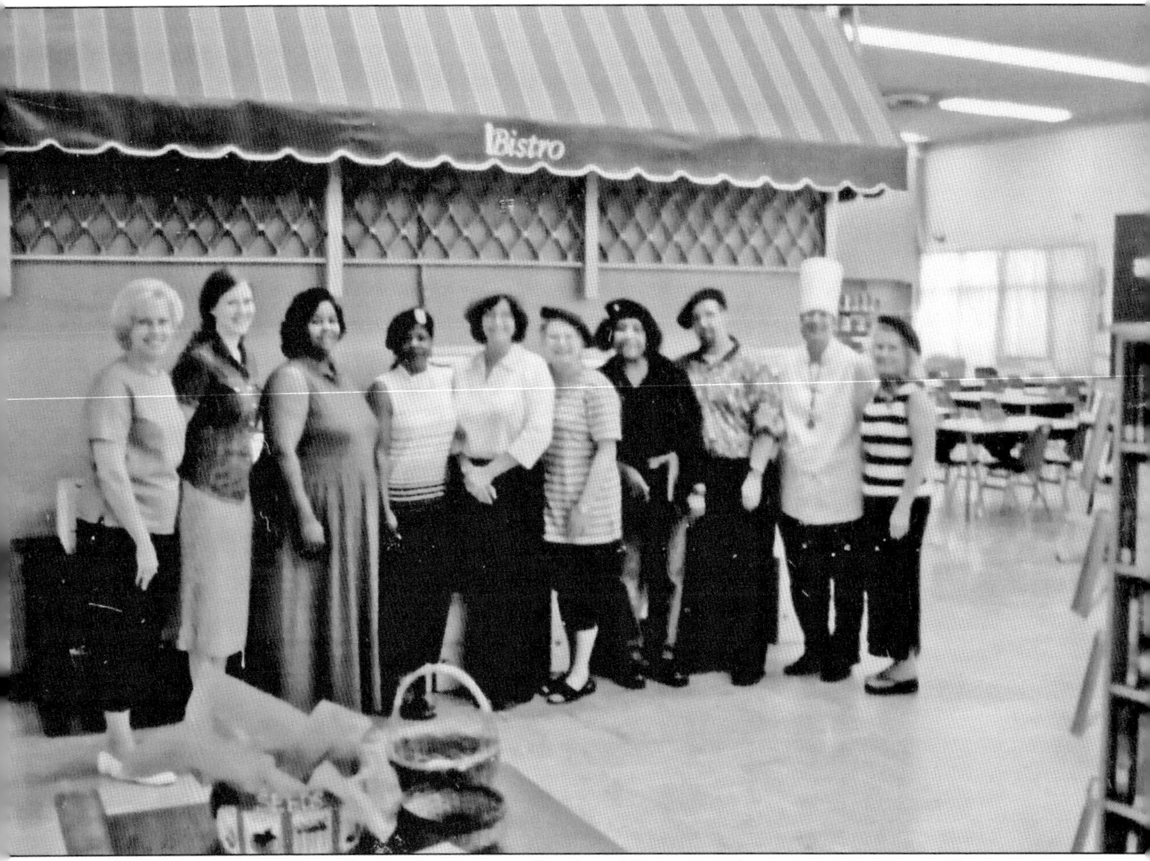

In late 2001, Gadsden Public Library was the first library in the state to acquire iBistro, Sirsi Corporation's enhanced public access catalog system. Patrons could see summaries, reviews, and cover jackets for titles, plus suggestions of related items. Personal access numbers allowed patrons to look at their records and put books on hold from their home computer. A self-check system that allowed patrons to check out books themselves was also installed. In April 2002, National Library Week was celebrated with an iBistro event. French refreshments were served to more than 500 patrons, and iBistro was demonstrated. Computers for public access to the online card catalog were located below the iBistro awning. Staff members pictured here, from left to right, are Dee Roper, Beth Latham, Gelaine Kelley, Tallulah Cash, Paula Spears, Paulette Makary, Lillie Jones, Kevin Graves, Sarah Pilkanis, and Anita Brooks.

Seven

Lee Howington
2002–2006

Lee Howington was appointed the library director in June 2002. For the 2002 fiscal year, the library served 315,000 patrons with a total circulation of 237,920. Use of electronic resources rose to 163,466 in 2003. Howington directed two monumental tasks: relocating the library and planning a new design to maximize use of existing space to reflect current library trends. In the renovation, the library received a face-lift for the exterior and a complete reconfiguration of the interior space to provide users with an inviting, user-friendly facility for showcasing the latest in information technology, while still housing traditional resources. Building modifications provided space for holdings of 300,000 items. Technology labs for children and adults were equipped with state-of-the-art equipment. Computer instruction could be offered by library staff in a new electronic classroom. Wireless technology allowed patrons with laptop computers to access the Internet throughout the building. Teens had their own dedicated space where materials and furnishings were selected especially for them. Patrons enjoyed the popular library where new movies, audio books, and multiple copies of best sellers were displayed in one convenient location for browsing pleasure. Comfortable indoor and outdoor seating allowed patrons to enjoy a snack or beverage and a wonderful view of the courtyard. Howington served as library director until October 2006.

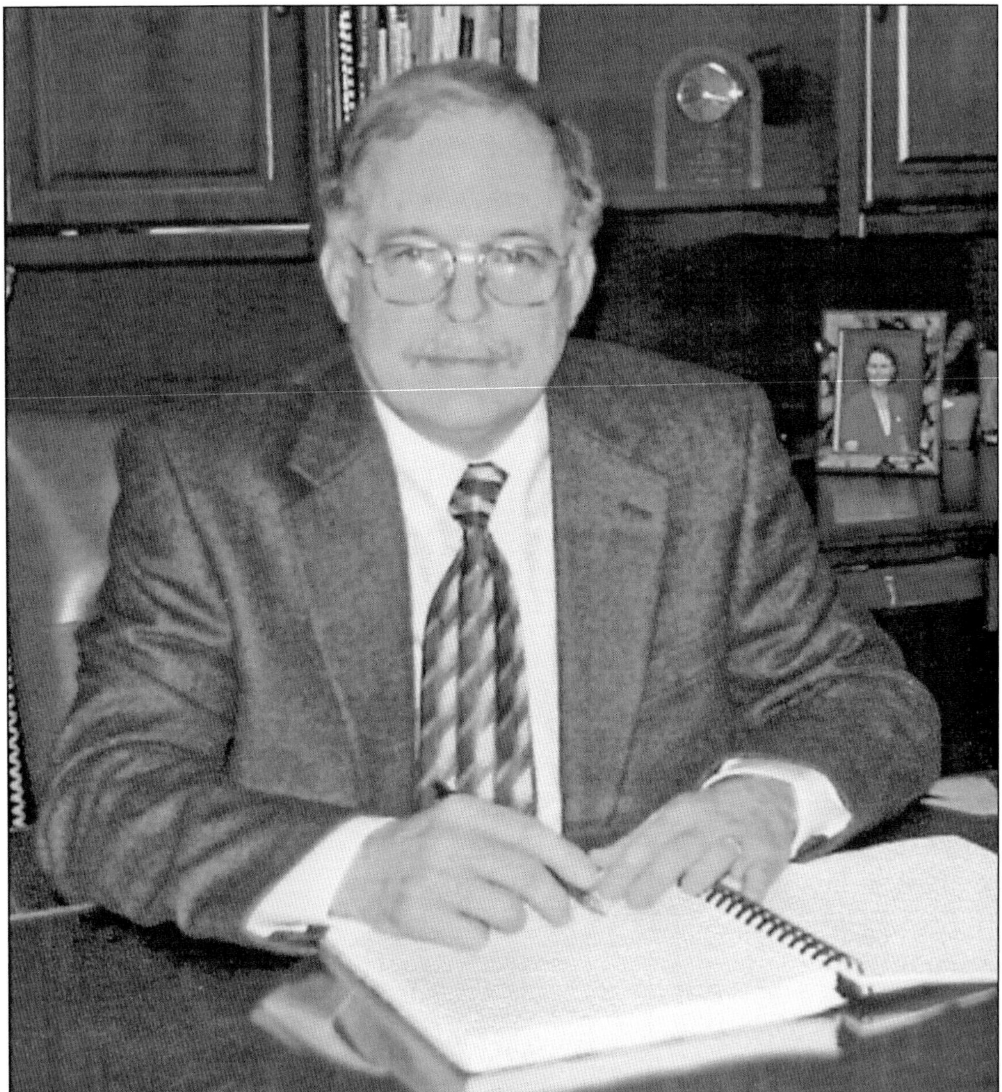

A native of Selma, Lee Howington received his Bachelor of Arts degree from Birmingham Southern College and a master's degree in library science from Florida State University. Howington came to Gadsden from Cartersville, Georgia, where he served as the director of the Bartow County Public Library for 18 years. He had a strong background in library construction, having overseen five library construction projects, including the building of two new facilities, as well as renovations and expansions. Prior to Cartersville, Howington was the director in Griffin, Georgia, from 1979 to 1984 and in Haines City, Florida, from 1978 to 1979.

The Alabama City branch was renamed the Hoyt Warsham Alabama City Library by resolution of the Gadsden City Council on October 1, 2002, with a dedication ceremony on December 11, 2002. Mayor Steve Means (left) is shown with Warsham.

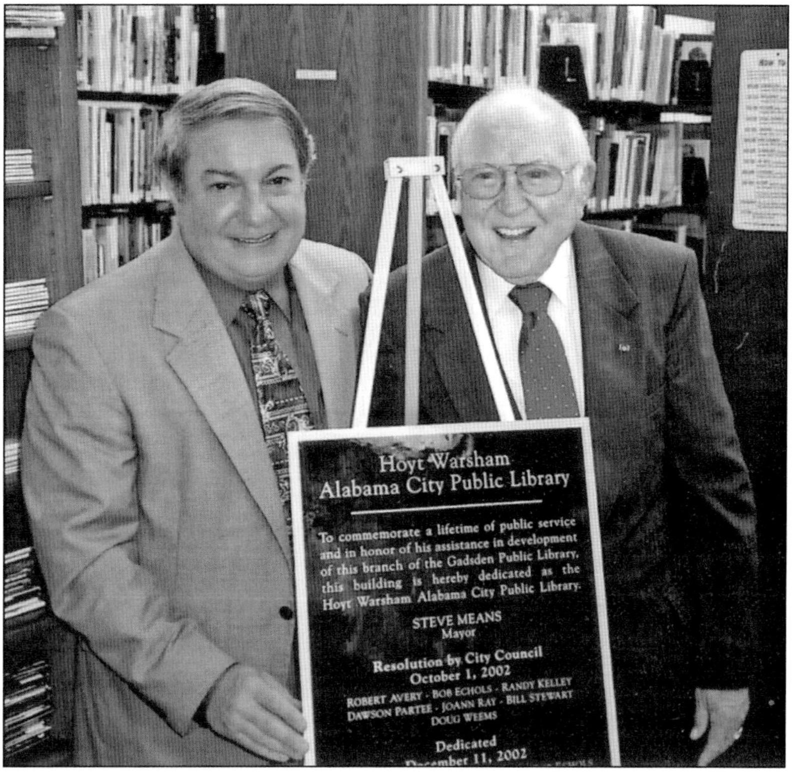

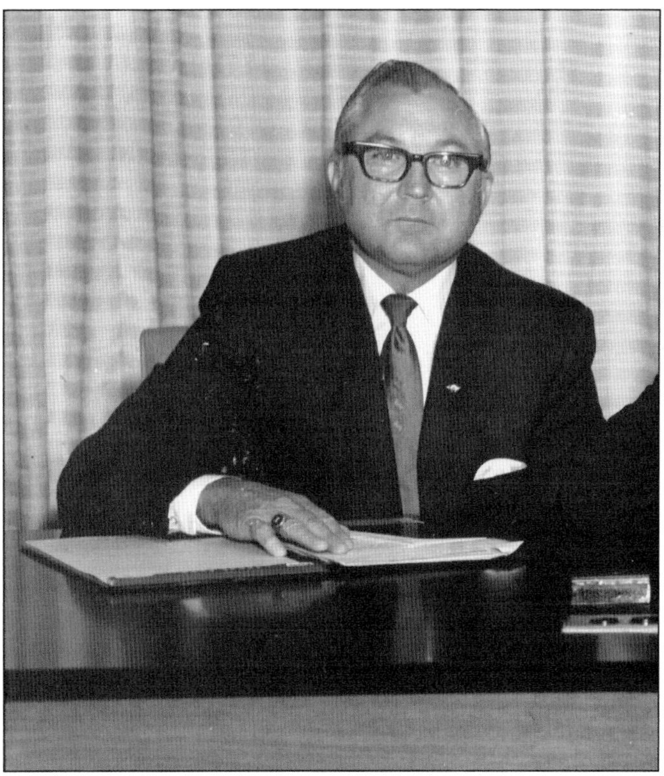

Hoyt Warsham lived in Alabama City and served Gadsden as public works commissioner from 1963 to 1970, working tirelessly to improve living conditions. Many new and improved services were implemented during his terms in office, including a new facility for Gadsden Public Library and expansion of the Alabama City branch.

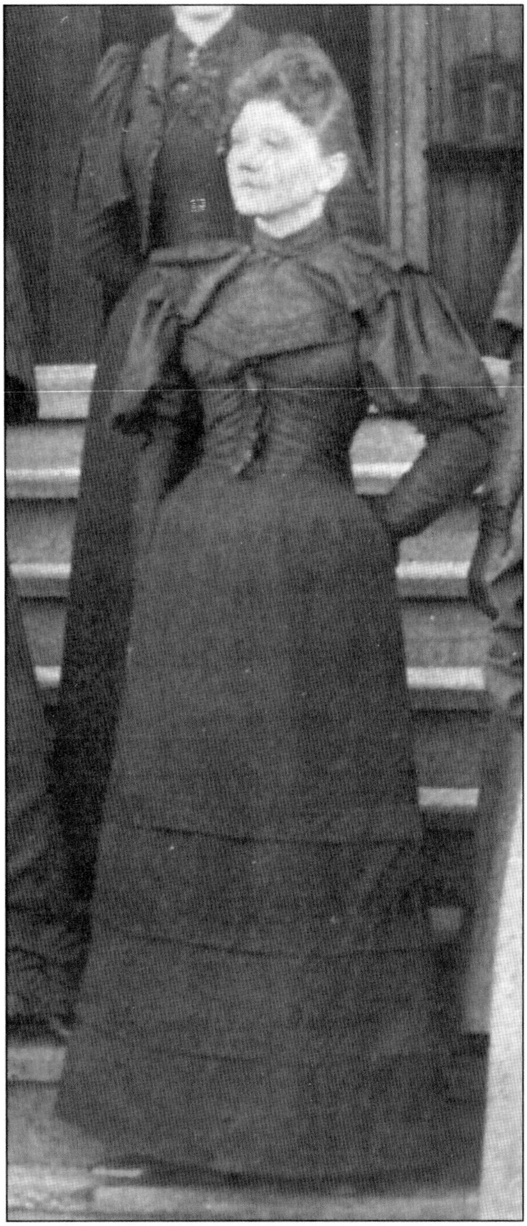

Unexplained noises, footsteps, and doors opening and closing were heard from the time the present library opened. For years, it was assumed to be the ghost of Lena Martin. Perhaps tired of being called "Miss Lena," the ghost got bolder, and in 2002, individuals researching in the upstairs locked stack area began reporting actual sightings. When seen, the ghost wore a black dress from the early-1880s period and had a black veil over her face. If so, it is logical to assume that it was not Martin, as she was a child in the 1880s and did not dress this way. Also, she never knew that the library would move to its present location. An 1880s photograph, made when Gadsden Normal School occupied this property, shows faculty members in front of the building. All who had seen the ghost identified her as Minnie Lay, pictured above. There are a few documents that mention Lay's participation in school functions. Otherwise, little about Lay except for one important fact: her classroom was located just about where the ghost was sighted.

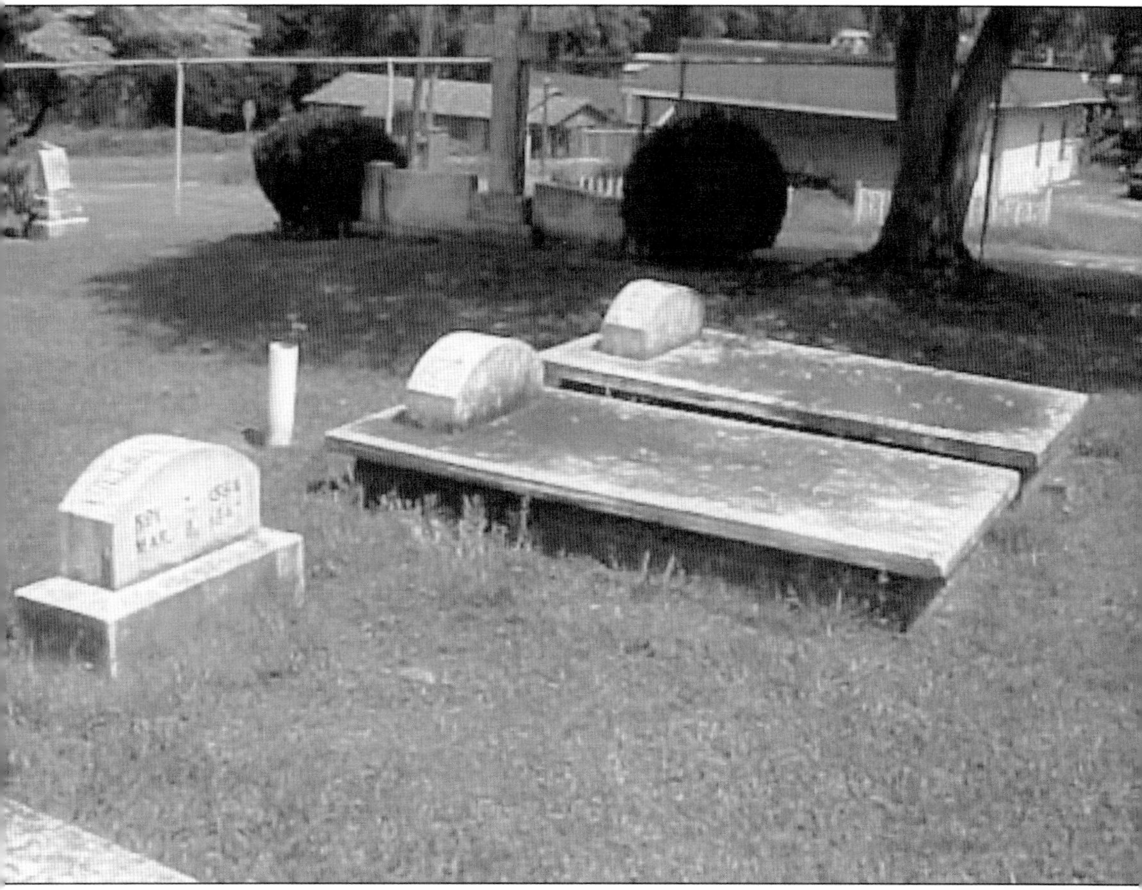

Minnie Lay was the sister of the famous W. P. Lay, who invented the hydroelectric power concept. Her sister, Sally Lay, married Henry Boswell Myers, and they had two daughters. Sally died in 1898, and in the following year, Minnie married Sally's husband and took care of the daughters. Minnie was born on November 7, 1864, and died on March 6, 1947. Pictured from left to right are the gravestones at Forrest Cemetery of Minnie Lay Myers, her sister, Sally, and their husband, Henry. A Mr. Johnny, a famous medium from Pascagoula, Mississippi, visited the library in 2003. From several photographs, he selected the one of the Gadsden Normal School faculty, and from it, he identified Minnie Lay as the ghost stalking the library. Mr. Johnny said he could feel her presence at the library but felt nothing when taken to Minnie's grave. Mr. Johnny said Lay will be seen again, but she is not the only ghost at the library. Readers must decide what to believe.

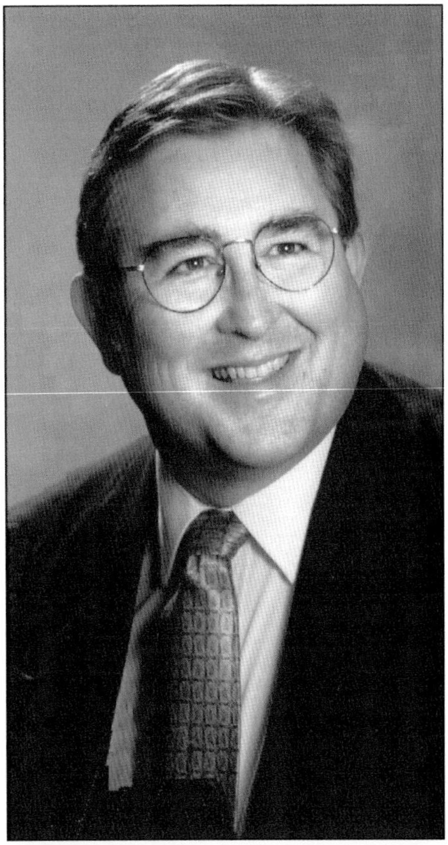

Local historian Danny Crownover researched the ghostly encounters at the library and reported his findings in the July 30, 2003, and August 6, 2003, issues of the *Messenger.*

In 2004, Mayor Steve Means and the Gadsden City Council appropriated $2.5 million for renovating the library's downtown location. Boatner Construction Company was awarded the contract with a bid of $1,849,118. An additional $250,000 was allocated for furnishings and landscaping in January 2006. Council members from left to right are (seated) Robert Echols and Jim Armstrong; (standing) Fred Huff, J. R. Countryman, Ben Reed, Walt Higgins, and Bill Stewart.

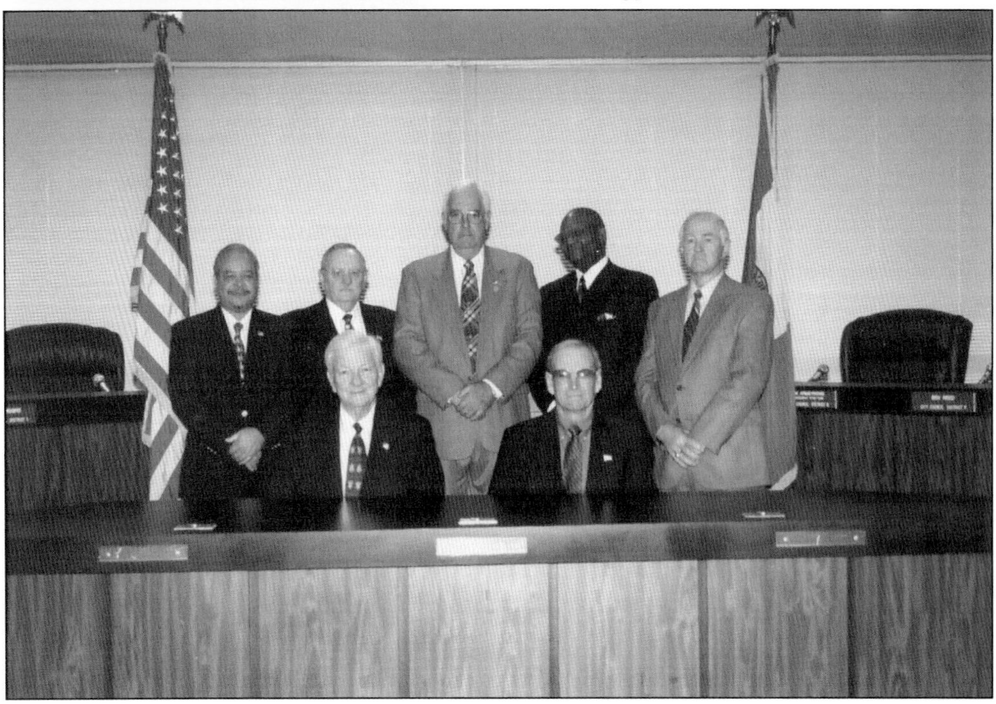

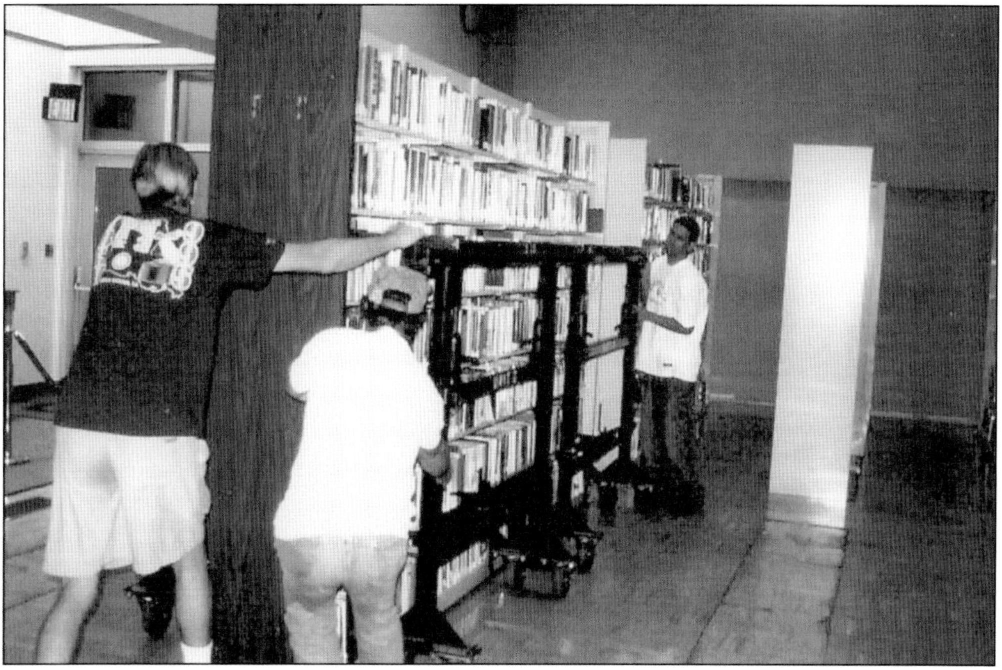

During renovation construction, main library services were moved by Hallett Library Movers to the Elliott Community Center, where a reduced number of books were made available.

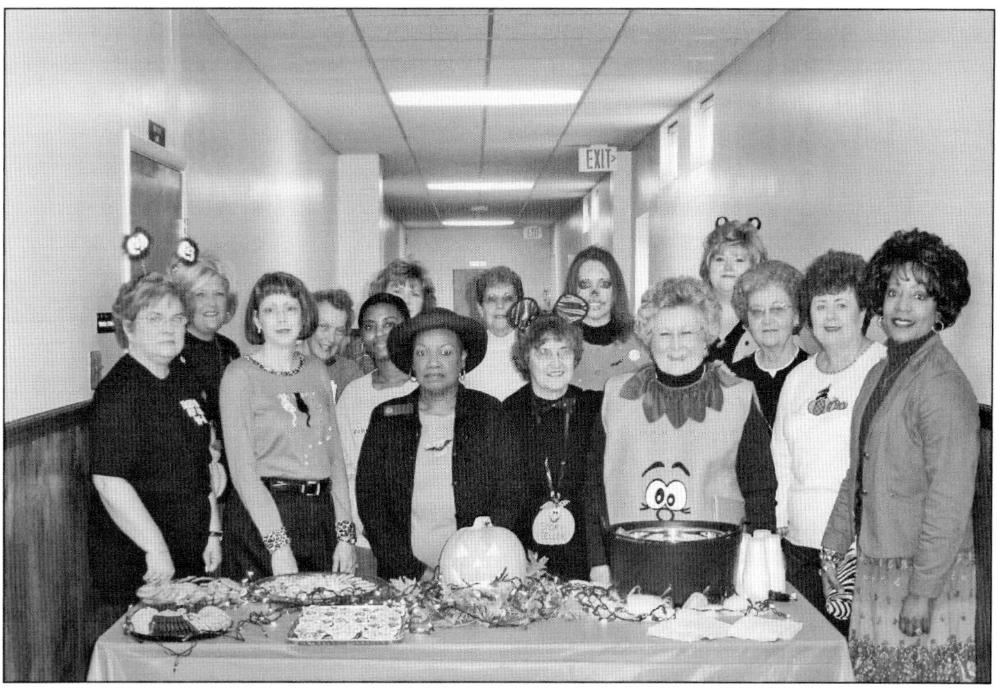

Altrusa International of Gadsden sponsored its fourth annual fall festival at the library in October 2005. A service organization focused on literacy, the Altrusa Club provided personal copies of books for children, and members read stories to them.

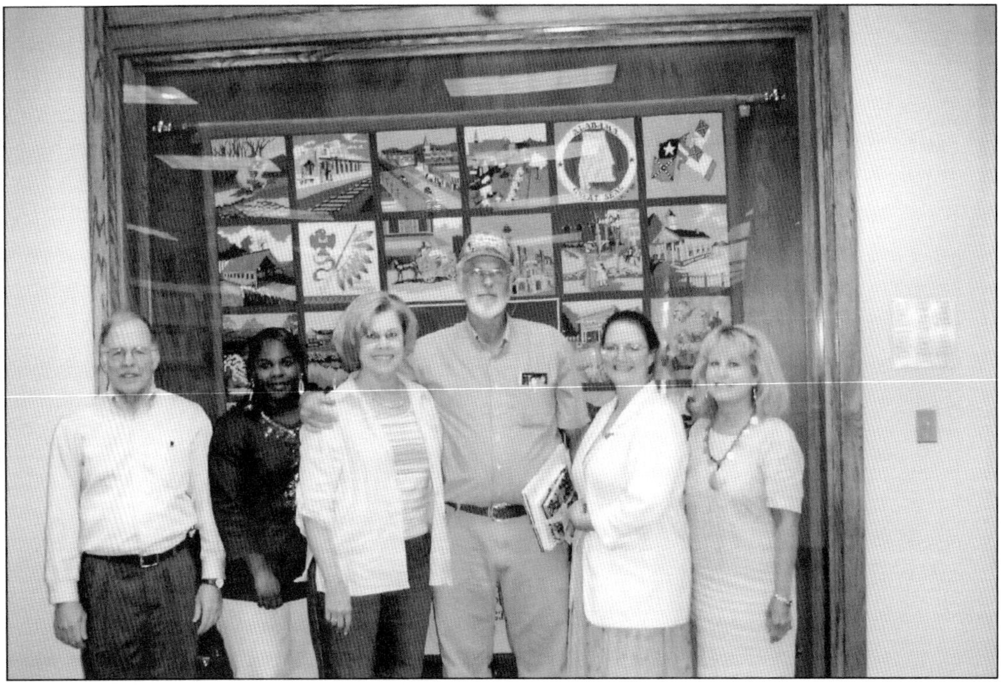

From left to right, Lee Howington, Tallulah Cash, Dee Roper, Boatner Construction job superintendent Tony McCain, Julie Dobbins, and Anita Brooks stand in front of a lit, custom cabinet designed for the genealogy department to display the needlepoint tapestry donated to the library in 1981 by the Gadsden Needlepoint Guild.

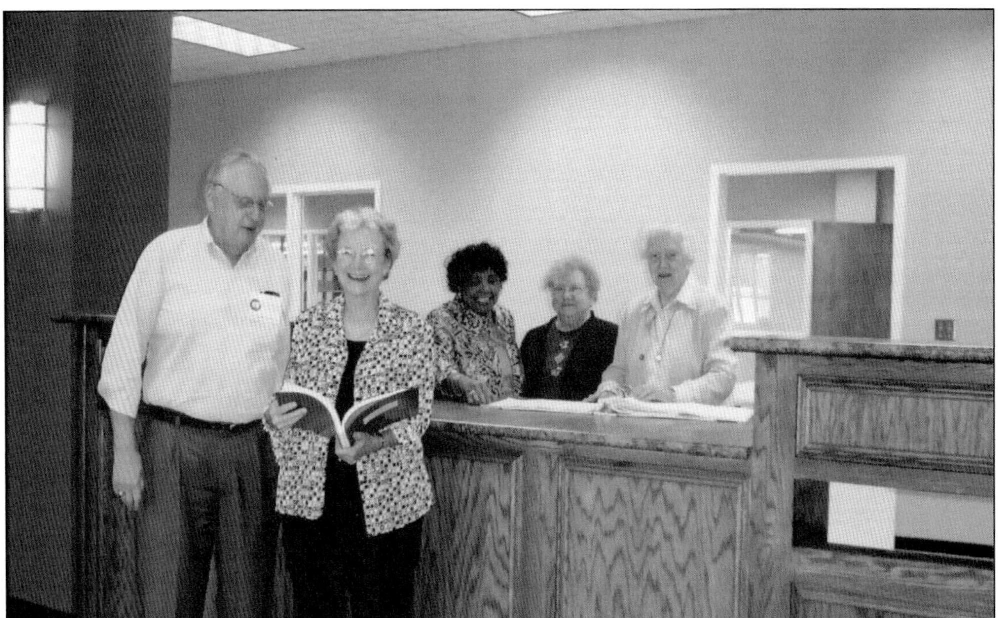

Library board members, from left to right, George Henderson, Bette Sue McElroy, Gesna Littlefield, Barbara Mote, and Hazel Oliver are shown at the new circulation desk while viewing the library renovation in April 2006.

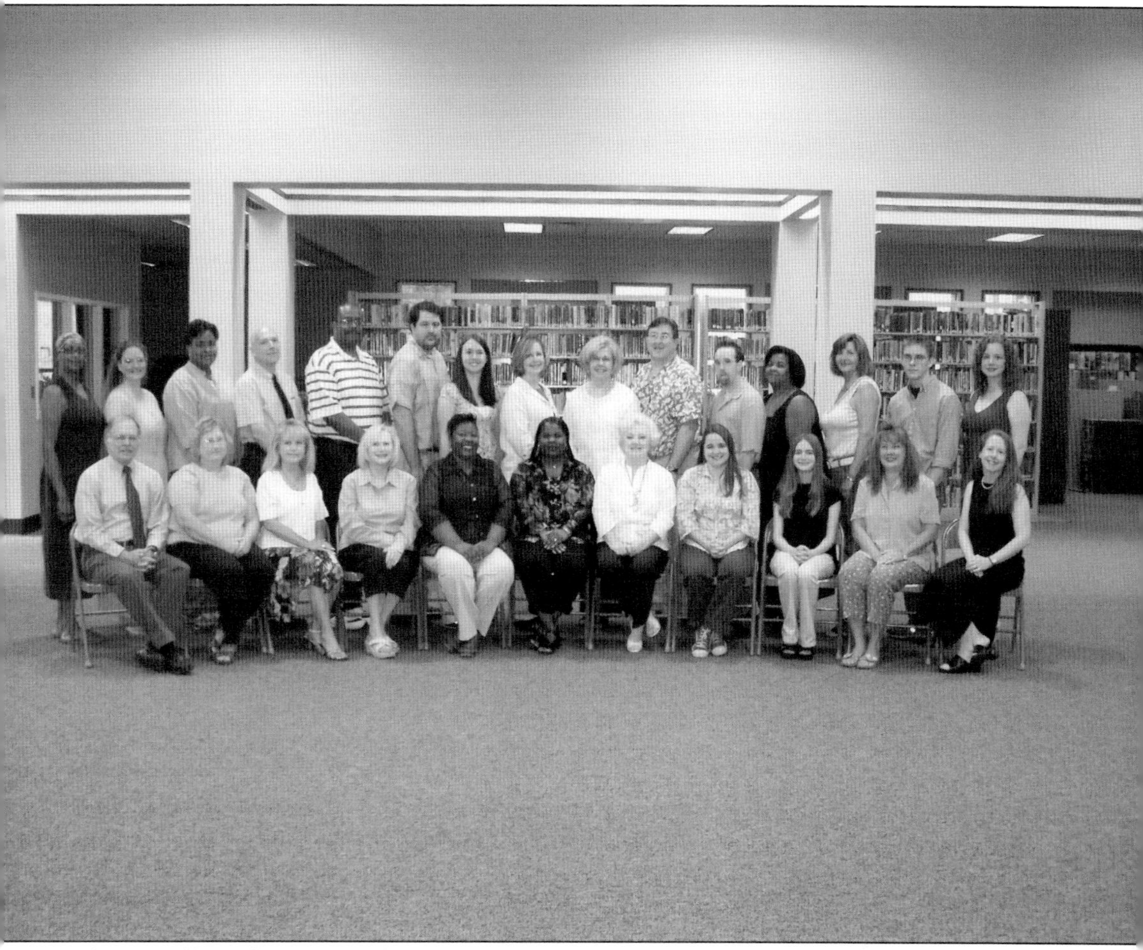

Library staff members pictured here in May 2006 from left to right are (seated) Lee Howington, Kay Henderson, Anita Brooks, Paulette Makary, Pauline Roberts, Tallulah Cash, Glenda Byars, Hilary Jackson, Melissa Moon, Pat Pearson, and Carol York; (second row) LaShunda Williams, Julie Dobbins, Amy Brisker, Louis Loveman, Tim Madden, Jacob Blackwood, Emily Osborn, Janice Johnson, Dee Roper, Danny Crownover, Kevin Graves, Gelaine Kelley, Paula Spears, Josh Carlson, and Amanda Jackson.

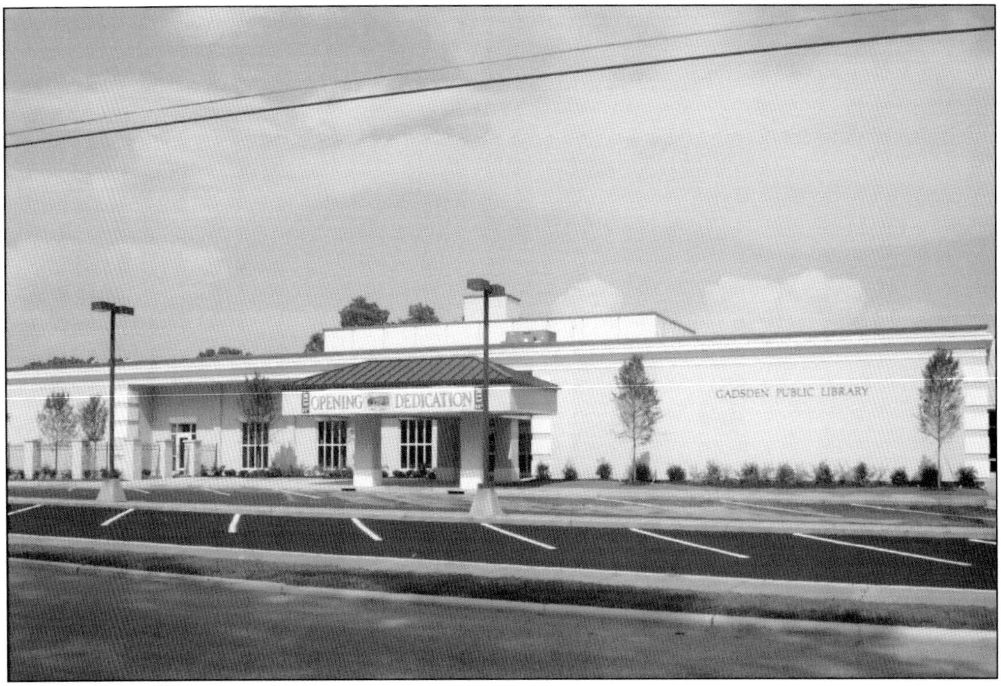

On July 11, 2006, hundreds attended a combined centennial celebration and opening dedication of the renovated library.

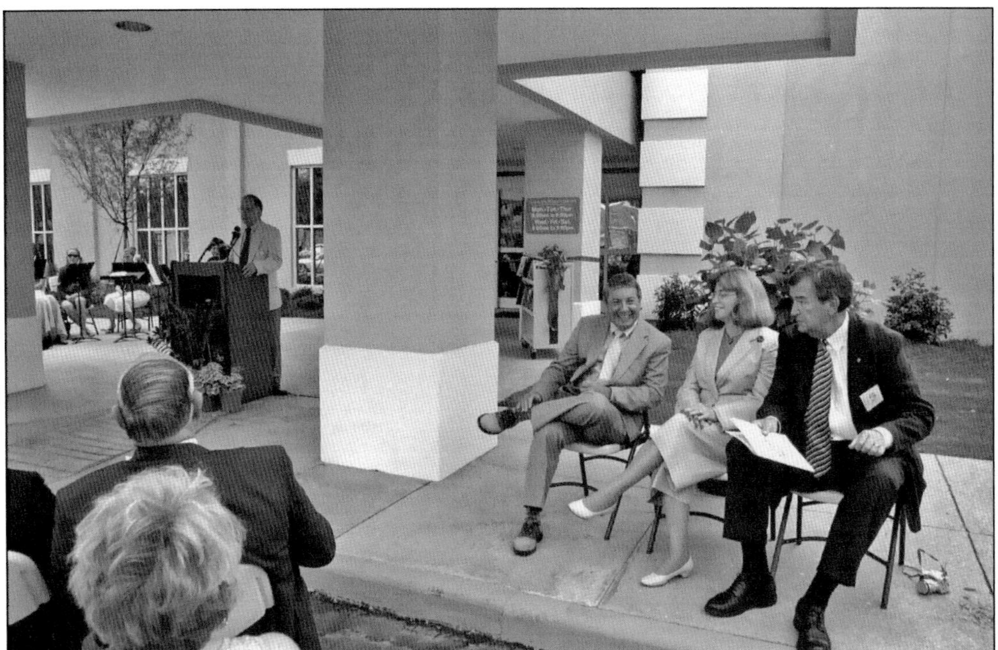

Lee Howington welcomed guests at the library opening. Pictured from left to right are (seated) Mayor Steve Means and former library directors Rebecca Buckner Mitchell and Bobby Junkins.

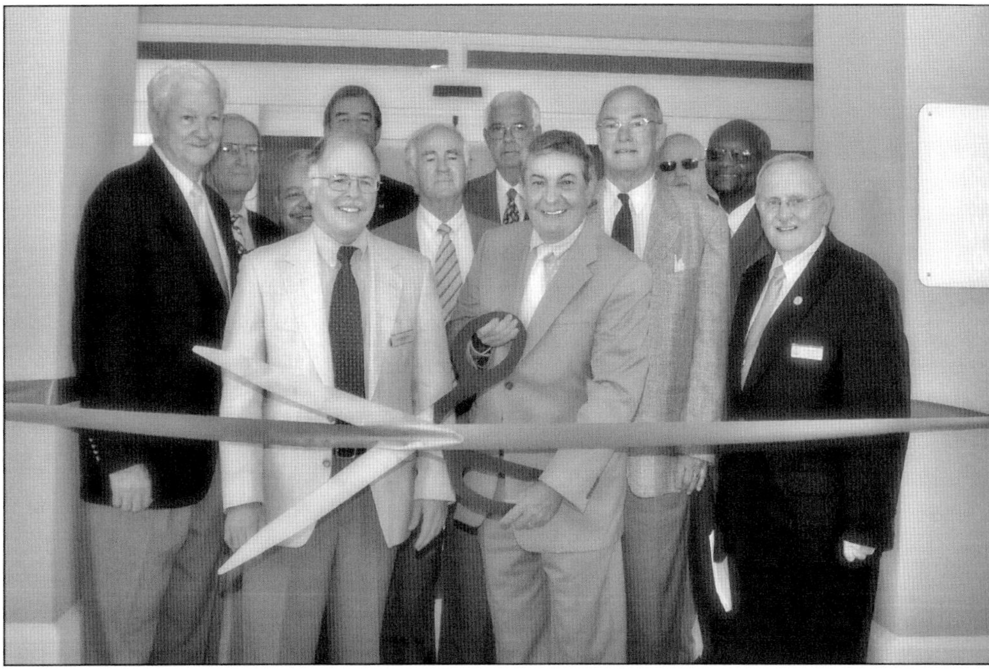

Participating in the ribbon-cutting from left to right are (first row) Lee Howington and Mayor Steve Means; (second row) Robert Echols, Jim Armstrong, Fred Huff, Bobby Junkins, Bill Stewart, Ben Reed, Ron Cannon, George Henderson, Walt Higgins, and J. R. Countryman. It was a sea of awed faces as the public had their first glimpse of the beautifully renovated interior of the library.

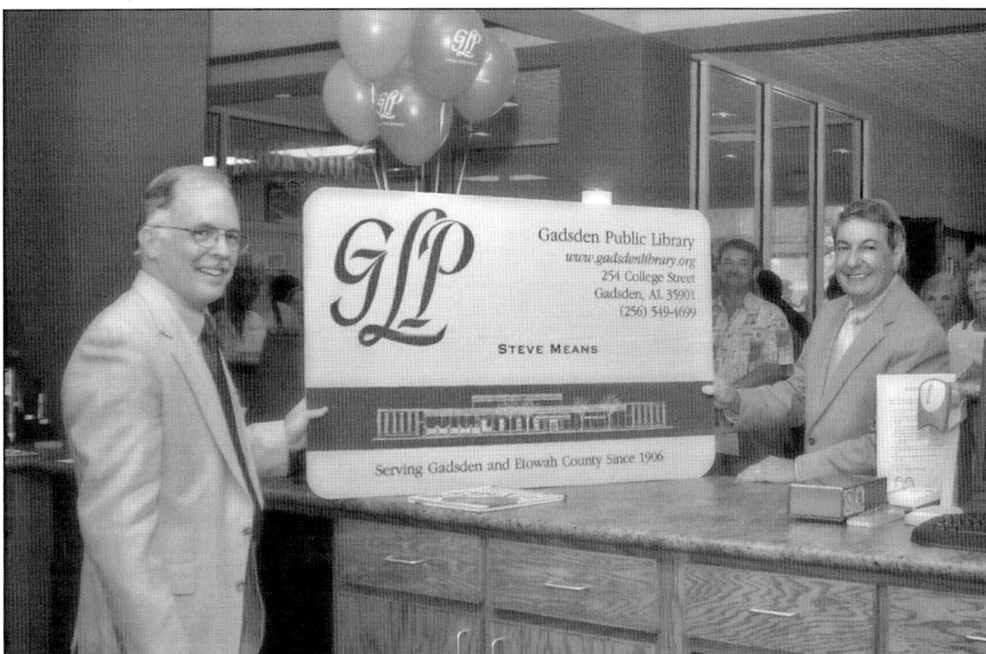

As a student in 1964, Mayor Steve Means was the last person to check out a book from the old Forrest Avenue location, so it seemed only fitting that he receive the first new library card from Lee Howington.

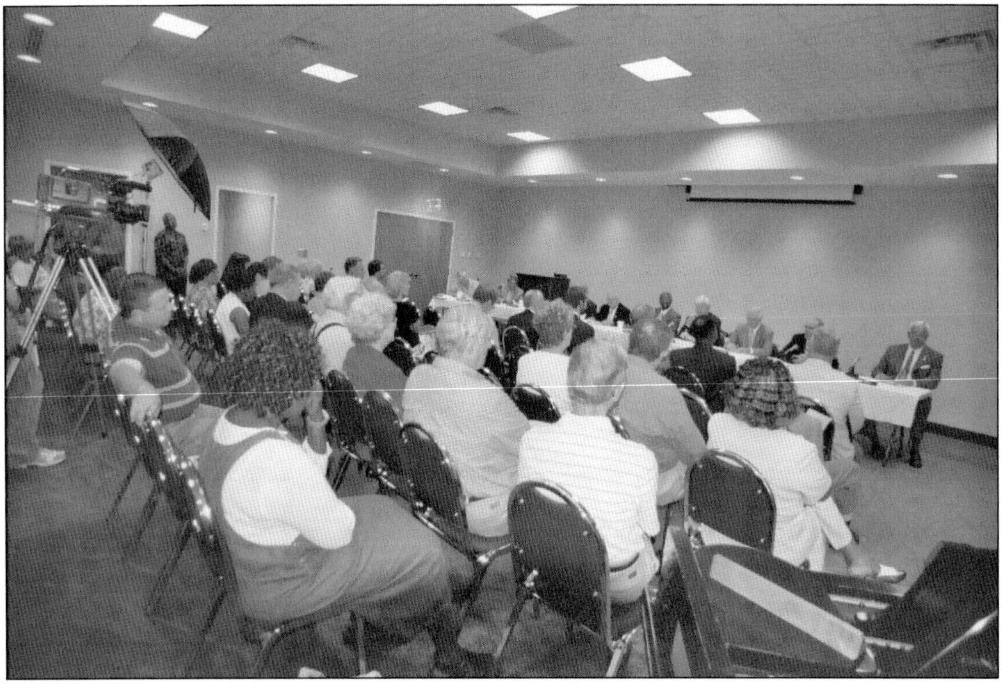

The Gadsden City Council enjoyed a change of scenery, holding the weekly council meeting in the Lena Martin Meeting Room.

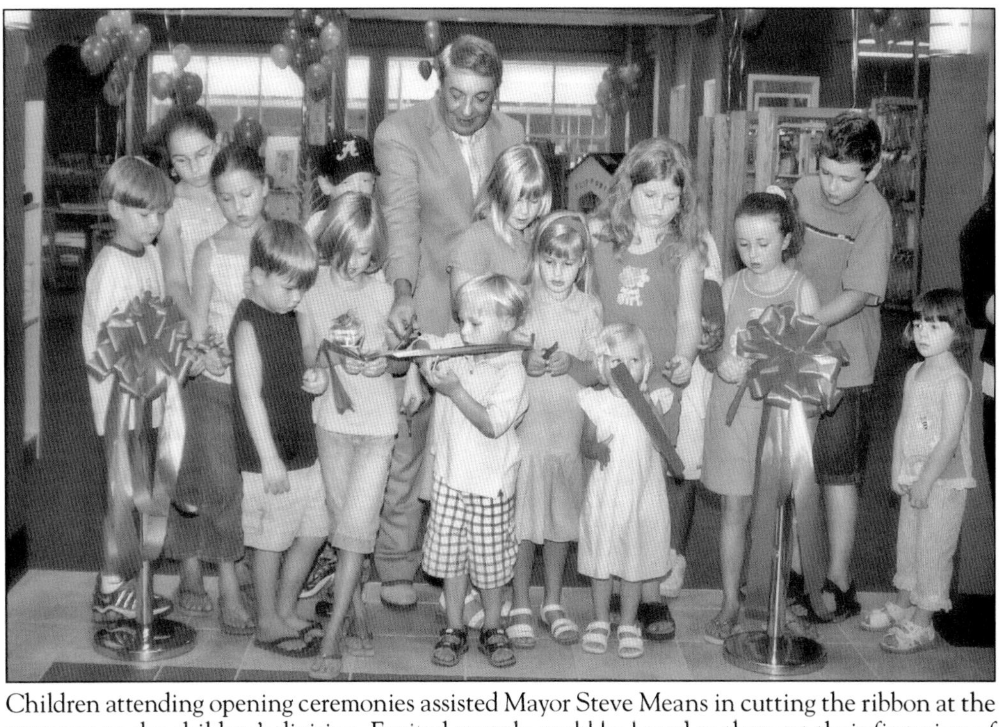

Children attending opening ceremonies assisted Mayor Steve Means in cutting the ribbon at the entrance to the children's division. Excited squeals could be heard as they got their first view of the bright, colorful children's library. The stimulating setting was designed to make the library an exciting destination for children.

A donation of $25,000 from the Alabama Power Company Foundation, in honor of William Patrick Lay, provided furnishings for the children's program room. Lay, a third-generation, Alabama riverboat captain, founded Alabama Power in Gadsden in 1906.

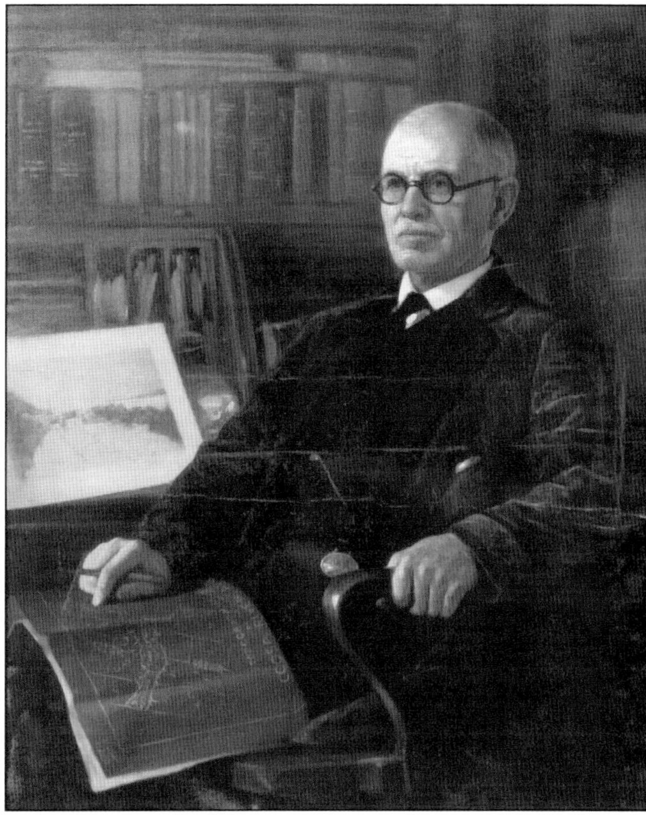

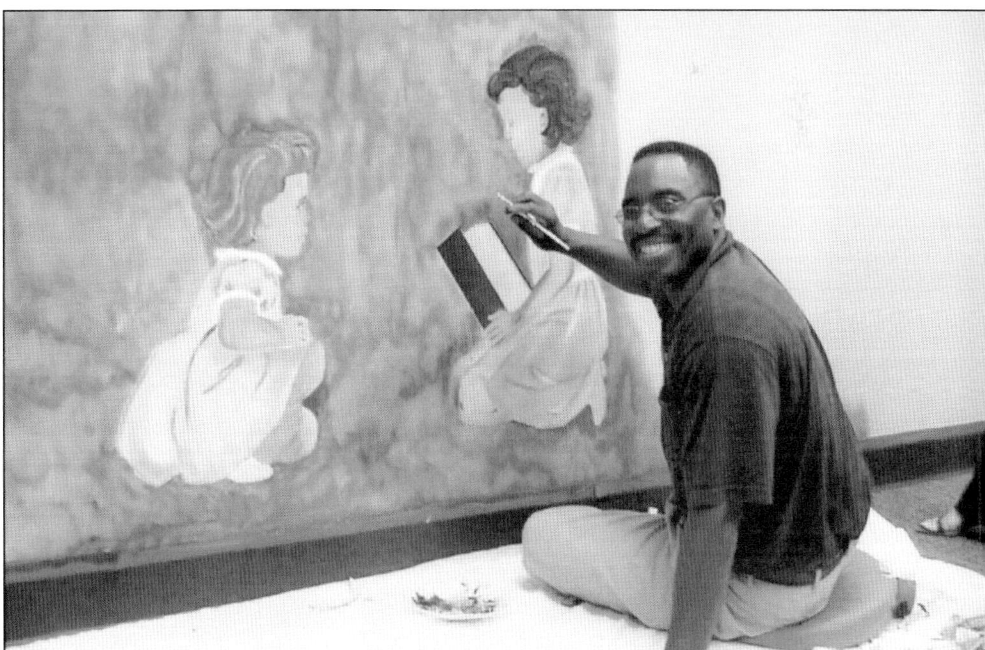

A mural in the children's program room was painted by local artist Tony Reddick, principal of Litchfield High School.

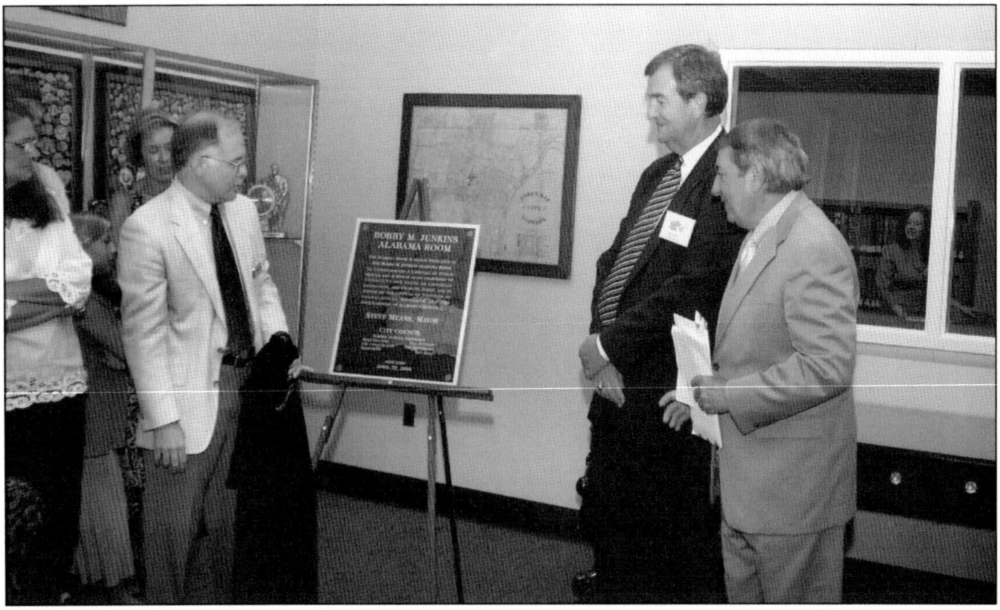

In tribute to a phenomenal past library director and current probate judge, the renovated Alabama Room was renamed by city proclamation on April 25, 2006, and in a ceremony held as part of opening festivities on July 11. A plaque, unveiled by Lee Howington (left) and presented by Mayor Steve Means (right), reads, "The Alabama Room is hereby dedicated as The Bobby M. Junkins Alabama Room to commemorate a lifetime of public service and in honor of his leadership to community and state as librarian, legislator, and probate judge, and in honor of his continued devotion to genealogical research and the safeguarding of Alabama's heritage."

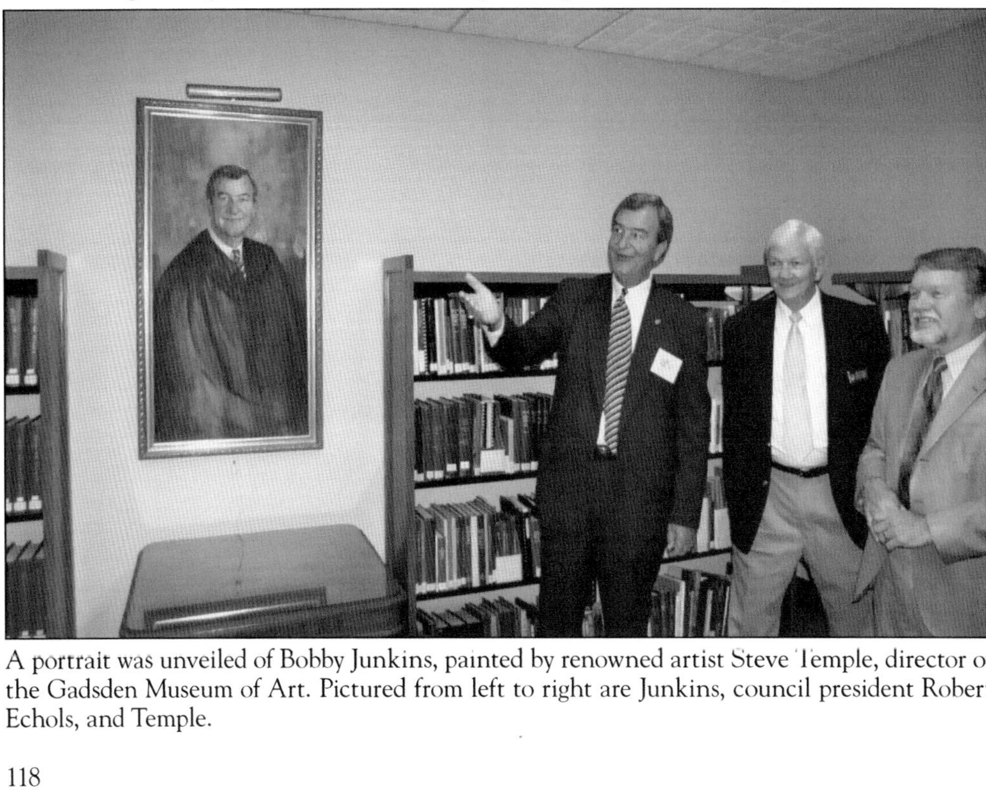

A portrait was unveiled of Bobby Junkins, painted by renowned artist Steve Temple, director of the Gadsden Museum of Art. Pictured from left to right are Junkins, council president Robert Echols, and Temple.

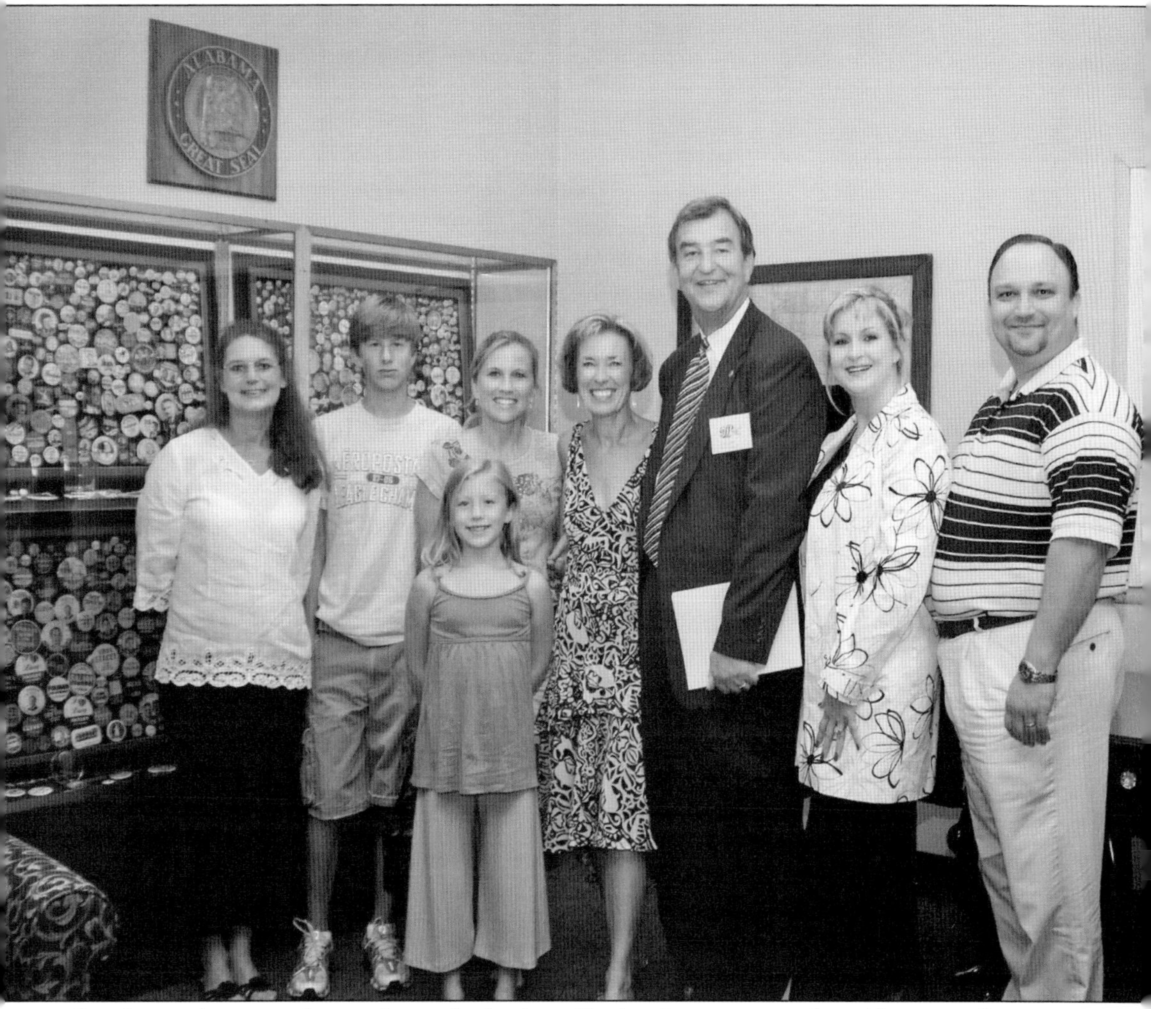

Family members, standing in front of a display of Junkins's extensive political button collection, from left to right are Judy Spears, Dillon Ward, Gracie Ward, Amy Ward, Susie Junkins, Bobby Junkins, Angela Junkins, and Jason Junkins.

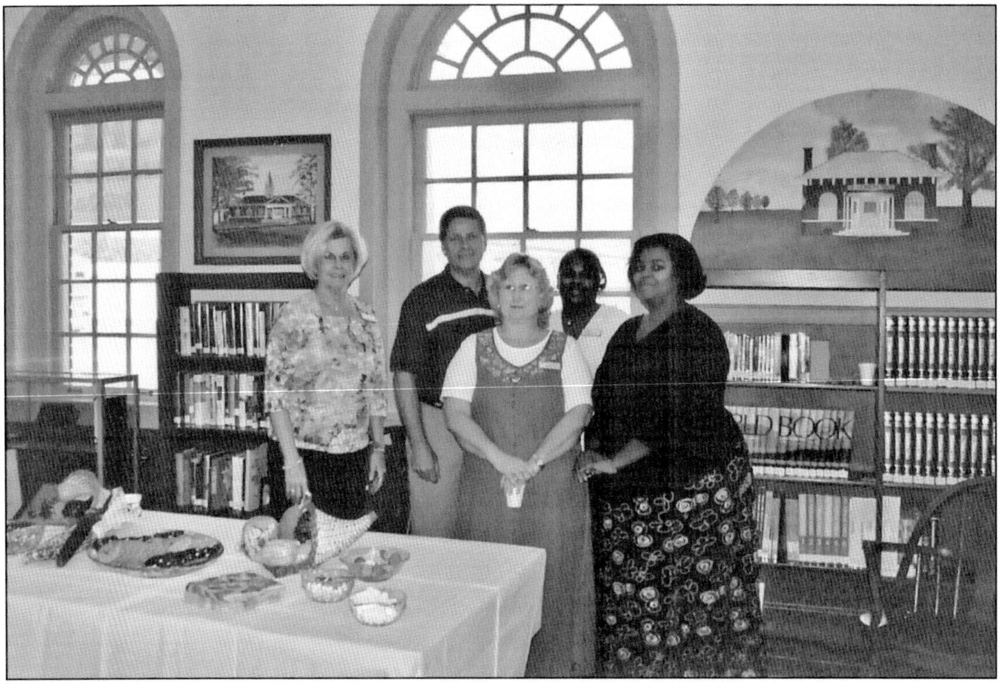

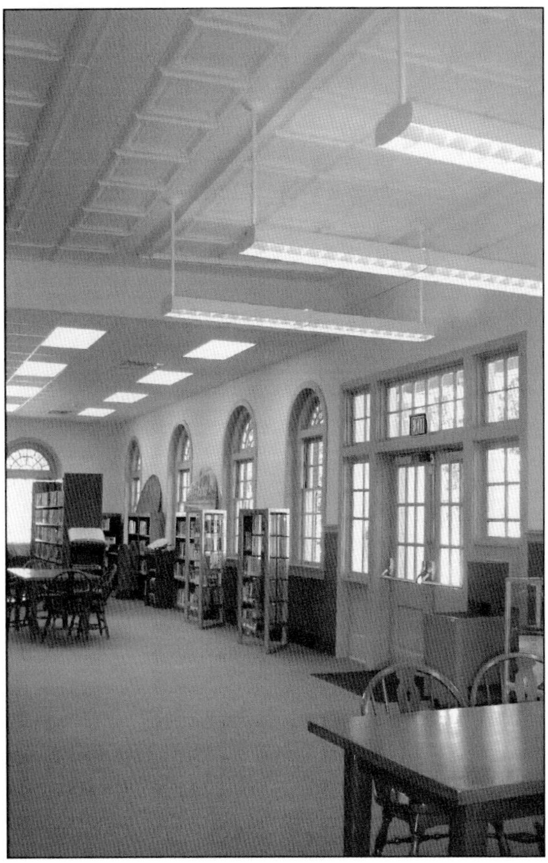

The Hoyt Warsham Alabama City Library was closed for six months for repairs and reopened on September 27, 2006. Pictured at the reception are, from left to right, Dee Roper, Sherman Guyton, Kay Henderson, Tallulah Cash, and Gelaine Kelley. Guyton was elected mayor of Gadsden and was inaugurated in October 2006.

During renovations to the Alabama City Library in 1958, the metal ceiling was replaced with acoustical tiles. Some of the original metal ceiling was discovered during the extensive interior renovation in 2006 and was incorporated into the design. Built in 1920, the library is the cornerstone of the Alabama City historic district.

Eight

Amanda Buckner Jackson 2006–Present

On September 28, 2006, Mayor Steve Means named Amanda Buckner Jackson as the library director. Lee Howington recommended Jackson for the director's position and took over Jackson's position of public services librarian. Jackson was only 27 when she became Gadsden's youngest library director. A poised public speaker, Jackson is often invited by civic groups to represent the library and promote its services. As director, Jackson plans to build on patrons' enthusiastic response to newly renovated library facilities, with usage expected to increase by 40 percent. Her focus will be on programs for people of all ages and ethnic backgrounds. Using federal funds provided by the Library Services and Technology Act, the Alabama Public Library Service awarded a $7,350 grant for expanding services to non-English-speaking persons, primarily to accommodate the growing Hispanic population.

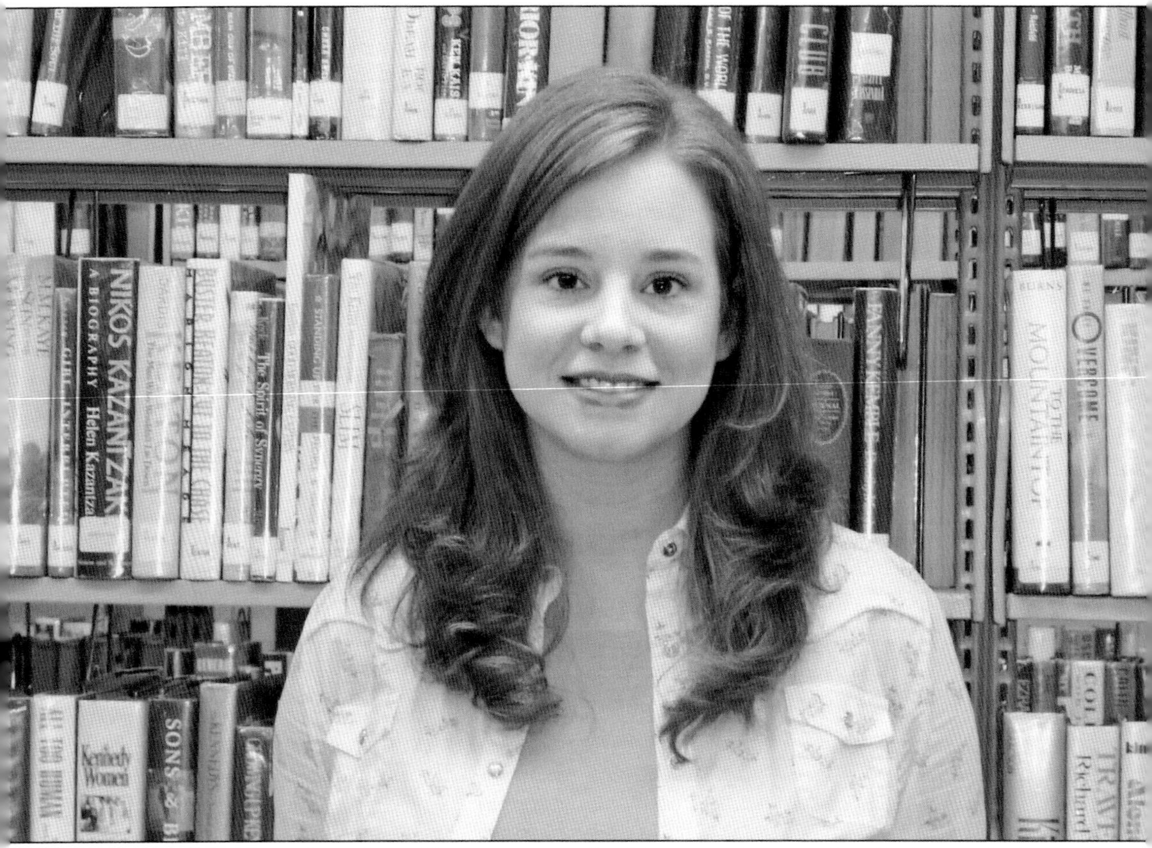

Amanda Buckner Jackson literally grew up in the library, as her mother, Rebecca Buckner Mitchell, was Gadsden's library director from 1988 to 2001. In an interview with *Gadsden Times* reporter Andy Powell, Jackson said her grandmother was also a librarian in Mississippi and started the library in the town where she lived. She said her family referred to libraries as "our family business." "Libraries to me are the heart of their communities. They are what feels good about their community," Jackson said. Jackson attended Emma Sansom High School before graduating magna cum laude from Jacksonville State University. She received her master's degree in library science from the University of Alabama. Prior to returning to Gadsden in 2005, Jackson worked for the Tennessee State Library and Archive as the children's services consultant.

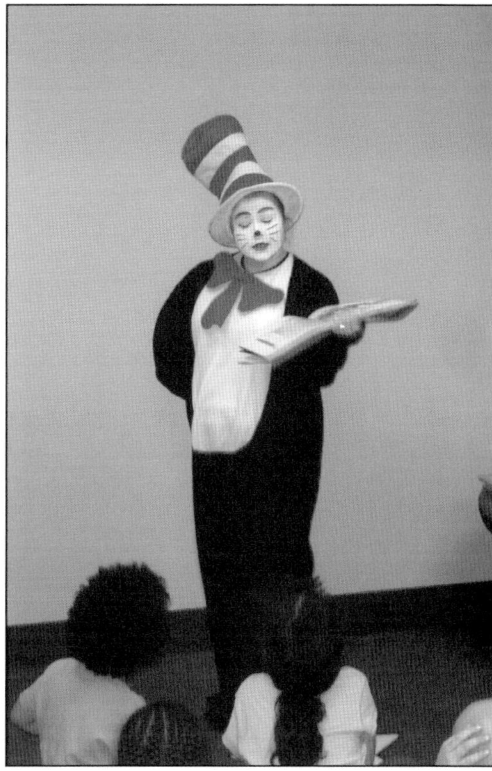

With an emphasis on programs, the library celebrated Dr. Seuss Day. Hilary Jackson is dressed as the Cat in the Hat (right), and LaShunda Williams is dressed as Daisy Head Maisy. Library staff members created excitement about reading when they visited local schools to read to elementary-grade classes.

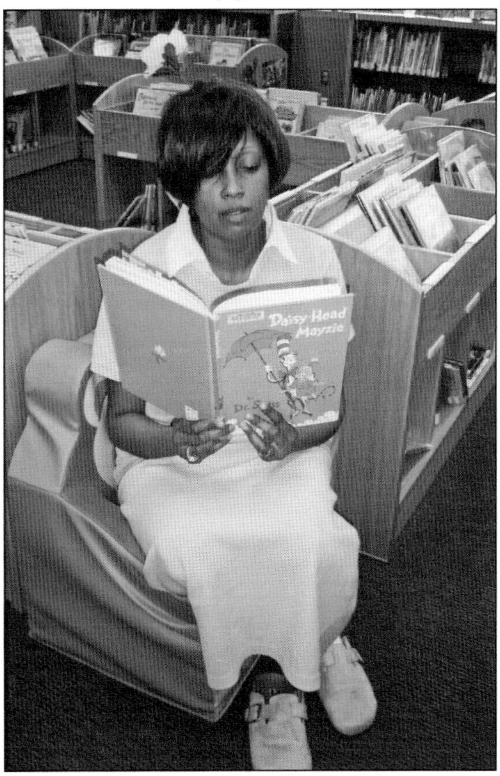

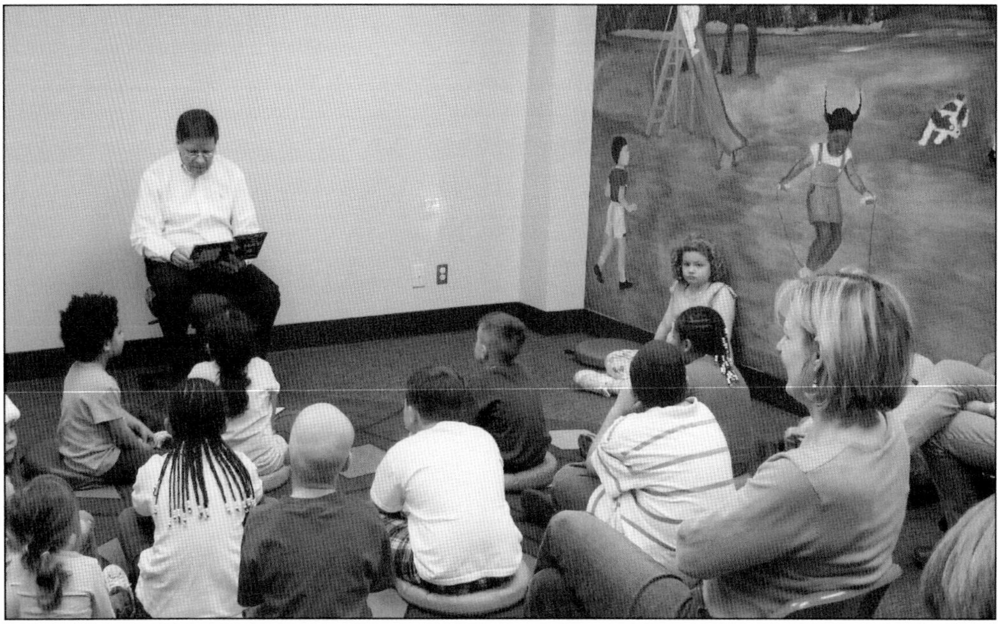

A popular program started by library director Amanda Buckner Jackson was the annual Celebrity Read Night, where local personalities were invited to read to children. Here Mayor Sherman Guyton reads *The Cat in the Hat* by Dr. Seuss to a group of children and their parents. Other celebrities included disc jockeys, football players, cheerleaders, and a former Miss Alabama. Jackson's daughter, Draven, can be seen on the far right sitting against the wall.

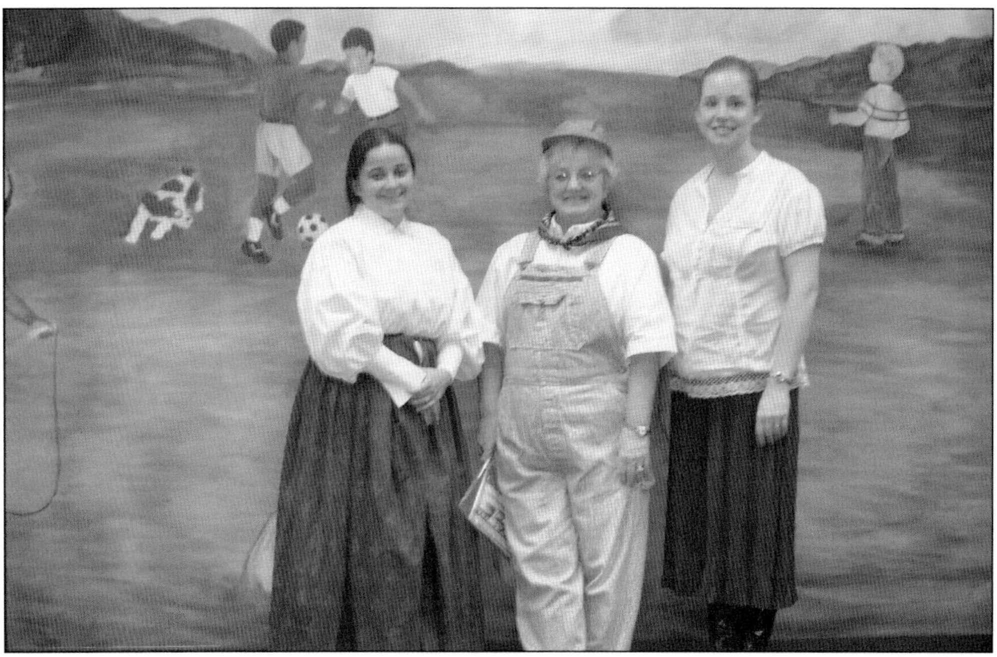

As the library continued its anniversary celebration, Hilary Jackson (left) and Amanda Buckner Jackson (right) wore centennial dress for family night. Glenda Byars (center) read *Choo Choo: The Story of a Little Engine Who Ran Away* by author Virginia Lee Burton, whose books have delighted generations of children.

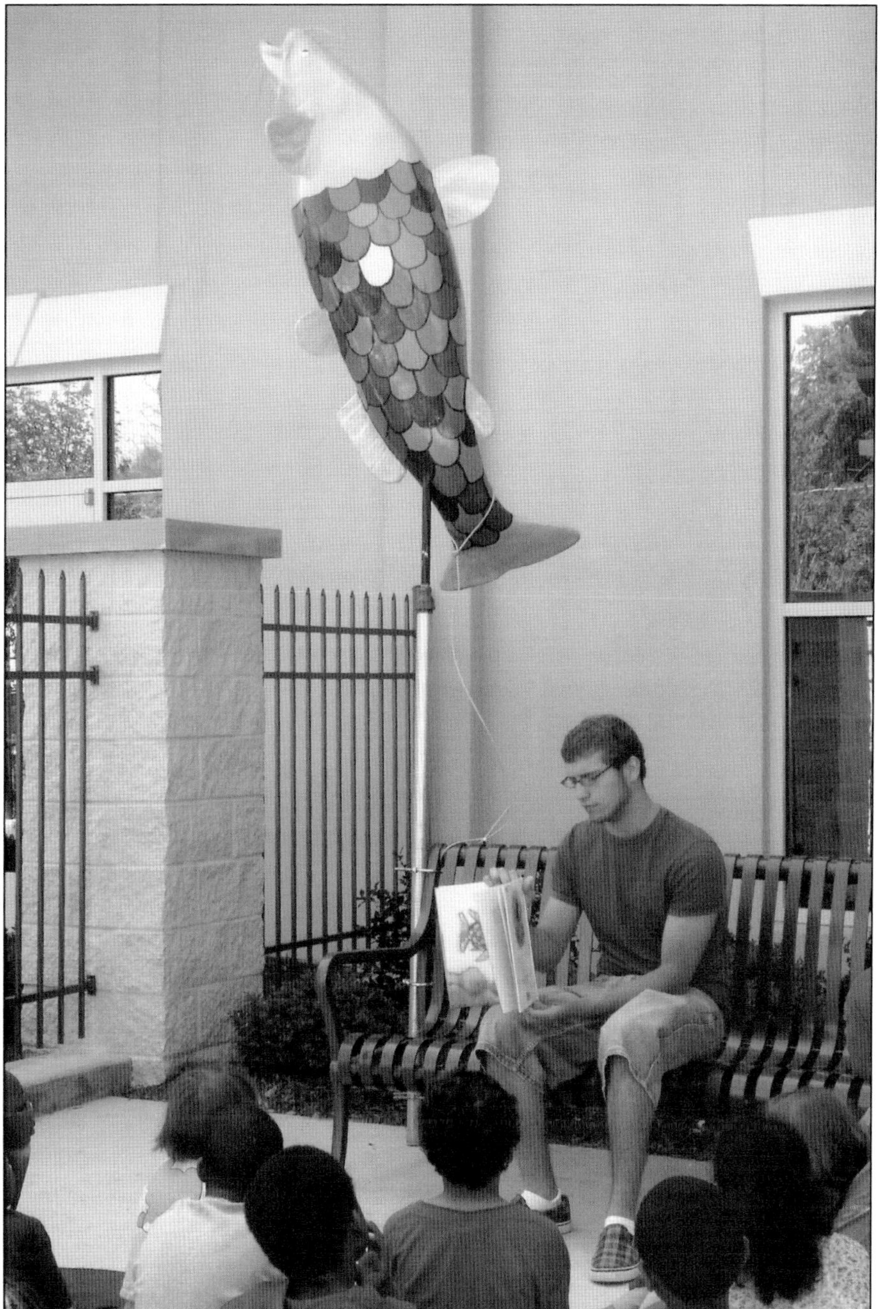

The year 2006 will forever be marked in history as the year Gadsden began its One Book, One Community reading promotion. Gadsden's project, aptly named Gadsden Reads, was a cooperative effort focusing on Daniel Wallace's book *Big Fish*, with events that included a screening of the film adaptation, scholarly lectures, and a two-day writer residency with the author. A visual art component was also developed, which consisted of 6-foot-tall fiberglass catfish sold to sponsors, painted by Alabama artists, and placed on Broad Street and at other businesses in town. At story time, Peter Martin reads Marcus Pfister's *Rainbow Fish* in front of the library's sculpture.

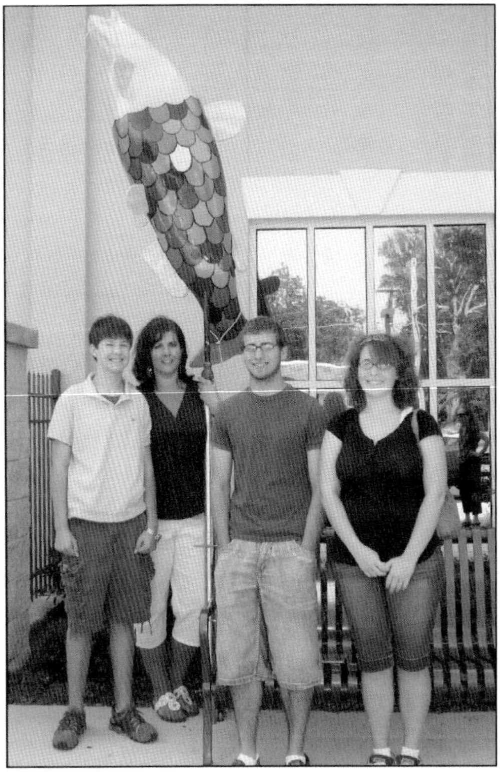

Artists Zach Brooks, Tami Brooks, Peter Martin, and Krystle Adcock used the book *Rainbow Fish* as their inspiration for painting the library's fish sculpture during Gadsden's One Book, One Community reading promotion.

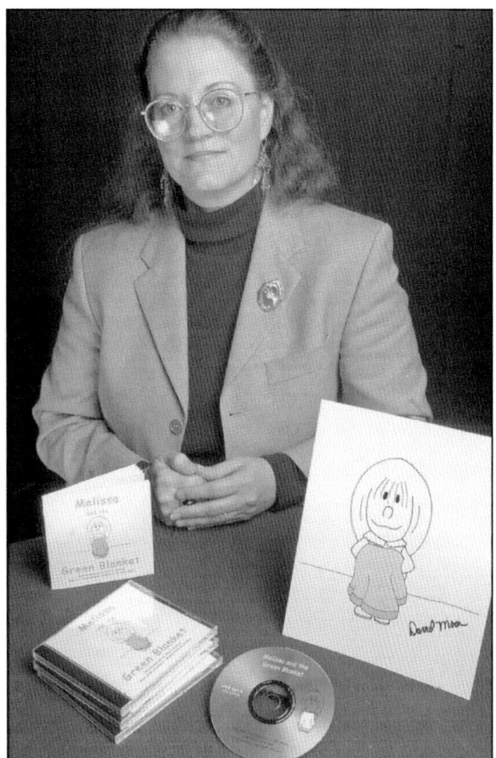

Local author and library employee Julie S. Dobbins released a children's CD/booklet in 2006. In December 2006, she and her husband, Craig Dobbins, presented a multimedia program of *Melissa and the Green Blanket* in the Lena Martin Room. The program included Julie reading the book, Craig accompanying on guitar, and a large-screen presentation of the pictures. (Photograph by Marc Golden, courtesy of the *Gadsden Times*.)

Late in 2006, the library announced that local best-selling author Linda Howard would be the featured speaker for National Library Week 2007 as Gadsden Public Library began its second century of providing educational, cultural, informational, and recreational enrichment to all citizens.

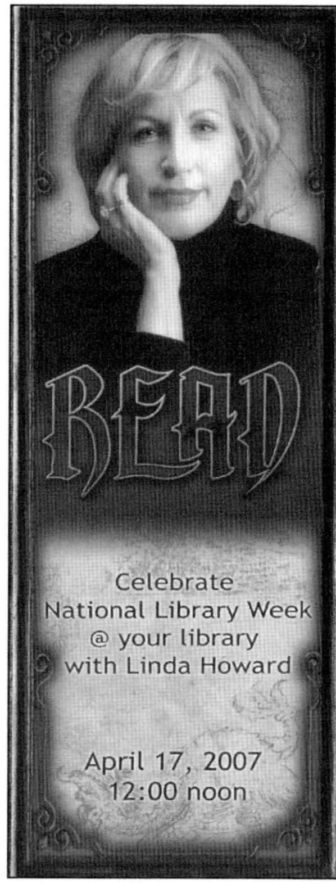

The Library History Committee consisted of, from left to right, (first row) Julie Dobbins and Bobby Junkins; (second row) Anita Brooks, Glenda Byars, and Danny Crownover. Each member of the committee contributed to *Gadsden Public Library: 100 Years of Service* in ways too numerous to count. Researching, writing, and editing this book was accomplished through the efforts of each member, but no one member can claim the finished work as their own. However, without their combined efforts, this book would have remained a dream. The committee hopes that the reality of that dream is an enjoyable experience for the reader.

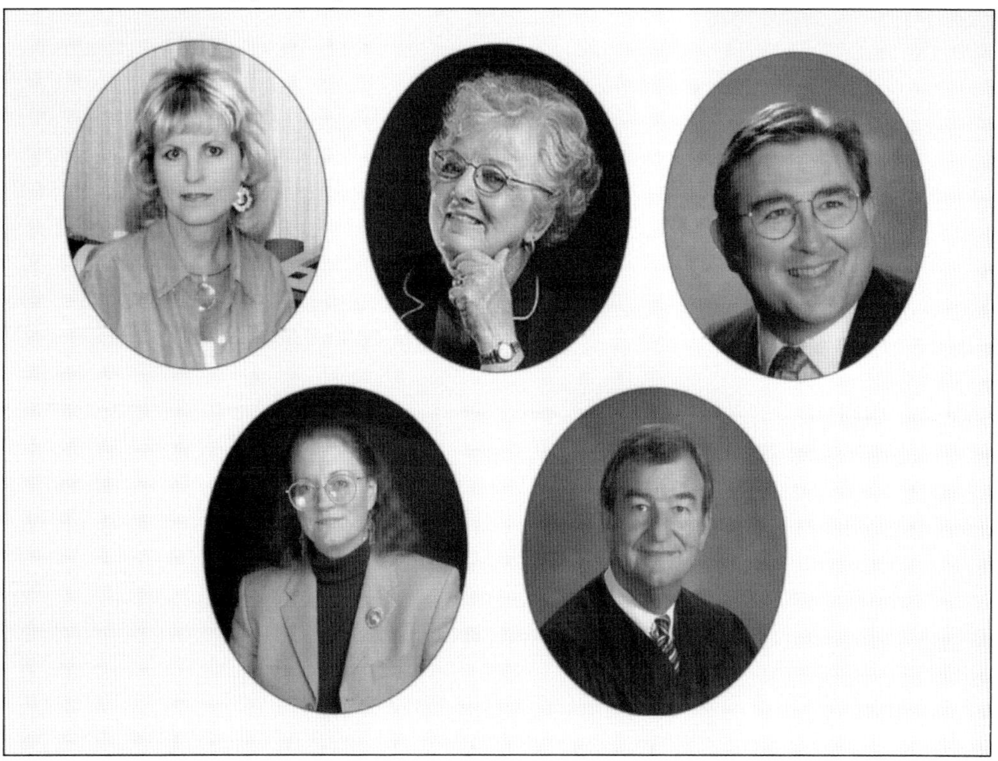